THE RECONNECTED HEART

HOW RELATIONSHIPS CAN HELP US HEAL

DR JONATHAN ANDREWS MAPS FCCLP

This book is a work of non-fiction. Unless otherwise noted, the author and the publisher make no explicit guarantees as to the accuracy of the information contained in this book and in some cases, names of people and places have been altered to protect their privacy.

WestBow Press books may be ordered through booksellers or by contacting:

WestBow Press
A Division of Thomas Nelson & Zondervan
1663 Liberty Drive
Bloomington, IN 47403
www.westbowpress.com
844-714-3454

Because of the dynamic nature of the Internet, any web addresses or links contained in this book may have changed since publication and may no longer be valid. The views expressed in this work are solely those of the author and do not necessarily reflect the views of the publisher, and the publisher hereby disclaims any responsibility for them.

Heart in Mind image by Chris Hardie. Heart Magic Eye by Paul Harvey.

ISBN: 978-1-6642-1564-1 (sc)
ISBN: 978-1-6642-1565-8 (hc)
ISBN: 978-1-6642-1563-4 (e)

Library of Congress Control Number: 2020924289

Print information available on the last page.

WestBow Press rev. date: 06/24/2021

To Millie, Isobel, Olivia and Zachary.

Beautiful and precious people.

May you know a deep, three-point connection all your days, and as a result may you sense honour, belonging, trust and worth.

CONTENTS

INTRODUCTION

How is your heart?

I'm not talking about the physical organ in your chest.

I'm talking about your psychological substance. I'm asking about how you are really going.

Here is a quick heart check:

- How do you feel about yourself?
- Do you feel ashamed, betrayed, worthless or alienated?
- Do others really know you?
- Do *you* really know you?
- What is your purpose in life?
- Is your purpose in life of a deep, almost spiritual significance?
- How would you describe your spiritual connection?
- Do you feel like you are making your own choices in life?
- Do you sense that life is under control or out of control?

After more than 20 years of work as a clinical psychologist, I've come to believe that the most helpful step we can take in life is to live with our hearts in our minds—that is, to live each day in conscious awareness of what we need to function well psychologically. The questions listed above all touch on areas of the heart. Neglecting these questions will compromise our inner sense of wellbeing and seriously limit our chances of flourishing in life.

Let me reassure you, though: if you found the heart check

difficult, you are not alone. In my experience, these questions are routinely overlooked by most people, irrespective of who they are and whether they are doing it tough or cruising along.

Even though many people neglect considering what is on their hearts, it would be uncaring of me, or any other person in your life, to normalise the difficulty that some of us have in answering these questions. Neglect of the heart is all too common in society, yet it is what most commonly brings people to therapy.

Most of the time, what brings people to therapy is that their hearts have been broken: broken by bad relationships and/or the absence of positive relationships. These sorts of relationships have led to a cracking of the individual's psychological foundation. Hearts are broken and people are left to recover from what I refer to as '*connection injuries*': betrayal, worthlessness, shame and alienation.

The purpose of this book is to reverse these injuries by facilitating a three-point connection:

- connection between you and the God of the Bible
- connection between you and others
- connection within you.

The book aims not just to remedy the four connection injuries, but also potentially to reverse them: to take you, the reader, into a space of trust, self-esteem, honour and belonging.

This book is not a list of the most recent discoveries, even though current research is referred to in it. Instead, it is a journey exploring one of the deepest psychological needs that all humans have: the need for connection. If we are to flourish and grow, and enjoy psychological balance and wellbeing, this need must be met. Only by keeping it in our awareness—that is, by keeping 'heart in mind'—can we increase the likelihood that this deep-seated need can be addressed.

The book is split into three parts:

Part One focuses on the heart and the importance of connection.

In Chapter 1, I will tell four stories. Each story has a different psychological injury, but emerges from the same problem.

In Chapter 2, the power of connection will be explored.

Part Two focuses on how relationships hurt.

Chapter 3 highlights how the impact of trauma varies according to the nature of the trauma, and how both *omission* and *commission* can have far-reaching effects.

In Chapter 4, we will consider how lack of connection (or the presence of *dis*connection) leads to changes (or 'injuries') at a heart level: instead of trust we feel betrayal; instead of high levels of self-esteem we experience low levels of self-esteem; instead of honour we feel shame; and instead of belonging we feel alienated.

In Chapter 5, we will look at how human beings are centrifugal in nature, and how this can help us understand our own hearts.

Having traversed the territory of connection and its consequences, we will be positioned to give a considered appraisal of our own history of relationships and how they have impacted us.

Part Three focuses on how relationships heal us.

In this part, we begin the journey of heart-level change by creating a three-point relationship:

- with God (Chapter 6)
- with others (Chapter 7)
- with ourselves (Chapter 8).

Chapter 9 highlights *how* we change.

Chapter 10 takes us to the cusp of healing. With our 'connection pyramid' intact and all three connection points consolidated, we are ready to enter into a new space in our lives where our hearts can be healed by new loving communities.

All through these three parts I will tell stories based on the people I've met. All personal details regarding age, gender and demography have been changed to protect the privacy of each person whose story I tell. I will ask questions to stimulate your thinking about how you might be able to restore connection and remedy the connection injuries that you might have.

Each time you see the following symbol, there will be an opportunity to connect with yourself and consider what is happening with you in your own heart and in your own relationships.

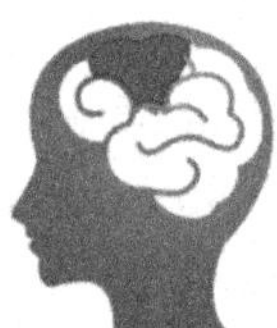

This symbol captures the idea of keeping your heart in your mind. It will become especially significant in the latter half of the book as we move beyond what the heart is and how relationships impact on it, and move towards how relationships may have hurt us, and how relationships might heal us.

As mentioned above, the goal of the book is to restore or strengthen the foundation of your heart. If you reach such a goal by reading this book, I will be overjoyed. It is more likely, though, that by reading this book you will begin this journey, a journey that will be life-changing, not because this book is remarkable, but because its message is timeless: by attending to our hearts we can change in a profound way.

Hearts break every day, but hearts also heal every day. Good relationships with friends and family, and a relationship with a good God, can change our hearts for the better. Changing hearts is God's core business. It is what he does best, and it is foundational in the process of drawing into him that this occurs—he gives us 'a heart of flesh' to replace our 'heart of stone' (Ezekiel 36:26). To bring someone's heart back to life is life-changing. This is the potential of the journey that we're now embarking upon.

I'd like to tell you about what I see as my role in the journey ahead.

My deepest desire is to remain connected with you as much as I can. To be connected with someone is exceptionally potent. To be connected, I will be trying hard to be with you on your journey, to share an understanding and to give you a sense of freedom.

I'll be trying hard to be with you by trying hard not to lead you—that is, I don't want to be out ahead of you. I don't want to move at a pace at which you don't want to go, so I encourage you to put down and pick up this book as it suits you. I don't want to be a parent or teacher; and alas, I have no pat answers for you. I don't have a simple 'fix' as such, and I won't be giving you *the* answer. I won't tell you what you feel and I won't tell you what you think. I won't even tell you what to do.

To be connected, I will also be trying hard to provide a good understanding of relationships and their consequences. As I describe the experiences of people whom I've met, and as I reveal some scientific findings, I hope that you will feel understood, and in being understood you'll feel less alone. If you say something like, 'He *got* me' when you finish this book, then my goal will have been achieved.

Similarly, if you understand yourself more or come to understand your friend or family member more, then this will also be a positive outcome. In order for connection to keep growing, depth of understanding must increase. Connection requires understanding and lots of it, and without understanding, connection will eventually die. You won't relate to everything that is shared, because we are all different, but I do hope that the territory regarding the injuries of connection is covered well enough in this book and that you find yourself or your loved one somewhere in it.

Connection requires not just understanding, but also freedom: freedom of behaviour and freedom of thought. What happens to connection when we are not free to decide who we are and what we are like? Connection with others deteriorates when the people we are with decide who we are and what we are like. You must be free to decide what is true about you. That is why I will refrain from telling you who you are, but I will ask you questions instead. Only when we are asked questions can we sketch out a personally-tailored account of our own truth. When the process is guided by you and you are in control of it, then you will feel like it really is true of you, not true of you according to someone else. For this reason, I most keenly want to provide you with your own space to decide what is true of you and what is not. When we have the power to decide what labels to put on ourselves, we are safe enough to continue talking.

Injuries of connection are perhaps the deepest and most disruptive of psychological disorders that I know. To be frank, there are psychiatric problems such as psychosis that wreak incredible havoc in people's lives, but as disturbing as these problems are, they can often be treated effectively with medication and on many occasions are transient. By contrast, injuries that relate to connection are only ever remedied by therapy and ongoing, stable relationships with others. Without these things, problems persist and unfortunately, we can go on getting re-injured.

These injuries are deep. They are not things that are quickly remedied, and they are not things that we can simply forget about and move on from. Facing what troubles us is the only remedy, and facing what troubles us requires effort and time. It is inconvenient *but* productive, painful *but* liberating. Sometimes the issues are resolved quickly; sometimes they are not. The key is that you have to feel in control of how deep you go with it. There are some things that you may want to face, but are too difficult to unpack. Leave them for later. There are some that will be easier for you to address, and you may like to tackle them first.

Injuries of connection can be profound, distressing and difficult to budge, but there is great hope. Relationships do hurt people, but relationships also heal people. It happens every day.

PART ONE

THE HEART AND THE IMPORTANCE OF CONNECTION

1

Four stories, all different; four stories, all the same

Sally was a beautifully presented, professional lady in her thirties. In reality, she was in a terrible way, but this wasn't obvious to me, especially early in our discussions. After we had met four or five times, I began to wonder whether she was going to talk openly about what was upsetting her. There had been small episodes of distress in several of our discussions, but they were only momentary.

Sally attended each visit in elegant attire. She wore heels and a long dress. Her hair was styled, and she had makeup on her face. She laughed freely and was engaging in conversation.

Week by week, visit by visit, she accumulated the courage to talk about the events that made her feel so terrible and inspired her to seek counselling.

As I got to know her more, the pauses in our conversations lasted a little longer. Finally, in the midst of a pause in our conversation, she looked out the window and said in a flat tone of voice that she felt 'dirty'.

When she left, I sat down and wrote the word in the middle of a new page. I just sat with the word. *Dirty.* It is a similar word to 'stained'. It is a crucial word, and I had to take this part of what she shared especially seriously.

For many of us, such words are just words. They seem to roll off our tongues and don't evoke anything much—a bit like saying the word 'awake', or 'paper'. But for Sally, using this word was not the same as it might be for others. Her reluctance to use it was understandable. When she said it, it dragged into the present an amalgam of horrible experiences from her past; experiences that she would prefer not to talk about. Talking about them made them real, and now the conversations we were having had her vexed. When she spoke about the dirty feeling, she sensed that a wave of symptoms were around the corner. She became so overwhelmed by these symptoms, so engrossed by them, that she ended up no longer being in the 'here and now' with me. She was in the 'there and then', around those people who had made her feel dirty and stained.

Ben was a big, solid fellow. Friendly and warm, he offered me a handshake when I first met him, and it felt like I was trying to shake hands with a dinner plate. Conversations can be hard with some people, but this was not the case with Ben. He knew how to connect, and I couldn't help but feel like I was being caught up in the energy of the rapport he so easily created. It was as if I was being taken along for a ride on a wave at the beach. There were twists, turns and drops.

People always come to counselling for a reason. Sometimes the reason eludes them a little, but it is there all the same. I'm always keen to make productive use of everyone's time, so towards the end of his first visit, I asked Ben what he wanted to achieve by coming to see me.

The joviality stopped.

He sat in a conflicted silence. He was upset with himself for taking so long to talk about his heart injury; he was upset because he was still upset. The struggle within him was not new.

When Ben was growing up, his dad was constantly away on business. As a result, time with his father was in short supply. On the odd occasions when his father was at home, he often recuperated in his study, watching the rugby, watching the cricket, watching whatever.

Ben was close to his mother. She was interested in him and liked to have fun. He was blessed to have a mother who knew how to relate to him. As was obvious to me, he had inherited his mother's large capacity for warmth.

When he was 12, his mum died of cancer. The fallout for the family was devastating. He had older siblings, and they all sought support from their friends in high school, but such resources and independence were not available to a pre-teen. He knew he couldn't talk to his father—his father wasn't disposed to doing that. Ben's feelings were powerful, and an audience was hard to come by. The very person he wanted to talk to was the very person who wasn't available to him any longer.

One evening, in the midst of grief, he caught an image of a scantily-clad woman on the internet. He clicked on the link, and for that brief moment, he thought of nothing else. The sadness departed. He felt attracted to someone, and he imagined that she was attracted to him. For a time he wasn't isolated; he wasn't alone. Then the images stopped, and the stew of tormenting sadness and hopelessness returned.

After his mum's funeral, his dad went back to work and back to watching television. His eldest sister moved out of home. Ben wanted to share with others how he was feeling, but he didn't know how to tell his friends. He wasn't even sure he had the words to express how he felt. Even if he could find the words, and even if he did have friends, he wondered whether they would want to listen. He sensed that they wouldn't know how to deal with his problems anyway, so he gave up trying to talk about the loss that he felt.

He missed his mother desperately. The old ache from that big loss rose up and rattled his large frame.

By the time Ben came to see me, he had been addicted to pornography for fifteen years. Like most addictions, Ben's struggle started as a coping strategy. It was a coping strategy with a fleetingly positive impact, but an impact all the same. Time slipped away and left him not only with the original injury of being alone, but also with almost endless iterations of powerlessness. He no longer controlled the use of the images; they controlled him. He felt lonely and worthless.

Tony was unusual—not in appearance or demeanour, but because most of the people I see have struggles early on in their lives, and Tony didn't. You might say he had a fortunate life: good family, good schooling and good health. He was an able-bodied man of good height. Even though his hair was greying a little, he retained a youthful vigour. He was a little uncomfortable in my presence, but not overly so. He certainly hadn't expected to be speaking to someone like me.

Tony had a career defined by a steady upward progression. He started work straight out of school in a mail office. He learned to turn up on time and work hard. He caught the train in to work with his dad across the Sydney Harbour Bridge. He laughed about how little he used to earn in those days, though it seemed a lot of money to him at the time.

His career seemed so uncomplicated. He got promoted in his early twenties out of the mail office and learned different roles. He stayed in the same company in which he started his career. He was greatly appreciated for the contribution that he made, and he was grateful to the company for the opportunities that it gave him. He worked as an accountant for more than thirty years.

Now, at the age of sixty, he had determined that this was the best time to slow down and spend more time with his wife. He was looking forward to doing some gardening and travel. At work, he received gifts and a standing ovation when he made his official goodbye. All the accolades were touching.

Having been granted his freedom, he began his retirement with a spring in his step. But after a short trip overseas, he found that his energy levels halved. His motivation was slipping, and a 'meh' feeling encompassed him. He simply didn't have a 'why' to his life.

'What do you think is your role in life now?' I asked.

My question appeared to stump him. 'I don't know. I guess that is just it,' Tony replied.

Tony went on to explain that he felt lost and was lacking purpose, but more deeply, he felt like he didn't belong. He felt flat. At church he would try engaging people in conversation, but he felt like he had little to contribute, so he would often take himself home early. When he was at a social gathering, he found himself talking too much about what he used to do. He dreaded that at any given time at a gathering, someone would ask him, 'What are you doing here?'

Samantha's experience was different. She didn't so much feel worthless as betrayed.

She had married William when she was in her early twenties. She was attracted to his confidence. He dressed well, and she often felt charmed by his attention. William was sure that other people were jealous of her, of him, and of what they had with each other.

Samantha had come from a family where her mum and dad were devoted to each other. They never strayed; they stayed loyal and connected. She brought that legacy of love and loyalty into her relationship with William. She was devoted to him, but more than that: she was devoted to the idea of marriage and all the principles that form that commitment. She was loyal to a fault. She could not have known that her moral and spiritual beliefs would conspire against her and turn her into a puppet for William.

The first time it happened, she was so shocked that she had no language and no way to orientate herself in its aftermath. It was so foreign to her. It startled and confused her, because what she encountered in her married life was unlike any exchange she'd experienced growing up.

It happened after Samantha's school reunion. She and William did not go to school together, and Samantha's school reunion invitation specifically stated that no partners were invited. Samantha left her house with a close girlfriend, anticipating a great night of seeing old friends.

During the night, a group photo was uploaded onto Facebook. It had Samantha standing next to her ex-boyfriend, a big smile on her face, his arm draped over her shoulder.

When she arrived home from the reunion, her husband asked whether he could talk to her. She agreed without hesitation. She asked him what he wanted to talk about. 'I want to talk about how you've hurt me,' he replied. She didn't once think that she had done anything wrong while at the reunion, so she was quite confused by the drama that unfolded. He wanted to 'sort it out', he said, but she wasn't sure what had to be sorted out. The temperature in the room began to climb. The yelling, pacing and pleading went on long into the night. William told her that she had ruined his 'reputation'.

Her convictions about what she did or didn't do wrong earlier in the night began to buckle under the weight of his monologue. In the torrent of words and emotion, she found her own judgement being washed away. The easiest thing to do would be for her to apologise. 'Have I perhaps been inconsiderate?' she wondered.

After the outrage came tears and apologies, then peace and tranquillity. It happened time and again after that. The best way, she thought, to prevent him from getting upset like this again was for her to do what he wanted. The best way to reduce his hurt, she thought, was to do less without him.

So she cut off all ties with her old friends. She washed away not only her own sense of right and wrong, but also her freedom. The pattern was always the same: he became hurt; he saw her as the cause; she lost her judgement when he became too emotional; and she, believing that she was the cause, restricted her freedom in the hope that he would no longer be distressed. First she lost her freedom of thought, then she lost her freedom of behaviour. Perhaps he was right. Perhaps all she needed was him, because they had something really special.

Something was amiss, though. There was an encroaching sense that something wasn't right within her and that the solution William was proposing wasn't helping. She noticed that before she went out for coffee with friends, she found herself walking on eggshells. She became more and more convinced that it was her responsibility to keep him at peace. Furthermore, she began to feel like she was to blame for any tension between them. Her mood went flat and her spiritual life lost its colour. She remained this way for the first ten years of their marriage, and no doubt she would have for the next ten years if he hadn't dragged her to the floor by her hair when she returned late one afternoon after meeting up with friends.

What do these four stories have in common?

It is clear that they have their differences: Sally felt ashamed, Ben felt worthless, Tony felt alienated and Samantha felt betrayed.

But even though these psychological injuries are different, they have a common origin. In a very real way, they are different manifestations of the same problem.

All four deep psychological struggles come from disruptions in *connection* with others.

In its barest form, connection refers to a 'binding together' of two entities. In this book, we will use the term to refer to a binding of one person to another, or of a person to God.

Sally, Ben, Tony and Samantha all suffered from disruptions in this binding process, and as a result they were all profoundly upset at a heart level.

What is the heart?

The word 'heart' has been used to convey a rich range of important meanings. The most obvious and easily understood meaning for us today is the organ in the chest that pumps blood around the body. Having a pulse is a sign of life, and life itself depends on our hearts functioning. Having a heart is foundational to our very existence.

The same word also refers to a part of us that exists within our physical body, but is itself not physical. If you were to open up the human body and examine it in an autopsy, you would never find your 'inner heart'—yet it is there, and it is real. We all have one.

The inner heart is not as easily defined as the physical heart. Its elusiveness results in many descriptions: our innermost core, the seat of our vitality, the source of our inclinations, our motivations; it refers to our purposes, our spirit, our soul and even our character.

We can see from the examples below that the English language is rich in expressions that use the word 'heart' to convey deeper concepts:

- A 'heart-broken' girl whose boyfriend has ended their relationship has found a shorthand way of saying, 'This incident has left me feeling devalued, directionless and lifeless.'
- Having a 'heart-to-heart' means having a deep and connected conversation with another person.
- Getting to the 'heart of the matter' means dealing with real or substantial issues being discussed.
- Having a 'change of heart' means having not only a change of mind, but a change of direction or a change of values.
- People who are 'heartless' are those who don't care and are disconnected.

The word 'heart' is as beautiful as it is versatile. It is an ancient word, one that is as old as the oldest book in the Bible. The Hebrew word *lebab* has been used for thousands of years to point to the deeper capacities that are characteristic of being human. These capacities include our will, our feelings and impulses, our characters and our inclination to form attachments with others. The heart is our control centre, and the centre of our inner life. It is the seat from which our thoughts, feelings, behaviours and physical symptoms come. The Greek word *kardia* is similar. It refers to the emotional centre of our being.

I will use a definition of 'heart' that draws from ancient roots but has a contemporary twist. It is the seat of our deeply-held personal truths, our uniqueness and our significance. Psychologically, it incorporates three of our most important needs:

- our need for positive nurturing relationships, also known as *connection* (connection builds our sense of self-esteem, trust, belonging and honour)
- our need for identity, or *direction* in life
- our need for *choice*, or a sense that things are under our control.

A fully-formed heart might look like what we see here:

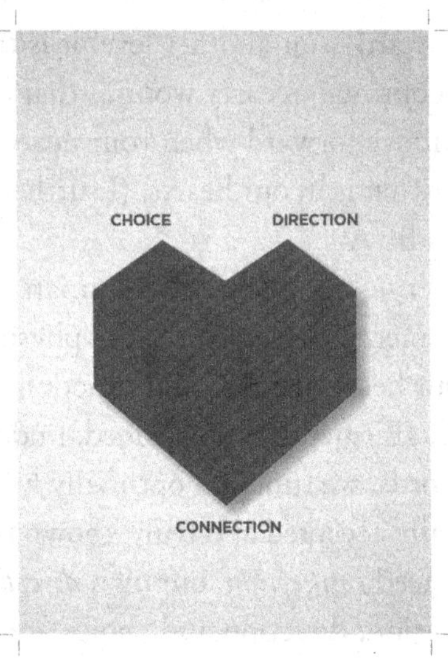

Figure 1. The three components of a full heart

The nature and needs of the heart

Children are taught quite early at school about caring for their physical being and the need to do what is necessary to stay healthy. They are taught to be active and eat well. They are taught to eat different coloured vegetables and to refrain from eating junk food. Lessons about the body are important and not to be overlooked.

By contrast, we are not so quick to focus on the need to care for what is in our hearts. Indeed, it is even possible to go through our whole lives without giving these needs much attention. Many of us are not even aware that who we are on the inside can be easily and seriously wounded by difficult life events. If we pass through times of deep, heart-level struggle, we simply assume that time will heal our pain.

This is why some are in the habit of saying, 'Time heals all wounds'; but it doesn't. When we say this, we underestimate the vulnerability of the heart and the vital role that it plays in our overall wellbeing. While understandable on one level—because we just have to keep moving forward—on another level it is tragic, because we will unnecessarily continue to carry wounds that never receive care. It is really hard to move forward when your heart is broken. We all have a need to face what is in our hearts. (I further address the need to do this in Appendix A.)

In a general sense, to be healthy human beings, we must have certain needs met. What is true of us physically is true of us psychologically. Our hearts develop and function fully when we are loved and accepted, affirmed, acknowledged, understood and given choices. In other words, we function optimally when we experience being unconditionally accepted and truly known by loving, actively caring people. We need *connection*, our own *direction*, and *choice*. If the needs of connection, direction and choice are not met, or if we experience treatment or events that are unloving, we will bear heart injuries that can range from mild to severe, and can range from brief to chronic.

The state of each person's heart is not set at birth and it does not remain static throughout the course of life. Who we are and the functioning of the heart changes as life progresses. Our experiences influence our hearts, and because our hearts are responsive to both negative and positive factors, they can be healthy and robust or they can be struggling or damaged, or fail to develop properly. Our hearts are intricately part of our entire being, and any compromise in their functioning can result in disruption to our functioning as people.

Over the last several decades, modern psychology has made many valuable advances in understanding the human heart. We not only know a lot more about its functioning and impact on our whole being, but there now exists a far greater body of knowledge about what can be done when things go wrong at this level.

That is what this book is about—heart restoration, from the bottom up. In Figure 1 above, you can see that *connection* is at the bottom. Connection is the foundation of the heart, and in this book we are in the business of securing this foundation.

Sally, Ben, Tony and Samantha all had their hearts broken by other people: Sally by relational trauma, Ben by grief and addiction, Tony by the loss of a role, and Samantha by an abusive spouse. Shame, worthlessness, alienation and betrayal come from ruptures in the connection process, and these ruptures create a fault line in the foundation of the heart. What these people have in common is a history of *dis*[1]*-connection*. You will meet all four of these people again in Chapter 4, when the four 'connection injuries' are examined, and you will meet them again at the end of the book.

Whenever we are hurt, our natural proclivity is to avoid anything that resembles the thing that hurts us. By coming to therapy, Sally, Ben, Tony and Samantha presented a puzzle: all four of them moved

[1] 'Dis' meaning 'do the opposite of', as in the word 'disallow'.

towards people even though people had hurt them. Knowingly or unknowingly, they all recognised one thing: they could not do without connection, because connection promises an answer. They had been hurt by people but they still sought people out. Relationships are the problem, *and* relationships are the solution.

Not everyone who reads this book will have been impacted in the same ways as Sally, Ben, Tony and Samantha, and not all readers will have been impacted to the same extent. You may, for example, have only a little in common with one or two of them, and there may be something else that isn't described by their experiences (for example, a particular descriptor like 'self-loathing' or an identity label that isn't covered in this book, such as 'I'm an idiot'). People are different and the injuries we have will vary. My hope is that you will find some of your experiences in this book, but I also want you to add your own if the shoe doesn't fit.

Some who read this book will only know a little of what it is to be impacted by others in negative ways. The injuries received have only been skin-deep, not heart-felt. If that is you, then this book will help you to understand and support other people in your life. All around us are friends, siblings, children, colleagues and other people who have been impacted by others in significant ways. All of them are in need of connection and understanding, and this book will help you to meet these needs. If you can learn how to do this for others, you hold out the promise of safety and healing for the people you love, and they are blessed to have you in their lives.

A full heart means knowing that we are of value as people, irrespective of our circumstances or of what we do, achieve or have. It means being able to trust, it means feeling honoured, and it means knowing that we belong. It means understanding who we are and living out our gifting and passions in a way that brings blessing to us and to those around us. A full heart knows direction, purpose and fulfilment because the whole of life is a true expression of our inner being.

Now we have a destination: a full heart. That is the goal; but how do we get there?

The way we get there is founded on the understanding that disconnection hurts and connection heals. This is the foundational take-home message of this book. To expand on this one step further, I would say that disconnection leads to connection injuries (betrayal, worthlessness, shame and alienation), whereas connection leads to a reversal of these injuries. Connection leads to trust, self-esteem, honour and belonging.

Simply put, when our hearts are broken, connection is how we rebuild and repair. For people of faith, the connection that we establish will be a three-point connection which provides a strategy to heal our brokenness:

1. Connection with God
2. Connection with others
3. Connection with self.

Now we have the road map: a three-point connection. By connecting in these ways, we can go a long way towards repairing injuries like those of betrayal, worthlessness, shame and alienation, and even go beyond that into a flourishing state.

These three types of connection—with God, others and self—will be examined more fully in 'Part Three: How relationships heal'.

Pause and review

- Connection refers to the binding of one thing to another. In this book we look at the connection between people, connection with ourselves and the connection between people and God.

- The heart is our control centre, and the centre of our inner life. It is the place from which our thoughts, feelings, behaviours and physical symptoms emerge.
- Connection is the foundation of the heart. Identity and a sense of control are also part of the heart, but they rise from this foundation. If we don't get enough connection or if we suffer disconnection, we can end up feeling betrayed, worthless, ashamed and/or alienated.
- These injuries can be reversed by cultivating better connection in three ways: with God, with others and with ourselves.

What one word comes to mind when you think of the state of your relationship with God?

What one word comes to mind when you think of the state of your relationships with others?

Out of 10, if 10 = really connected, to what extent are you connected with yourself?

Your answers to the above questions give you your starting point. We know the destination that we're heading towards (restoration of trust, self-esteem, honour and belonging) and we have set our pathway towards it, seeking a profound, three-point connection with God–others–self to help resolve hurts and flourish. We know that connection—safe, caring, intimate connection—will feed our hearts.

Why choose that as our pathway? Will it really be helpful?

The reality is that we choose it because it is who we are, and we choose it because connection has a power that will benefit all of us. This power is the focus of the next chapter.

2

The power of connection

James Frazier Reed's wife was seriously unwell. Life wasn't easy for either of them, but it was especially difficult for her. The winters were harsh in Illinois, and, like any decent human being, James wanted to change their situation to make living easier for his wife. If his wife was going to recover from her health difficulties, they were going to have to move.

The year was 1846.

Like the Israelites over 3000 years before him, James wanted to make it to a land of promise. He was a man of passion and adventure by disposition. He came up with an idea, and spoke with the families around him. His enthusiasm was infectious. Before long, friends and neighbours had signed up to go with him and his family. On 16 April, nine wagons set out from Springfield on what would be recorded as one of the most tragic journeys in American history.

In a little under a month, the party reached Independence, Missouri, the starting point for the California Trail. In the winter of 1846–7, 87 pioneers became stranded in the Sierra Nevada mountains. The weather changed. Storms came. Only 47 survived the freezing temperatures. They became known as the 'Donner Party', named after George Donner, the leader of their group.

James Frazier Reed was not a part of that group at the time. He had been banished after he stabbed another teamster, John Snyder, to death.

The party wanted to hang him, but after his sick wife pleaded for his life, the group agreed to send him away. He took off to Sutter's Fort. After a brief rest he tried to return to the group with supplies, but was prevented because the snow was too deep. The winter had set in and sealed the fate of most of the party. He made several attempts to help the party with the help of others, and was eventually reunited with them and his family. He died of natural causes at the age of 73 in San Jose. He had been involved in ventures in gold prospecting, real estate, exportation of natural produce, and serving, somewhat ironically, as a lawman.

Now, I don't know whether we can say that the Donner Party victims didn't 'die in vain'. I've never liked that phrase. It is a phrase often used by someone trying to gloss over tragedy. But I admit that there are times when my stance on this is challenged. The death of Jesus was not in vain, for example. And what happened to the Donner Party is also, perhaps, one of those times.

Almost 150 years later, a group of researchers got together to examine all available diaries of people who were in the Donner Party. From those diaries, the researchers were able to determine that, after the factors of age and gender were controlled for, social connection was the most accurate predictor of survival in those harsh conditions. Strong, quality ties—that is, good binding or connection with others in the group—increased the likelihood of an individual surviving; conversely, poor levels of connection increased their risk of death.[1] It is challenging to realise that for humans, connection is not simply something nice to have or something to 'enjoy on weekends'. It is the very thing that can underwrite our survival when survival is threatened.

The claim being made here is a big one. Connection is so important that our very lives depend on it. There are times when we are oblivious to its importance and we are numb to its significance and its beauty. Every now and again, the mist clears and we can see just how profound it is. It is true that connection helps with survival,

[1] DK Grayson, 'Donner party deaths: a demographic assessment', *Journal of anthropological research*, vol. 46, no. 3, 1990, pp. 223–242.

but it also helps every other thing in life. It helps our bodies, our brains, our behaviour and our mood as well.

Connection protects bodies, brains, behaviour and mood

Cardiovascular disease (CVD) is the number one cause of death globally. The World Health Organization (WHO) says 'more people die annually from CVD than from any other cause'.[2] According to meta-analytic reviews[3], an inverse relationship has been found between social involvement and many of the markers of cardiovascular disease, such as hypertension, high body mass index, unhealthy waist circumference and inflammation.

In fact, the state of your relationships in your middle years is a better predictor of your future health than your cholesterol. Robert Waldinger, chief investigator of the Harvard Grant Study of Adult Development (a famous longitudinal study which I will refer to again later), has given one of the most popular TED Talks ever. It is entitled 'What makes a good life?' In his talk, Waldinger states:

> When we gathered together everything we knew about them ['them' being the large group of men who were studied] at age 50, it wasn't their middle-age cholesterol levels that predicted how they were going to grow old. It was how satisfied they were in their relationships. The people who were the most satisfied in their relationships at age 50 were the healthiest at age 80.[4]

---

[2] World Health Organization, *Cardiovascular diseases (CVDs)*, 17 May 2017, viewed August 2017, <http://www.who.int/mediacentre/factsheets/fs317/en/>.

[3] A meta-analysis is a review of many works of scientific research.

[4] R Waldinger, *What makes a good life? Lessons from the longest study on happiness*, 2015, viewed November 2020, <https://www.ted.com/talks/robert_waldinger_what_makes_a_good_life_lessons_from_the_longest_study_on_happiness>.

Have you ever been to a General Practitioner for a check-up, and instead of them taking a blood sample to check your cholesterol, they asked you about your relationships? The science suggests that such a strategy might be quite appropriate.

If you, like me, are a tad sceptical by nature, you might find yourself saying, 'Yeah ... but if we feel isolated we are prone to eating more or smoking more, and that could explain why isolation or disconnection puts us at risk of cardiovascular disease.' This seems to be a worthy consideration. However, many studies have controlled for the impact of lifestyle factors, including smoking and physical (in)activity, and they *still* see an impact of disconnection on the biological heart.[5]

The bottom line is that disconnection impacts negatively on our physical health, and this is not because of things that are commonly associated with loneliness: it is *because of the loneliness*. The independent contribution of loneliness has been quantified, with researchers noting that loneliness or social isolation is linked to a 29% increase in the risk of having a heart attack and a 32% increase in the chance of having a stroke.[6]

Connection plays a part in protecting us from multiple health problems that we routinely face throughout life, not just CVD. Recent evidence confirmed that the operation of our immune systems depends on our level of connection with other people. In 1997, Sheldon Cohen and his colleagues in Pittsburgh gave 276

---

[5] J Holt-Lundstad & TB Smith, 'Loneliness and social isolation as risk factors for CVD: implications for evidence-based patient care and scientific inquiry', *Heart*, vol. 102, no. 13, 2016, pp. 987–989.

[6] NK Valtorta, M Kanaan, S Gilbody, S Ronzi & B Hanratty, 'Loneliness and social isolation as risk factors for coronary heart disease and stroke: systematic review and meta-analysis of longitudinal observational studies', *Heart*, vol. 102, no. 13, 2016, pp. 1009-1016.

healthy adults a virus and monitored them for the development of the common cold. They measured mucus secretion, mucus clearance and amount of viral replication. They found that those with more diverse types of social ties were less susceptible to common colds, they secreted less mucus, they were more effective in ciliary clearance of their nasal passages, and the virus replicated less in them. In this study, those with the least diverse types of social ties were 4.2 times more at risk of having a bad cold than those who had the most diverse social ties. They concluded that diverse social networks were associated with greater resistance to upper respiratory illness.[7]

Social integration, especially when bolstered by having a strong sense of purpose, has been shown to activate the genes that fight pathogens in the body, and deactivate the genes that are linked to inflammation in the body.[8] Researchers in the field have concluded that social integration reduces the risk of chronic diseases and an early death by changing the way our genes are expressed.[9]

Not only does connection protect us from premature death, from cardiovascular disease, and from colds and other viruses, but it turns on genes that defend us from viral attacks and turns off

---

[7] S Cohen, W Doyle, DP Skoner, BS Rabin & JM Gwaltney, 'Social ties and susceptibility to the common cold', *JAMA*, vol. 277, no. 24, 1997, pp. 1940–1944.

[8] BL Fredrickson, KM Grewen, SB Algoe, AM Firestine, JM Arevalo, J Ma & SW Cole, 'Psychological wellbeing and the human conserved transcriptional response to adversity', *PLoS ONE*, vol. 10, no 3, 2015, pp. 1–17.

[9] Ibid. You might think, 'Well, when you are more connected you are happier, so maybe being happy is what leads to a more favourable gene expression.' The researchers in the paper cited above stated that 'Hedonic wellbeing showed no consistent CTRA association.' (CTRA – conserved transcriptional response to adversity – refers to the way in which genes can increase inflammation and reduce antibodies in the body when we face adversity). So what they are saying is that being happy alone won't bring about a reduction in inflammation: you have to be happy *because* you have a sense of connection and purpose in your life.

genes that lead to inflammation. All of this strongly suggests that connection helps us physically. It is as if our bodies just cry out for it.

This is all well and good; but do you know what? There are more benefits to come.

When we do not have sufficient connection, we often summon the energy to reach out to other people for it. For most of us, we use the energy to good effect. We make a phone call or send a text and arrange a catch-up. The connection we achieve undoes the loneliness, and we bring ourselves back into normal functioning, fending off negative feelings.

However, some of us in this situation begin to withdraw, and a depressed mood looms on the horizon. This withdrawal, combined with commonly reported decreases in energy in people who are depressed, renders the sufferer even less likely to reach out to others. As depression grabs hold, suicidal thinking increases according to the degree of loneliness felt by the sufferer. This relationship between suicidal feelings and loneliness is true for both men and women[10], and is true whether or not social isolation is defined objectively (i.e. living alone) or defined subjectively (e.g. feelings of loneliness).

Connection can prevent depression, but the good news is that it can also lead us out of it. Dr Tegan Cruwys and her colleagues from the University of Queensland found that social identification—that is, feeling part of a group—predicted a faster recovery from depression. They have recommended that health practitioners

---

[10] A Stravynski & R Boyer, 'Loneliness in relation to suicide ideation and parasuicide: a population-wide study', *Suicide and life-threatening behavior*, vol. 31, no. 1, 2011, pp. 32–40.

facilitate social participation for depressed people, because the strategy is both clinically effective and cost effective.[11]

Loneliness, which is the absence of connection, is not just linked to depression. It is also linked to anxiety. Lack of connection can be seen in a variety of anxiety problems but is most clearly seen in people who fear evaluation from others. Social Phobia is a common anxiety condition that leads people to avoid social situations out of anxiety that they will be judged or scrutinised by others. According to Beyond Blue, approximately 11% of the population suffers from it in a diagnosable way in their lifetime. No doubt many more people than that endure the symptoms of Social Phobia, but the distress that they feel is not enough to cross a diagnosable threshold. More women than men suffer from it, and it typically begins in adolescence.[12]

When people suffer from Social Phobia, they live with a pervading self-consciousness. Even if they don't avoid people, or even if they can't avoid people, they often curb what they disclose to others out of fear of over-exposing themselves to the glare of social scrutiny. When asked how they are going, they say, 'Good.' And that is it—no more information, no opening up or personal revelation. A question such as, 'And how are you?' may follow to promptly turn the focus of the conversation back onto the other person. At these times, the glare has been averted, but the avoidance that gave them relief sold them a lemon: they remain unknown and lonely. They get anxious, so they avoid revealing themselves to others. When they avoid revealing themselves, no-one can know them. When no-one knows them, they can have no assurance of love and acceptance.

---

[11] T Cruwys, SA Haslam, GA Dingle, J Jetten & NJ Hornsey, 'Depression and social identity: an integrative review', *Personality and social psychology review*, vol. 18, no. 3, 2014, pp. 215–238.

[12] Beyond Blue, *Social phobia*, 2019, viewed September 2019, <https://www.beyondblue.org.au/the-facts/anxiety/types-of-anxiety/social-phobia>.

As well as being a risk factor for mood disorders, social isolation is also linked to personality disorders such as Avoidant Personality, Antisocial Personality, and Borderline Personality. As a consequence or as a creator, disconnection is entwined with an array of enduring personality issues that are distressing and restrictive.

Beyond the physical benefits, and beyond the mood benefits, being connected with others helps your brain develop, it protects your brain as you age, and it helps you act in more pro-social ways.

In a review of literature, researchers set out to determine the association between connectedness and the brain. They concluded that connection affects the 'rate and fate' of neural development. What this means is that if you are connected, your brain is more likely to grow more neurones more quickly.[13] Fish, birds and mammals are just the same: researchers have observed that when they have enhanced social environments, there is rapid cell growth in those brain regions associated with memory, communication and social interaction. In short, when we are connected, our brains grow.

These findings cast a shadow, though. The phrase 'rate and fate' also refers to how, in the absence of connection, our brains do not do well. In a large-scale study it was shown that loneliness predicted greater cognitive decline and increased risk of dementia, even after controlling for the effects of education, gender, age, and other health-related factors.[14]

---

[13] S Cacioppo, JT Capitanio & JT Cacioppo, 'Toward a neurology of loneliness', *Psychological bulletin*, vol. 140, no. 6, 2014, pp. 1464–1504.

[14] RS Wilson, KR Krueger, SE Arnold, JA Schneider, JF Kelly, LL Barnes & DA Bennett, 'Loneliness and risk of Alzheimer disease', *Archives of general psychiatry*, vol. 64, 2007, pp. 234–240.

Let's return to our hypothetical routine check-up with our doctor. Our cholesterol has been checked, because monitoring and lowering cholesterol is the standard course of action to prevent CVD. If the level is high, our physician then tells us to exercise some more and watch our diet. We then ask our doctor about how we might protect our brains as we get older, and we get the same recommendations—exercise, eat well—plus a few extras: keep on reading and learning. Great ideas, though perhaps, again, it would also be good to get a relationship check, because good connection is a potent way of preventing cardiovascular disease *and* cognitive decline.

So we know that connection helps our bodies, our moods and our brains. Yet there is another question we can ask: does connection with others change the way we behave towards others? Not surprisingly, connection with others helps us to develop safer ways of relating. When we connect with other people, particularly with regard to their feelings, it leads us to act more compassionately towards them.

When researchers interviewed men who assault their partners, they found that they were inclined to 'minimise others' negative views of themselves and dissociate themselves from their partners' physical and emotional injuries'.[15] The role that emotional disconnection is playing in domestic violence is evident here. The absence of emotional connection maintains poor behaviour towards others, because in the mind of the perpetrator, the views of others don't count and the injuries that their victims suffer aren't that bad. They have completely opted out of trying to understand and empathise with the experience of the person who is hurt. Being unable or unmotivated to connect with others maintains violent behaviour. Understandably, therapy for domestic abuse perpetrators often involves facilitating a connection with how the abuser sees the abused, and helps the abuser feel the

[15] S Goodrum, D Umberson & KL Anderson, 'The batterer's view of the self and others in domestic violence', *Sociological inquiry*, vol. 71, no. 2, 2001, pp. 221–240 (p. 221).

suffering of his or her victims. To put it in a more elegant way, therapy for perpetrators of domestic violence involves training the perpetrators to better connect with their victims.

When the researchers mentioned above did the same interviews with age-matched men who did *not* assault their partners, they found the opposite. Non-abusive men 'consider others' negative views of themselves, and they describe a deeper understanding of their intimate others' problems'.[16]

It is clear that when we are connected at a deep level, the benefits flow centrifugally outwards from our heart, benefiting many areas of our functioning: our moods change, our brains change, our behaviour changes and our bodies change. Figure 2 provides a visual summary of where we have been.

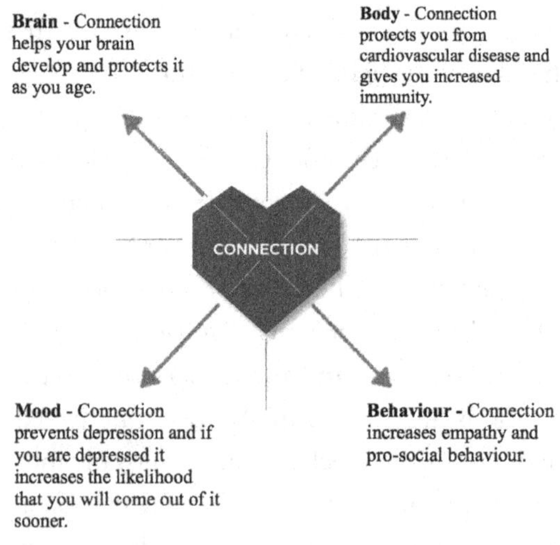

Figure 2. The positive impact of connection

[16] ibid.

The experience of researching and writing on this topic may be similar to your experience of reading it … the message is as consistent as it is relentless. Connection leads us to flourish across many domains of functioning, and disconnection leads to decay in those same areas of functioning. Whether it is for your mood, your brain, your body or your behaviour, connection with others has a power to safeguard you from a whole range of difficulties. So pervasive is the impact of loving connection that Professor Bessel van der Kolk, the Founder and Medical Director of the Trauma Centre in Boston, Massachusetts, states that 'Being able to feel safe with other people is probably the single most important aspect of mental health.'[17]

Many of us have taken a stand against smoking. We give a no-nonsense talk to our teenagers about it, how it isn't going to help them, how it will hurt them. 'Keep that up and it is going to kill you,' we say. Our political representatives readily acknowledge how destructive smoking is. Every year they spend millions of taxpayers' dollars broadcasting the risks via all types of media. They fund community groups to set up hotlines to support those who want to quit the habit, and they demand that horrific pictures be put on cigarette packets so that people will know the shocking consequences.

What if we all understood that the level of threat posed by social isolation is a risk equivalent to cigarette smoking? If we did, then we would not feel so comfortable with our own lack of connection or the lack of support for others who are disconnected.

We need an attitude change. We need to prioritise connection and safety in ways that we have not done before. Imagine if we all

---

[17] B van der Kolk, *The body keeps the score: brain, mind and body in the healing of trauma*, Viking, New York, 2014, p. 79.

sang and lived out the Rodgers and Hammerstein anthem adopted by Liverpool Football Club: 'You'll never walk alone'. As I type out the words, I can hear in my head the footballers singing it …

> When you walk through a storm
> Hold your head up high
> And don't be afraid of the dark …
> Walk on, walk on
> With hope in your heart
> And you'll never walk alone
> You'll never walk alone.

What a message; what a powerful, life-giving message. 'You'll never walk alone.'

Connection: a non-steroidal anti-inflammatory

How does something as simple as positive relationships have the power to benefit us on so many levels? The complete story is not yet understood, but it appears that connection calms our bodies, helping to reduce inflammation.[18] Just as connection is a necessary and constructive influence in our lives, disconnection, whether brief and obvious or chronic and subtle, is always going to be an unwelcome complicating factor, regardless of our situations and ages. Our systems become inflamed by it.

'Well, okay,' you might say, 'it is just like taking an aspirin, so why don't you just take an aspirin?' This may be a good counter-argument. Aspirin's role in reducing the risk of cardiovascular events has already been established, and now it appears as though it might

[18] GL Hermes, L Rosenthal, A Montag & MK McClintock, 'Social isolation and the inflammatory response: sex differences in the enduring effects of a prior stressor', *American journal of physiology-regulatory, integrative and comparative physiology*, vol. 290, 2006, pp. 273–282 (p. 273).

prevent cancers.[19] Not only that: aspirin holds some promise for the treatment of depression.[20] So why not just take the actual pill? Aspirin, like connection, can reduce inflammation, and you could save yourself the time and effort that is involved in getting to know someone and being known by someone. Well, to be honest, this may be true, and the same could be said for eating salmon or getting regular exercise.

However, with or without aspirin/exercise/salmon or any other helpful intervention, connection will continue to have its impact above and beyond other interventions. We are tied to others and there is nothing we can do about that. We impact and are impacted by others every day. It is simply a part of being human. Solutions such as aspirin/exercise/salmon are helpful and we should all consider them, but if that is all we do, we will be ignoring the reality that we are made for relationships, and to push on in life remaining indifferent to this need will not only set us up to fail, but will set us up to fail to contribute.

I recommend that you consider adopting any of the health strategies that have just been suggested. You can eat fish, take aspirin and go running. All of these will be helpful; but connection will trump all of these options, because it will do something that none of these things will ever be able to do for you.

---

[19] PM Rothwell, JF Price, FG Fowkes, A Zanchetti, MC Roncaglioni, G Tognoni, R Lee, JF Belch, M Wilson, Z Mehta & TW Meade, 'Short-term effects of daily aspirin on cancer incidence, mortality, and non-vascular death: analysis of the time course of risks and benefits in 51 randomised controlled trials', *The Lancet*, vol. 379, 2012, pp. 1602–1612.

[20] This approach has occurred because of a different view that some researchers are taking on major depression. Instead of thinking that depression is caused by lower levels of neurotransmitters like serotonin, some consider that depression may be an inflammation response to distress. Logically, some practitioners have begun using non-steroidal anti-inflammatory drugs (NSAIDs) like aspirin: see JG Rahola, 'Somatic drugs for psychiatric diseases: aspirin or simvastatin for depression?', *Current neuropharmacology*, vol. 10, 2012, pp. 139–158.

I'm not asserting that connection is a better remedy than other ones, though that appears to be a safe conclusion. What I am asserting is that connection will give you what those other remedies are unable to. There is no aspirin that will make you belong; nor is there any salmon that will free you from shame. There is no exercise that will render you worthy, or help you to recover from betrayal.

The impact of connection is incredibly powerful. It goes beyond healing by transforming us into something greater than what we thought was possible. It moves us from receiving to giving. It promises a world of meaning, purpose and hope. Connection sets us up for freedom, for generosity, for a focus on others. Connection sets us up for multiple benefits, especially if we are connected early on in our lives.

Connection in the early years

We need connection throughout our lives, although our need for it fluctuates according to our development and our circumstances. During times of struggle or conflict, we need more of it. During times of integration, equanimity and purpose, we may need less of it. We always need it, but our need for connection ebbs and flows in the course of a lifetime. However, there is one period of life when our need for it is universal and obvious.

Our need for connection is especially important during the first few years of life. When a baby arrives in this world, its brain is only forty weeks into its long period of development. Our brains grow in small ways all through our lives, but the basic architecture will only be complete in our early to mid-20s. At birth, the right hemisphere of the brain is predominant in our functioning. The left hemisphere is also developing, but the focus of construction and functioning is in the right hemisphere.[21] The right half of the brain is concerned with the self in relation to others, with the emotions and with the body, and it seeks to put together the big picture about ourselves and our place in the world.[22]

When we arrive in the world, we are entirely dependent on others. Not yet equipped to resolve distress by ourselves, our natural disposition is to depend on carers to resolve any distress that we experience. When we are hungry, our carers feed us. When we are cold, our carers supply warmth. When we are frightened, our carers protect and reassure us. The resolution of our distress resides in the curiosity that comes with the loving care provided for us. All sensible and loving parents know the guessing game that occurs when an infant cries. They go through the checklist: Is she cold? Is he hungry? Does she need her nappy changed? Does he just need to be held? The caregivers hear and see the distress of an unmet need, and provide a solution.

Tragically, some children's dependence on carers is not met with a positive response. Lack of support, or even negative responses, distresses these children further. They have no-one to soothe them, their stress continues chronically and they have no way of regulating the powerful emotions that linger. It is for this reason that one of the most common ongoing psychological problems in people who have

---

[21] The differences between our hemispheres has been overstated and popularised for the convenience of coaches and human resource training the world over. Scepticism is warranted; however, disregard for the small but real differences between the hemispheres is unwarranted. From Roger Sperry, who first cut the bridge between the hemispheres of patients suffering epilepsy, through to Michael Gazzaniga and many other high-profile researchers who have studied brain lateralisation, the differences between the hemispheres have been scientifically documented and, frankly, the findings are intriguing. If you have time, search for 'Gazzaniga and split brain patient Joe' on YouTube. It features Alan Alda from *M*A*S*H*. You'll love it.

[22] The left hemisphere develops later in the developmental cycle. It likes to pull things apart rather than put things together. It is 'logical, linear and linguistic': see I McGilchrist, *The master and his emissary: the divided brain and the making of the western world*, Yale University Press, London, 2009.

suffered disconnection in their early years is emotional regulation difficulties.

Little children learn very simple beliefs about life. These beliefs can remain preverbal and unspoken for decades. From the treatment they receive as infants, they develop beliefs, and these beliefs will influence them indefinitely. They can be toxic or helpful, and they can remain unconscious or made conscious later in life as people reflect on their early years and what their caregiver relationships were like.

A consistently positive and nurturing response from a caregiver teaches a child that when they are near others they receive safety, connection, warmth, understanding and freedom. Proximity to others brings security. Experience forms positive beliefs about themselves and other people.

Many of us are blessed to have had conscientious and nurturing caregivers. Because of them and their actions, we are more likely to have a sense of who we are, see our own needs as legitimate, have control over our emotions, and see others as a resource to move towards. Children who have experienced this form beliefs like 'When I'm with people, that is when I'm safe.'

However, if children cannot rely on their caregivers, over time they form beliefs like 'When I'm with others, I am unsafe', 'When I'm near others I'm alone' or 'When I'm with others I get no understanding and have control taken from me.' It is no wonder that some prefer to be by themselves. For these people, proximity to others brings insecurity. For people who have learned these lessons, other people aren't potential answers for having needs met; rather, they may be reminders of neglect, or that they aren't worth time and effort.

The quality of the connection that we receive early in our lives has a long-lasting impact. Our vulnerability, and the heightened activity of our brain's right hemisphere at this time, makes us more sensitive to both connection and disconnection. If circumstances are favourable—that is, we achieve safe and loving connection in our early years and into our adolescence—we become established for a better life. If we fail to have connection in childhood and adolescence, it is harder to establish ourselves in this way. In many respects, early connection for human beings is fateful.

This brings to light a common misunderstanding about resilience. Most parents will try to teach techniques or introduce strategies to help their children bounce back from adversity and challenges. This seems very sensible, but it is often difficult to get children to use the strategies at the time when they are distressed, because it is at those times that they are rendered unable to think. None of us thinks clearly when we are upset, especially when we are young. If we really want to have resilient children, we need to love them over a long period of time. When children receive connection and understanding from an early age, they become easier to soothe, better able to soothe themselves, and, as a result, will either not require resilience techniques or will create techniques of their own.

Bessel van der Kolk, whom I mentioned earlier, highlighted how love underpins resilience by referencing a longitudinal study by Alan Sroufe entitled the *Minnesota Longitudinal Study of Risk and Adaptation*. Summarising the findings, van der Kolk stated that:

> Sroufe also learned a great deal about resilience: the capacity to bounce back from adversity. By far the most important predictor of how well subjects coped with life's inevitable disappointments was the level of security established with the primary caregiver during the first two years of life. Sroufe informally told me that he thought that resilience in adulthood could be

> predicted by how lovable the mothers rated their kids at age two.[23]

The importance of connection in the formative years (from when we are born through to the beginning of adulthood) is not being adequately realised and addressed. As a society, we are often not meeting the needs of our young people. It is sobering to learn that two-thirds of 12–13-year-olds in Australia have experienced low warmth or high levels of hostility from their parents, placing them at risk of mental health difficulties in their adult years.[24] Connection, or lack of it, in our early years not only puts us at risk of bad things, but puts us at risk of not getting the good things. We know that good cardiovascular health, good immune functioning, positive mood states and good brain functioning depends on high connection, but we haven't emphasised that happiness and success as adults also depends on high levels of connection earlier in our lives.

In 1938, a study began that still continues today. It is one of the longest running longitudinal studies we have. I mentioned this study, the Harvard Grant Study of Adult Development, earlier in this chapter when I quoted from Robert Waldinger's TED Talk. It has examined the physical and emotional wellbeing of over 200 men at Harvard in their undergraduate years. The researchers have tested and interviewed the participants every few years to monitor and record their wellbeing. George Vaillant, the director of the study for more than three decades, is still following the remaining men from the study, who are now in their 90s. Vaillant has concluded that a happy childhood, moreover a childhood saturated in love, is a source of lifelong strength and success. Loving relationships early

[23] van der Kolk, op. cit., p. 161.

[24] S Guy, G Furber, M Leach & L Segal, 'How many children in Australia are at risk of adult mental illness?', *Australian & New Zealand journal of psychiatry*, vol. 50, no. 12, 2016, pp. 1146-1160.

in life, for example, increased the likelihood of having a higher rank when a man entered the army to fight in WWII. It also increased the likelihood of a higher ceiling level income between the ages of 55–60. Love from parents was a better predictor of future happiness and proved to be a better predictor of flourishing in later life than body type, birth order or social class.

Like a newly planted sapling, we get off to a good start when we are planted in the right soil. Safety, love and connection are like sunlight, good soil and water. When all of these good nutrients are in adequate supply early, we are destined to grow big and healthy, strong, robust and full of life. Establishing strong roots early on, we develop strong limbs and stretch out and up into the sky.

As we consider this, many of us will exhale. Some will exhale out of relief because we were well cared for by loving people. Knowing that we have been cared for gives us reason to hope for our future. But some of us will exhale not as people who are relaxed, but as people who are consigned to the way we are because we weren't loved when we were young. We don't say 'Phew'; we say 'Argh'. We think, 'That ship has sailed' and that there is nothing that can be done.

I have good news. That ship has *not* sailed.

Do not be discouraged

It is quite clear from both academic and anecdotal evidence that having strong and safe connection with a caregiver sets a person up for a good life. Missing out on connection when we are young may lead to ongoing challenges.

However, it doesn't mean that all hope is lost. It is what goes right in the present that counts.

As the Harvard Grant Study continued over decades, it became evident that in spite of bad events and disconnection during the early years of some participants, many of those participants recovered and did well in their adult lives. What happened in those early years did not always determine what happened in middle and later life.

How is that? What is it that determines that one person does well, and another doesn't? Vaillant and his colleagues found that positive ongoing relationships in adult years protected these men from the impact of previously negative events. That is to say, childhood injuries do not set in stone our direction in life, because they can be overridden by present-day connectedness.

I'll give you an example.

At the age of 40, Daniel Garrick, a participant in the Harvard Grant Study, described himself as 'mediocre and without imagination'.[25] He had worked hard to get himself through university and then tried his hand at acting, but neither in the professional nor in the relational realm did he feel that he was enjoying himself or making progress. But as he got older, he became less reserved and more expressive, and as an older man he played major roles in the theatre, and remarried late in life. George Vaillant wrote:

> Since age eighty, Garrick has enjoyed the highest possible mood scores. He did give up biking at seventy-six due to multiple aches and pains; nevertheless, at eighty-six his only medicine was Viagra 'as needed'—twice a week, he boasted.[26]

Whether he became connected and that led him to take Viagra or whether he took Viagra and 'Viagra-associated' activities led him to feel more connected is a moot point. Needless to say, though, facing others and involving himself in close relationships was good for him. He had 'the highest possible mood scores' because he learned to

---

[25] GE Vaillant, *Triumphs of experience: the men of the Harvard Grant Study*, Belknap Press, Harvard University, 2012, p. 234.

[26] ibid., p. 237.

connect in his adult years. He died at the age of 96. Looking back on this man's life, George Vaillant's words ring true: 'What goes right is more important than what goes wrong.'[27]

Play. Fun. Laughter. Sharing. Some are tempted to think that our need for connection belongs only to our younger years, and that as we get older it no longer matters; but it isn't a need that only the young possess. The impact of isolation, no matter what our age, screams to us that connection is not something we can easily dismiss. We simply cannot sustain ourselves in loneliness, no matter what age we are. Michael Yapko, internationally renowned clinical psychologist and author, writes:

> The quality of your relationships affects your potential for happiness and success more than any other factor, even your level of intellect or economic status. No matter how smart you are, if you don't get along well with others, you can't enjoy the emotional and physical benefits that come from warm relationships with caring people. No matter how much money you have, you can't buy genuine love.[28]

Connectedness matters at every stage of life. Even if our early lives were marred by a shortage of connection, we are not determined by this when our present-day relationships are accepting and supportive. Relationships have the power to restore the foundational parts of our hearts, and give us a better sense of self, no matter what stage of life we are in.

---

[27] ibid.

[28] M Yapko, *Depression is contagious*, Free Press, New York, 2009, p. 25.

There is a medical centre in the suburb next to where I work called Ubuntu Medical Centre. I drive past it every day. It sits on a major road that feeds into a tunnel that takes many people into Brisbane city on their early morning commute. *Ubuntu* is a maxim of South Africans of African descent. It is a word that references a significant aspect of what it means to be human. The Reverend Bongani Finca defines *ubuntu* as: *we are what we are, because of other people.* He states:

> We don't live in isolation, we live in a community. That sense of community is what makes you who you are, and if that community becomes broken, then you yourselves become broken. And the restoration of that community, the healing of that community, cannot happen unless you contribute to the healing of it in a broader sense. Basically that is it. *Ubuntu* is that I am because of others, in relationship with others. I am not an island of myself, I am part of the community, I am part of the greater group.[29]

'I am because of others.' It is difficult to be more concise than that.

Connections make us, and disconnections break us. Human beings have the power not just to dehumanise, but to humanise. Relationships hurt but relationships heal. Whether positive or negative, others are the making of us. We are because of others. Even when we have missed out on connection in the early years, we can afford to have hope, because the things that have hurt us—people—are the same things that can lift us up. 'We are because of others' is a statement about present-day relationships just as much as it is a statement about previous relationships. Now, and into the future, other people hold the potential for positive change if we can

---

[29] Cited in CBN Gade, 'What is *ubuntu*? Different interpretations among South Africans of African descent', *South African journal of philosophy*, vol. 31, no. 3, 2012, p. 493.

engage with them in safe and loving ways. Present-day relationships are potent and hold the hope for the restoration of our hearts.

The philosopher Raymond Gaita has written about the transforming power of connection. In the early 1960s he worked for three months in a psychiatric ward with patients who had chronic psychiatric conditions. One day, a nun appeared on the ward who had a lasting impact on him. He witnessed firsthand the power of one person to humanise another. Gaita wrote:

> In her middle years only her vivacity made an impression on me until she talked to the patients. Then everything in her demeanour towards them—the way she spoke to them, her facial expressions, the inflexions of her body—contrasted with and showed up the behaviour of those noble psychiatrists. She showed that they were, despite their best efforts, condescending, as I too had been. She thereby revealed that even such patients were, as the psychiatrists and I had sincerely and generally professed, the equals of those who wanted to help them; but she also revealed that in our hearts we did not believe this ... I admired the psychiatrists for their many virtues—for their wisdom, their compassion, their courage, their capacity for self-sacrificing hard work and sometimes for their bedsides. In the nun's case, her behaviour was striking not for the virtues it expressed, or even for the good it achieved, but for its power to reveal the full humanity of those whose affliction had made their humanity invisible. Love is the name we give to such behaviour.[30]

[30] R Gaita, *After Romulus*, Text Publishing, Melbourne, 2010, p. 57.

It is worth repeating Gaita's last sentences because of the power and clarity of his words: 'her behaviour was striking [because of] its power to reveal the full humanity of those whose affliction had made their humanity invisible. Love is the name we give to such behaviour.'

The significance of this isn't small. Love is the making of us. Love humanises us and makes us real.

Ubuntu—'I am because of others'—is not only applicable in Africa. It is applicable to people everywhere: it is applicable in Russia, the United Kingdom, the United States, China and Oodnadatta (a remote town in outback Australia). It is applicable to those who are well and flourishing, as well as those afflicted by suffering. We shape and define each other. Love humanises us, and lack of love dehumanises us.

If we look out for and carefully nurture them, safe relationships have the potential to create great changes in us and in others. Our horizontal connections with other people and our vertical connection with God represent real opportunities to grow and become stronger.

In 2004, Joan Kaufman and her colleagues from Yale University gathered together 101 children. Of these 101 children, 57 were chosen because of their relational history. Those children had parents or caregivers who had abused them and/or failed to attend to their needs.

Their caregivers were at times in custody or under the influence of drugs or alcohol. The children were so badly treated by caregivers that they were removed from their homes by the state. The remaining 44 children in the study were used as a control group so that comparisons could be made.

Kaufman and her fellow researchers went on to examine those children who were genetically at risk of developing mental health difficulties. Having identified these children in *both* groups, they went on to quantify the level of depression in the children.

In one way, what Kaufman and her colleagues found is what they expected: children who were genetically at risk of depression were twice as likely to suffer from depression when they had been mistreated as those who were genetically at risk but not mistreated.

It sounds like a fait accompli for these children. If you are a sensitive person and you go through tough times, it is possible that you will end up with a mental health condition.

Fortunately, there was good news to come. And I hope this piece of information speaks to you and gives you hope.

The researchers also found that if a mistreated, genetically at-risk child had one trusted adult with whom they connected—I repeat, just *one* adult— for even as little as once per month, the impact of the abuse was only modest. The mistreated children who were supported had their level of emotional upheaval reduced to the same level that was found in the genetically vulnerable children who had never been abused, and it only took one caring adult. Just one. Once a month. That is all it took.

Hello Dr Kaufman,

I'm still a little astounded.
Can you confirm for me my reading of your paper (titled "Social Supports and serotonin transporter…")?
My reading of your paper is that the presence of positive supports (EVEN as little as ONCE A MONTH?) reduced the risk associated with maltreatment almost equivalent to the genetically at risk children who had not been maltreated?
I can't see that represented in a graph on the paper. Is there a graph?
Was it really once a month?
I do appreciate your time. Thank you so much.

Dr Jonathan Andrews MAPS FCCLP
Clinical Psychologist
Brisbane, Australia

Figure 3. Kaufman correspondence 1

I was so astounded by this finding that I wrote to Dr Kaufman. I wanted to get her reassurance that I was reading her paper correctly. I doubted that what I was reading was accurate; or, more precisely, I thought it likely that I was reading it inaccurately.

'I'm still a little astounded,' I wrote. 'Can you confirm for me my reading of your paper?'

Then I was further astounded that she wrote back. As with any good researcher, her words were considered, but the message was clear. 'That they [the sensitive children who had been maltreated] could identify one such positive resource was key, and then that they had ongoing contact was also essential.'

Hi Jonathan - Some contact with an important person definitely made a difference .. but the more contact the better. Most of the children were still in foster care at the time of the study, so contact with long standing positive supports is often limited. That they could identify one such positive resource was key, and then that they had ongoing contact was also essential. The children who could not identify any such support were most vulnerable to depression following child maltreatment.

All the best, Joan

Figure 4. Kaufman correspondence 2

The impact of one caring adult all but wiped out the mental health impact of the abuse. The wise words of psychiatrist George Vaillant again ring true: 'What goes right is more important than what goes wrong.'

Carly was (and remains) a lovely person. A petite lady in her late 20s, she always presented well. Even though she smiled and seemed ready to laugh, I got the impression that she was also slightly aloof. She worked at a university part-time and in the hospitality industry providing services for the disadvantaged. She came to me early in the new year saying that she was 'flat'. Her energy levels were low and she was finding it hard to concentrate.

At Christmas time she had gone on holidays with two other people. These two were a couple. So there she was in an exotic location, excluded. 'I felt like the third wheel,' she said. As she spoke about the holiday, she tried to hold back tears.

Sadly, the feeling remained when she came home from the holiday. She tried to keep the feeling at bay by exercising constantly, listening to music and being around others, but she couldn't shake the feeling of abandonment and not being understood. The feeling of isolation was creeping around in the background of her every experience, and she was finding it hard to stop the feeling pouring out into her daily life.

Unfortunately, feelings have a life of their own and they spring forth at times that are not of our choosing. At night she became haunted by a memory of being lost in a car park when she was a toddler. Older feelings and experiences crept forward into the present and tormented her each day. She knew that she had to face these feelings.

Towards the end of one particular session, I asked her whether anyone had ever apologised to her for what she missed out on in her childhood. She said that they hadn't. I said, 'Carly, I want to say that I'm sorry this happened to you. It was wrong that it happened. It should never have happened. I regret that you got this sort of treatment, and you didn't deserve it.'

She gave something of a chuckle then looked off to a corner of the room. I knew her well enough at this stage to ask, 'Carly, what is going on?'

'What?' she said.

'You have been telling me how isolated and abandoned you felt because others don't understand. But when I share with you what is understanding, you chuckle then switch off. What is that? What happened to our connection?'

She knew what I was getting at. She knew why I was confronting her. She was disconnecting at the very time connection was occurring. She was discarding the very solution that she dearly wanted. It wasn't her fault. She was simply living by the script that her early relationships had taught her—'people neglect people' was her core belief, so when they came near she had to freeze and flee. I couldn't let the present moment disintegrate into more of the same morass of isolation. I invited her to expand on what happened in that moment when she chuckled—what she felt, and what she thought.

We spoke about the confusion she felt when I apologised; how she knew that what I said was what she wanted, but how she found it difficult to accept and trust. She apologised, but I reminded her that even though she was being gracious, I was not at all offended and I understood that it was a habit that she had formed when people came close to her—that she became scared and couldn't trust. She said that she so dearly wanted to hold onto the words, but they seemed to slip away from her. I couldn't help but think that it was the opposite: she wanted to trust the words but *she* seemed to slip away from *them*.

I had to confront her about this, because what happens in the present must go right. What happens in the present is important. What goes right is more important than what goes wrong.

Joan Kaufman and her colleagues noted that:

> the negative sequelae associated with early stress are not inevitable. Risk for negative outcomes may be modified by both genetic and environmental factors, with the quality and availability of social supports among the most important environmental factors in promoting resiliency.[31]

[31] J Kaufman, Y Bao-Zhu, H Douglas-Palumberi, S Houshyar, D Lipschitz, JH Krystal & J Gelemter, 'Social supports and serotonin transporter gene moderate depression in maltreated children', *PNAS*, vol. 101, no. 49, 2004, pp. 17316–17321.

If I were going to help Carly bounce back from adversity, I had to keep the quality of the connection really high. We had to keep our conversations high in understanding and safety.[32]

The good news is that connection is not just for the vulnerable—it works well for everyone. It doesn't just rescue us from the impact of bad things, like it did for my patient Carly or for Daniel Garrick in the Harvard Grant Study: it enhances the good things and propels us into a flourishing state if we are already doing okay.

Professor Shelly Gable at UCLA illustrated how constructive positive connection can be. In a research experiment she showed that when we communicate good things that have happened to interested people, there is an increase in positive feelings and a sense of wellbeing that goes *above and beyond* the impact of the positive event itself.

Say, for example, your friend gets an 'A' on a test at school or university. She comes over to your house and you say, 'Wow! You killed it! Tell me all about it. Take me through it. I want to know your whole experience from beginning to end.' She senses that you are motivated to hear and you are excited for her. This is what Gable's research found: your friend's joy derived from telling you about her success will exceed the joy that she derived from achieving an 'A' in the first place.

I'm still taken aback by this research—by its simplicity and significance. There is a catch, though. The 'above and beyond' impact occurs only when we communicate with people who are keenly interested; only when the listener is *actively* and *constructively*

[32] After a couple of minutes of discussion she told me that she discarded my comments not because she didn't believe that I meant what I said, but because she found it so hard to believe what I said. She found it hard to comprehend that others would think that it wasn't all her fault. She believed from an early age that she was to blame for her isolation.

involved in the disclosure. It did not occur in the study when the listener was passively involved ('That's nice, dear'), nor did it occur when the listener was destructively involved ('Tell someone who cares'). It occurred only when the listener was positive and wanted to know about the event.

The benefits weren't just for that moment, though. When active and constructive listening occurs in family and friendships as a pattern over time, good things happen. People who do involve themselves in these sorts of exchanges in ongoing ways report higher levels of intimacy, and higher levels of satisfaction in their relationships.[33]

When genuine and interested connection is made, we are provided with the opportunity to be understood and humanised in the process. Others will only really understand when we reveal ourselves to them, but it is only possible to reveal what is on our hearts when we sense that it is safe enough to do so. When we are connected and understood, a sense of wholeness can be achieved.

Pause and review

- Connection protects us from harm, it humanises us and it sets us up for a good future.
- The impact of connection is expansive. It improves the functioning of our bodies, our brains, our mood and our behaviour.

---

[33] SL Gable, HT Reis, EA Impett & ER Asher, 'What do you do when things go right? The intrapersonal and interpersonal benefits of sharing positive events', *Journal of personality and social psychology*, vol. 87, no. 2, 2004, pp. 228–245.

- No matter what our history of connection may be, it is present-day connection that helps us. This is great news for all of us, and we can afford to have hope for the future because of it.

We have established the important and powerful role of connection in healthy growth and functioning. We now turn to the repercussions of the absence of connection and the presence of disconnection. It stands to reason that if connection is essential in our lives, then the withdrawal or reversal of it will have serious consequences.

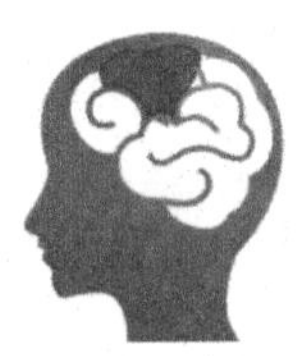

What is your connection history? How would you describe it to a friend?

Who were you connected to growing up? Who were you disconnected from? When did that occur?

Are your current connections characterised by safety and intimacy?

Who in your life is 'actively' and 'constructively' interested in you?

PART TWO

HOW RELATIONSHIPS HURT

3

Omission and commission (people hurt people)

In the 1990s there were Magic Eye pictures all over the place. Book stores and newsagents would sell them and school kids would cover their books with them. They would appear in shop windows and kids would stand like zombies staring at them waiting for a three-dimensional image to appear. Some kids would shriek because they saw something; other kids would shriek in frustration because they could not see anything. The challenge was to stare into the centre of a picture, but stare through what you initially saw, trying to find another image beyond the obvious one—to see through the superficial to something hidden.

Figure 5. Magic Eye heart image

The challenge for us is to do the same. Have a go at the image above. What do you see? Stare into the centre, as if you are looking through it. Make the flowers go a little blurry, then move the page slowly towards you and then away from you, looking for new links between different features. Keep experimenting this way until the three-dimensional image emerges. It may take a couple of minutes.

When interacting with people we need to look through the obvious as well. We need to stare through the behaviours, the thoughts, the emotions, and the physical reactions to a deeper reality. Only then will we see reality beyond the superficial. Only then will we see the heart.

The most significant thing that a psychologist brings to a counselling session isn't a tool like a new behaviour or a way of relaxing. It is the recognition of a pattern that they see before they use the tool. Psychologists are pattern finders, or pattern recognisers. This is a skill that I hope you develop a little by reading this book. The patterns that we observe are created by unseen influences that give rise to them. Unspoken motivations, inner drives and unarticulated hurts cannot be observed directly, but they can be uncovered by us when we see that there are common patterns leading to the way we interpret situations, the physical expressions of our bodies, our feelings and the ways we behave. These are the more obvious expressions of the unseen heart. By looking through the seen, the unseen becomes illuminated. In the same way as the Magic Eye picture above, we are waiting for the heart to emerge.

Many people I know are great pattern recognisers, and they aren't psychologists. They can see a pattern in someone else's behaviour and can efficiently uncover the sensitivity that has led to it. You may be one of them.

I invite you to test your skill as a potential psychologist. Let's see if you can uncover a hidden pattern. I'm going to reveal to you a series of facts that have been established by research about trauma. As each finding is disclosed, ask yourself, 'What is the pattern that is emerging? What is the hidden story?' The real story is found in the unobservable factors, and we want to link these hidden factors up with the facts that are presented to us.

Ready?

Fact 1

Natural disaster[1], such as an earthquake, impacts on vast numbers of people, but oddly the level of psychological penetration is low. That is to say, it is tough to endure the life-threatening nature of an incident such as an earthquake, but what are usually more difficult to resolve are the human issues arising from the event. For example, if you weren't considered after the event, or people ignored your plea for help or, worse still, took advantage of you when you were helpless, these issues often become harder to deal with than the actual disaster.

Fact 2

The extent of traumatic stress that people endure is at least partially a function of perceived intentionality. For example, if you fall over at school and break your ankle, the extent to which you are damaged at a psychological level is at least partly determined by your appraisal of whether or not you were deliberately pushed by another student.

Fact 3

The severity of trauma is firstly a function of dose, but secondly a function of social support following the traumatic event. Hence, when

---

[1] Tsunamis, bushfires and hurricanes belong to the realm of 'natural disasters'. They impact on vast numbers of people, are terrible to endure, and are very difficult to bounce back from. We wouldn't wish them upon anyone. Yet they do not impact on everyone uniformly. Some traumatic incidents are harder to take than others, but even in those traumas that appear catastrophic, some people appear to bounce back. What is going on? How do we make sense of disparate information in the literature? As frightening and destructive as these incidents are, trauma has to take a particular form for it to be penetrating and damaging to us at heart level. To put it bluntly, natural disasters are impersonal and tend to affect high numbers of people but have low penetration: they aren't as upsetting as personal forms of trauma.

you look at the frequency of Post-Traumatic Stress Disorder (PTSD) in New York City following 9/11, the frequency of PTSD decreases the further north you move up Manhattan Island. That is to say, the closer to the trauma you are, the more likely you are to develop PTSD. However, even if you are directly exposed to the traumatic event, the likelihood that you develop PTSD will be determined by whether or not you have a partner to go back to, whether or not you have a secure job, and whether or not you return to a safe environment where you can sleep, eat and be part of a community.[2]

Fact 4

Lastly, there is a curious difference in the occurrence of PTSD between World War II (WWII) and the Vietnam War. There was a lower incidence of PTSD in WWII veterans compared with the Vietnam veterans, but why?

Jeffrey Lieberman, former president of the American Psychiatric Association, noted:

> In World War II, America was preemptively attacked at Pearl Harbor and menaced by a genocidal maniac bent on world domination. [In that war, and in contrast to the Vietnam War,] [g]ood and evil were sharply differentiated, and American soldiers went into combat to fight a well-defined enemy with clarity of purpose.[3]

Lieberman pointed out that when trauma strikes, a sense of 'clarity and purpose' can buffer us against the distress that we endure. 'At

---

[2] CR Brewin, B Andrews & JD Valentine, 'Meta-analysis of risk factors for post-traumatic stress disorder in trauma exposed adults', *Journal of consulting and clinical psychology*, vol. 68, 2000, pp. 748–766.

[3] J Lieberman & O Ogas, *Shrinks: the untold story of psychiatry*, Weidenfeld and Nicholson, London, 2015, p. 254.

least I was doing the right thing' is a belief that helps us to endure suffering, but such moral clarity didn't exist in the Vietnam War.

Yet it was not only the moral incorrectness of that particular conflict, but what was commonly coupled with that perception that was upsetting for the veterans. Beliefs about moral incorrectness created a different reception when soldiers returned home. During and after World War II, soldiers were welcomed home as heroes because they went to fight the 'genocidal maniac bent on world domination'. This wasn't the case for veterans returning from the Vietnam War. In Australia, as in the United States, Vietnam veterans returned to large numbers of people who were vocal in their disapproval of them. For some, these returning soldiers weren't considered to be titans; they were considered to be traitors. There was no gratitude for the sacrifices that they had made or the suffering that they had endured. They saw and had to do horrific things in the name of service, but ended up in public disgrace.

Nowhere is the contrast between WWII and Vietnam veterans better captured than in the Cold Chisel song lyric 'There were no V-Day heroes in 1973'. Instead of the tickertape parades experienced by WWII veterans, the Vietnam veterans were met with indifference and, at times, contempt. This rupture in respect and compassion for returned soldiers is likely to be one of the more significant reasons for the increased incidence of PTSD in Vietnam veterans.

How did you go playing psychologist? What is the theme running through these findings? What was the pattern that you observed? What hidden reality was emerging?

Have a look and see if your conclusion is the same as mine.

The sinister thread that weaves its way through the research relates to the vulnerability we have to each other. When trauma is personal, it is very difficult for us; when it is impersonal, it is easier. What the literature on trauma adds is that even in the context of extremely challenging experiences, it is the human elements within and after these events that have the capacity to disturb us deeply at a heart level. Human beings are extraordinarily sensitive to other human beings. We can be traumatised by being exposed to the pain and anguish of others, and we can be deeply disturbed by the unsupportive or intentionally unkind reactions of others, especially when we are struggling. Poor or negative reactions from others has great power to break us down and radically undermine our hearts.

We are sensitive to both disconnection and connection at all times, though perhaps more so during times of need. When we are hurting, we look out for connection. If you are immobile after breaking a leg, it is not just medical and practical issues that need attention—you need to ask whether or not people are connected to you. If your marriage has broken up, you need to ask yourself not just about how you are coping, but about who is caring for you. If you lose your job, you need leads to help you find more work, but you also need to ask whether or not you are meeting up with people who love you. If you are under pressure at work, you need to ask yourself if you are drinking too much to alleviate stress, but you also need to ask, 'Who am I catching up with?'

The practical needs of a person in each of these situations will, of course, need to be addressed, and real care for people will always consider these needs. Food and shelter are important, but my central point is that practical solutions may not have as much impact as love and care from people with whom you feel safe.

The importance of connection is difficult to overstate. Similarly, the absence of connection is really significant. I don't mean disconnection—I mean the absence of any connection: no love, no tenderness, no rapport with others. We are wired for connection with others, so what can we expect when this is 'omitted' from your life? You would be right to guess that omission has significant psychological consequences.

Omission: the absence of connection

Mother Teresa is known worldwide for her work amongst the destitute in India, particularly around Calcutta. She was intimately aware of the devastation wrought by poverty. Early in her career, during the Bengal famine of 1943, approximately three million people lost their lives due to starvation, malnutrition and disease. No doubt this galvanised Mother Teresa's devotion to those who lived without material things. Until her death in 1997, she devoted her life to serving the impoverished.

Knowing her commitment to the poor and outcast, one of her most famous quotes seems, at least to me, to be quite unexpected. For one who was so well known for helping those who didn't have much food or shelter, we might have expected her to say, 'To be without food is terrible', or 'To be without shelter is terrible.' But that is not what she said. What Mother Teresa clearly said was:

> The moment I pick up a person who is hungry, give him a plate of rice, I've removed the hunger. But the person who is hurt, who is lonely, who feels rejected, unwanted, unloved, I think that's the much greater poverty, much greater disease, much great[er] painful situation of today … and I think a destroyer of peace and unity.[4]

Being without food or shelter didn't rate as the most terrible poverty—it was living without connection. Her words testify to the fact that to live without love can have a profoundly detrimental effect upon us. It is easy to comprehend that leaving our physical needs

[4] Permission to use this quote granted via private correspondence with the Mother Teresa of Calcutta Center, <https://motherteresa.org/copyright-information.html>.

unmet will have a negative impact on us, but the simple absence of connection may be even more terrible.

Omission occurs when no-one takes an active, loving interest in us as unique individuals. Omission is different from 'commission'. Omission is the lack of something good. Commission is the introduction of something bad. Omission of connection equates to the absence of love. When someone hasn't connected with us, it is not that we have had bad things done to us; instead, it is that we haven't had good things done for us.

Loving behaviour from others is essential for our hearts to develop, and the consequences for children who suffer omission can be particularly serious. In 2010, over 500,000 cases involving the neglect of a child were reported in the USA, accounting for 78% of all maltreatment cases reported.[5] In 2015–2016, 11,403 substantiated cases of neglect were reported in Australia. This was the second most common type of maltreatment recorded in that time period (24.9% of all substantiations).[6] The only form of maltreatment that was higher than neglect was 'emotional abuse'. In that time period, 20,339 substantiated cases of emotional abuse were reported (45% of all substantiations). Interestingly, the definition of 'emotional abuse' included 'emotional deprivation'—that is, 'omission'. So together,

[5] National Scientific Council on the Developing Child (JP Shonkoff, P Levitt et al.), *The science of neglect: the persistent absence of responsive care disrupts the developing brain* (Working Paper 12), 2012, viewed on Centre on the Developing Child Harvard University website, <https://46y5eh11fhgw3ve3ytpwxt9r-wpengine.netdna-ssl.com/wp-content/uploads/2012/05/The-Science-of-Neglect-The-Persistent-Absence-of-Responsive-Care-Disrupts-the-Developing-Brain.pdf>.

[6] Australian Institute of Family Studies, *Child abuse and neglect statistics*, Child Family Community Australia (CFCA) Resource Sheet, June 2017, viewed December 2019, <www.aifs.gov.au/cfca/publications/child-abuse-and-neglect-statistics#table3>.

neglect and omission are likely linked to 70% of all substantiated cases of child maltreatment in Australia.

Omission occurs more commonly than commission, but it is surprising to many that the level of distress and impairment caused by neglect can actually exceed the level of distress and impairment caused by the more obviously nasty forms of abuse. The authors of a 2012 Harvard University report on the developing child noted with clarity that 'deprivation or neglect can cause more harm to a young child's development than overt physical abuse'.[7]

Mother Teresa's comments ring true. It is not the absence of food or shelter that is really damaging, even though these absences are difficult. It is to be without love that is the terrible poverty. Treatment that is detached, uninterested and 'switched off' teaches children negative beliefs about themselves, life and the world. It is these beliefs that will affect their behaviour, their expectations in life, their wellbeing and their mental health. Because long-term neglectful behaviour becomes the child's 'norm', the child may not realise for many years that things have gone terribly wrong, and the road to understanding and being healed from this type of insidious, non-dramatic relational injury can be complex and long.

When we think of neglect we, understandably, think of children. Adults retain a sense of agency, so when we are neglected by others as adults, maybe we can act on it to bring about a solution. There are times, however, when even adults can't find solutions, either because our mood relegates us to dimly lit rooms, or because circumstances dictate to us our isolation. Even when the omission occurs later in life, it can still have significant impact.

On the last day of July in 2009, three Americans were hiking in Northern Iraq near the Iranian border. The three friends were

[7] National Scientific Council on the Developing Child, op. cit., p. 2.

captured by Iranian soldiers under suspicion of being American spies. One of the three, Sarah Shourd, was on a break from her teaching position in Damascus, Syria.

Sarah was arrested and put in jail. For 410 days she was in solitary confinement. She was told that it was for her own good. It didn't take long before the impact of the isolation began to make a serious impact.

> After just two months my mind began to slip. I would spend large portions of my day crouched down on all fours by a small slot in my cell door listening for any sounds that might distract me from the terror of my isolation. I suffered from insomnia, nightmares, hallucinations and emotional detachment. I often had violent panic attacks. More than once I completely lost control and began screaming and beating at the walls of my cell until my knuckles bled. I started to realise that there was a slow disintegration of my personality, my sense of who I was … You are existing in this kind of vacuum.[8]

Living without others is torturous. The absence of connection fractured Sarah deeply. She said that she 'existed in a vacuum' but that is almost understating things. It seems more accurate to say that she unravelled and almost *ceased* to exist in that vacuum. Extreme isolation leads people down a rabbit hole towards what looks like an inevitable fate of psychological decomposition.

Terry A. Kupers is a Professor at The Wright Institute and author of a book entitled *Prison Madness: The Mental Health Crisis Behind Bars and What We Must Do About It.* There are an estimated

---

[8] S Shourd, *The Iranian Government locked me in solitary confinement for 410 days*, American Civil Liberties Union, 17 July 2013, viewed August 2016, <https://www.aclu.org/blog/speakeasy/iranian-government-locked-me-solitary-confinement-410-days-today-my-thoughts-are?redirect=blog/prisoners-rights/iranian-government-locked-me-solitary-confinement-410-days-today-my-thoughts>.

80,000 people in solitary confinement in the United States today, representing only 2–8% of the total population of prisoners. Kupers reported in an article that 'on average, 50% of US prisoner suicides happen among [those] prisoners who are in solitary confinement'.[9]

Ominously, in Australia, many states are 'unable to provide figures' regarding the number of people who are in what we call 'segregated custody' because figures 'constantly fluctuate'.[10] What feels ominous to me is that not only are we unable to be transparent about those things, but we are also unable to label what we are doing. Instead of saying that we put the prisoner in 'solitary confinement', we resort to using a euphemism to help ease our own discomfort—we call it 'segregated custody'.

It may be the case that unruly prisoners are put in 'segregated custody' away from other prisoners because they display unsafe behaviour and have pre-existing mental health problems. So there is a case to be made that these prisoners were already unstable before they went into solitary confinement. However, there is no getting away from the fact that solitary confinement leads even healthy people down a pathway of disintegration, where suicide appears to be a solution to the unbearable loneliness.

Shourd described her experience of solitary confinement as if it were leading to an inevitable fate:

> The only thing left to do is go crazy —just sit and talk to the walls … I catch myself [talking to the walls] every now and again. It's starting to become a habit … Sometimes I go crazy and can't even control my anger anymore … so it is frustrating and I just lose it. Screaming, throwing stuff around … I feel like I

[9] TA Kupers, *Cruel and unusual treatment of WikiLeaks suspect*, CNN, 16 March 2011, viewed September 2016, <http://edition.cnn.com/2011/OPINION/03/16/kupers.bradley.manning.prison/index.html>.

[10] G McKeon, *Life on the inside: how solitary confinement affects mental health*, ABC News, 8 October 2014, viewed September 2016, <http://www.abc.net.au/news/2014-10-08/solitary-confinement-mental-health/5789062>.

> am alone, like no one cares about me—sometimes I feel like, why am I even living?[11]

The monstrous consequences for omission are evident in this quote: 'I feel like I'm alone … no one cares …' You can see how the isolation is tied intimately to its consequences. She doesn't just say, 'I feel like I'm alone' and that is it; she quickly adds, 'no one cares'. Unfortunately, the damage does not stop there.

Like a cup overflowing, the damage spills from 'others don't care' into other areas of her heart. When we are alone, we can often feel uncared for and this impacts on our sense of identity: Shourd said 'I felt completely lost … There was a disintegration of my personality, my sense of who I was.' The damage in the 'direction' sector of her heart has spilt over into the young woman's sense of hope and her sense of future: 'Why am I even living?' she asks. As illustrated in Figure 1 in Chapter 1, when the basement of the heart is fractured, then the other components of the heart become affected. In the example of Shourd above, we can see how omission steals something from us that we would have otherwise felt if we were loved. Lack of warmth prevents the other sectors of our heart being filled up: our sense of direction is lost and we lose a sense of hope.

If the integration of a human personality is brought about by connected people, then disintegration is the breaking down of that personality because of the absence of those relationships. People cannot live in vacuums—they disintegrate and decompose in them.

It is not enough just to have or be in relationships. As we have discussed, the sorts of connections we need to have are those

[11] Human Rights Watch and the American Civil Liberties Union, *Growing up locked down*, 2012, available at <https://www.hrw.org/sites/default/files/reports/us1012ForUpload.pdf>.

brought about by active and constructive, safe and dependable people.

Some time ago, the English paediatrician Donald Winnicott highlighted that the development of a human being depends on the child's mother being able to 'mirror' her child.[12] Effective child-rearing requires, as mentioned previously, that the mother or father give form to the child's wishes and needs by organising them for the infant. It is through the attunement and organisation processes of the parent or guardian that a child learns about what they want and why they are distressed. The child cries, the mother begins her checklist. Is the child hungry? Is the child tired? The emotion rises up, is heard and considered, then responded to. Without the child knowing, the caring mother models to the small child how to care. The mirroring process is important in the remedy of loneliness.

Loneliness is a perception about the quality of our relationships. Loneliness cannot be understood by considering objective markers—like how many times you played with others this week. Indeed, it is common for people to be in relationships and still feel lonely. Loneliness is the feeling or sense of being isolated, or not being part of relationships. When our experience is not understood and 'mirrored' back to us, the quality of our relationships suffers.

Loneliness is, unfortunately, all too common. In one nationally representative survey of over 3000 people in the United States, over one-third of respondents who were over the age of 45 reported feeling lonely. This proportion was larger than it was for younger age groups (below 45), but also larger than it was for older people (25% of those who were 70 or over reported feeling lonely).[13] This is a huge number

---

[12] DW Winnicott, *The maturational processes and the facilitating environment: studies in the theory of emotional development*, International Universities Press, 1965, cited in L Cozolino, *The neuroscience of psychotherapy: building and rebuilding the human brain*, WW Norton & Co, New York, 2002.

[13] American Association of Retired Persons, *Loneliness among older adults: a national survey of adults 45+*, September 2010, viewed November 2019, <https://assets.aarp.org/rgcenter/general/loneliness_2010.pdf>.

of people, and only some of those people who reported being lonely actually lived alone! It is a cold and tragic truth that a large number of lonely people are actually either married or living with others.[14]

Australia also has large numbers of people who report being lonely. According to a 2009 paper, 35% of Australian men and 29% of Australian women report that loneliness is a significant issue in their lives.[15] The pattern in Australia is similar to the United States: in our middle years, we reach a low point of social support, but generally this improves as we get older. This is the pattern for both men and women, though it appears that men might be especially at risk during that time and their loneliness decreases more steadily as they age.

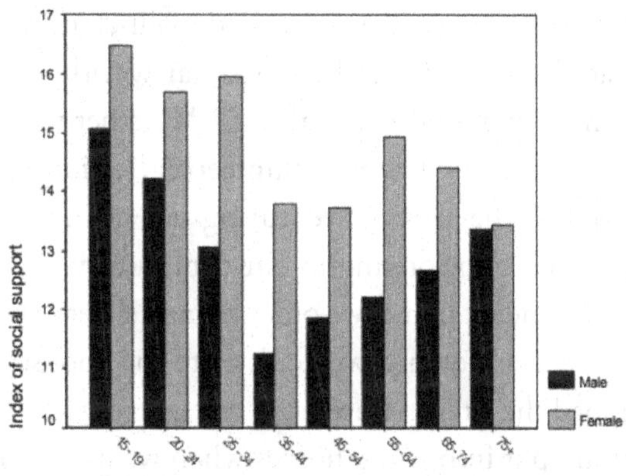

Figure 6. Personal support and friendship by sex and age among people aged 15 to 75+ [16]

[14] CM Perissionotto, IS Cenzer & KE Covinsky, 'Loneliness in older persons: a predictor of functional decline and death', *Archives of internal medicine*, vol. 172, no. 14, 2012, pp. 1078–1084.

[15] A Franklin & B Tranter, *Housing, loneliness and health* (Final Report No. 164), Australian Housing and Urban Research Institute, Melbourne, 2011.

[16] M Flood, *Mapping loneliness in Australia* (Discussion Paper No. 76), The Australia Institute, Manuka, 2005, viewed May 2019, available at <https://www.eurekastreet.com.au/Uploads/File/611/15mappinglonelinessPDF.pdf>.

Oddly, loneliness being at its worst in our middle years is not universal. While loneliness is a problem in many countries, the European pattern may be the opposite to that in Australia and the United States. In Europe there are higher levels of loneliness among adolescents and older people compared to those in middle age. It appears safe to say that the pattern of loneliness across the life span varies according to country and/or culture.[17]

Many Christian people see that the church has a role here in connecting people, and that the loss of faith may be robbing our community of the opportunity to be better integrated socially and spiritually. This may be true, but more broadly what we are seeing is a loss of trust in community groups as the provider of such things.

Andrew Leigh, the academic turned politician, has cogently shown that at the same time that personal wealth has grown, a sense of community has been shrinking.[18] Whether it be decreased interest in Scouts, Lions Clubs, volunteering, unions or sporting clubs, we have lost the sense of venturing out of the family home and finding a sense of belonging to our community. We download videos on the internet at home, we order home delivery and never get to know the restaurant owner, we don't go to the bookstore because we can download the latest release from Amazon onto a Kindle. Our grandparents are put in nursing homes when we used to have them with us at home. We've run out of time to speak to our neighbours because we spend too much time at work.

The overall picture in our society is one of growing disengagement from one another. If you add to the picture that, on average, smartphone users pick up their phones 39 times per day, and use their smartphones for, on average, just under three hours a day[19], we are looking like very isolated people indeed. Unlike

---

[17] K Yang & C Victor, 'Age and loneliness in 25 European nations', *Ageing and society*, vol. 31, no. 8, 2011, pp. 1368–88.

[18] A Leigh, *Disconnected*, University of New South Wales Press, Sydney, 2011.

[19] A Alter, *Irresistible: why we can't stop checking, scrolling, clicking and watching*, Penguin, London, 2017.

our grandparents, we are less involved in the community, more engrossed in technology, and as a result we are more and more prone to loneliness. Electronic connection via social media simply doesn't cut it. Adolescents these days are connected more electronically, and even though they're 'more tolerant and less rebellious' they're also 'less happy and completely unprepared for the real world'.[20]

It is not technology per se, however, that is the problem. It is what technology takes us away from that is the problem. This is stated clearly by Professor Jonathan Haidt from New York University: '... time spent using electronic devices was not generally harmful for highly sociable kids'.[21] But if technology stops us from being sociable, then we are in trouble. In light of the threat that technology poses, it leads us naturally to one obvious question.

What can we do about being lonely?

There are many strategies that can help to reduce loneliness. I'm going to suggest that we start with a few very simple strategies: put down the phone, look someone in the eye, find a reason to smile and listen for soothing tones.

Simply looking each other in the eye can make a big difference. Failure to make eye contact, or perhaps, worse still, failing to look with interest into someone's eyes, diminishes our sense of connectedness. When there is no eye contact or when there is no interest shown in the eyes of the person who gazes at us, we feel like we have been 'looked through'. The Germans have a phrase for this—*wie Luft*

---

[20] This is a quote from the superbly titled book by JM Twenge, *iGen: why today's super-connected kids are growing up less rebellious, more tolerant, less happy—and completely unprepared for adulthood—and what that means for the rest of us*, Atria Books, New York, 2017.

[21] G Lukianoff & J Haidt, *The coddling of the American mind: how good intentions and bad ideas are setting up a generation for failure*, Allen Lane, USA, 2018, p. 153.

behandeln—which translates as 'looked at as though air'. When we are looked at in this sort of way, it can be quite hurtful. Researchers experimented with this on students at a university. They had a researcher gaze through students when they passed them on the campus. When they interviewed the students after the event, the students said it left them feeling like they didn't belong and gave them a feeling of being ostracised.[22]

So we need to be with someone who is safe and wants not to look through us, but to make eye contact with us.[23] Yet we also need to respond in different ways. One crucial way is to use the opportunity to smile. The reason for this is that using our facial muscles in this way immediately enhances our emotional responsiveness to positive things.

For example, in one experiment, university students were asked to rate, on a ten-point rating scale, a selection of Gary Larson's *The Far Side* cartoons.[24] Participants in the study were allocated to one of three groups: each participant would either hold a pen in their mouth with their lips, hold a pen in their mouth with their teeth and not their lips, or hold a pen in their non-dominant hand. The key to understanding the experiment is to observe how the facial muscles mimic a smile when the participants were holding the pen between their teeth without their lips touching the pen. Contrasted to this was the group who were asked to hold a pen in their mouths with only their lips. All of the muscles that would normally be used to hold a smile in place were deactivated in this group. You might want to give it a try yourself now if you are finding it hard to imagine this experiment!

---

[22] ED Wesselmann, RD Cardoso, S Slater & DD Williams, 'To be looked at as though air: civil attention matters', *Psychological sciences*, vol. 23, no. 2, 2012, pp. 166–168.

[23] You do not have to maintain constant eye contact. I give a simple rule to people: when you are talking, you don't have to maintain eye contact all of the time; when you're listening, you probably do.

[24] F Strack, LL Martin & S Stepper, 'Inhibiting and facilitating conditions of the human smile: a nonobtrusive test of the facial feedback hypothesis', *Journal of personality and social psychology*, vol. 54, no. 5, 1988, pp. 768–777.

  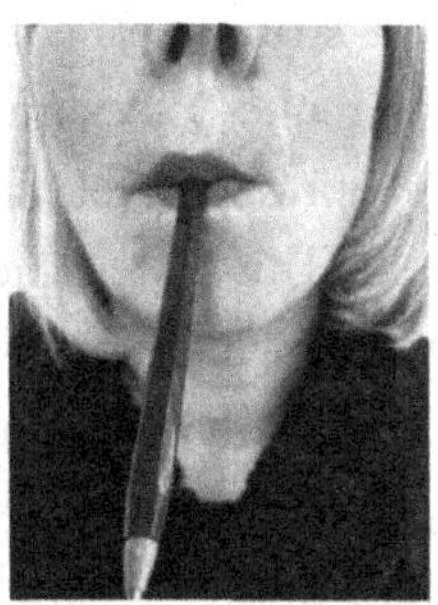

Figure 7. Inhibiting and facilitating conditions of the human smile

Upon completing a variety of tasks, the participants in each group were asked to rate the selection of cartoons from '0' (not at all funny) to '9' (very funny). What they found was that cartoons were rated least funny by the group that had their smiling muscles inhibited (holding a pen in their lips) and were rated most funny for the group that had their smiling muscles facilitated (holding the pen in their teeth). The conclusion was that by smiling you're facilitating the affective (that is, emotional) aspects of positive experiences, but interestingly this has very little to do with the cognitive. That is to say, people who smile enjoy more positive feelings, and the smile leads directly to the positive feelings, not via a thought like, 'I notice that I'm smiling, that is good.'

I am hoping you will regularly put down the phone, make more eye contact and look for opportunities to smile. However, moving closer to someone else can create alarm and the body will often make us aware that we are in danger. So we are going to need to do something extra. Learning to exhale a little longer on each breath will be helpful[25], tensing up and then letting go of physical tension will be constructive, but I'm also going to ask you to listen out for the sounds of empathy—the same sounds that you would have heard

---

[25] Singing or playing a wind instrument are great ways of exhaling in slower, more controlled ways.

from a caring mother when you were young, or the same sounds *you* might make, for example, when playing with a dog. These tones of voice represent safety, and are crucial parts of the Social Engagement System. This system, according to Stephen Porges[26], once it fires up, competes with the mobilisation symptoms—the accelerating heart rate and shallow breathing. It also competes with the immobilisation system—the energy drop, the appetite drop, the shame and hopeless feelings that come with being stuck. Hearing caring and empathic tones of voice competes with both of these physiological systems. In short, it is hard for the body to hear empathy and feel either frightened or defeated at the same time. It will typically forsake one for the other. Either the connection will win, or either of the mobilising or immobilising systems will win.

This is where it gets exciting. Our eyes, our faces and our ears are all configured to get the best out of our relationships. There is one crucial ingredient that we must have if we are to remedy loneliness. We can only find a remedy for loneliness when the quality of the relationship is high. The bottom line is that we must try to understand, and try to be understood.

We know that loneliness involves a poverty in the quality of our relationships. The only way to improve the quality is to increase the depth of our relationships, and the only way to increase that is to ensure that all parties are connected with and understood. We cannot, and others who keep our company cannot, hope to feel connected without being truly understood.

We become lonely when we cannot see ourselves being reflected back to us in the voices of people who are close. It is the absence of understanding and connection in people around us that puts us in danger of becoming lonely. We need to see that they understand; we need to see that they 'get' us—in effect, we need to see something of our own reflection in the way that they comprehend us.

---

[26] SW Porges, *The polyvagal theory: neurophysiological foundations of emotion, attachment, communication and self-regulation*, Norton, New York, 2011.

Keen interest from a caring person is important, but their understanding depends on our willingness to disclose information about ourselves. Humans need understanding but we can't hope to be understood without being prepared to reveal the truth about ourselves. Lack of sharing is the death knell of intimacy. This absence injury—this omission of love—is responsible for making so many sad, and is our responsibility to fix. To be understood, we need to share and—this is the key—we need to see that what we have shared is clearly understood and valued.

We need to be motivated to remedy the loneliness, but we and others need to have the right attitude: the truth that you share will primarily be established by you. We need to be understood, and given that we are the ones with the greater level of access to our personal thoughts, hopes, intuitions, images, memories, fears and feelings, we will be the ones to reveal them. We will be the ones who get to establish the truth about ourselves, and to do that we'll need to be around someone who asks questions and listens. We are the source of information. We are the guide. Ours is the story that needs to be told, and it can only be told by us. Caring others may help in the assembly of this information, but it is almost impossible to do without us. To do this better, or to help others to do this better, we will look at some ways we might go about this in Chapter 8, 'Connection with self'.

Milan Kundera wrote a novel entitled *Ignorance* about two Czech citizens, a man and a woman, who emigrate to avoid communist occupation.[27] Josef moves to Denmark and Irena goes to France. When the communists leave their homeland, they both return to the Czech Republic and are reunited. They talk of what it is like to be back with friends and family after a 20-year absence.

[27] M Kundera, *Ignorance*, Harper Collins, USA, 2003.

Irena says to Josef:

> 'The worst thing is, they [her friends and family] kept talking to me about things and people I knew nothing about. They refused to see that after all this time, their world has evaporated from my head. They thought with all my memory blanks I was trying to make myself interesting. To stand out. It was a very strange conversation: I'd forgotten who they had been; they weren't interested in who I'd become. Can you believe that not one person here has ever asked me a single question about my life abroad? Not one single question! Never!'
>
> …
>
> 'And what about in France?' he says. 'Do your friends there ask you any questions?'
>
> She is about to say yes, but then she thinks again; she wants to be precise, and she speaks slowly: 'No, of course not! But when people spend a lot of time together, they assume they know each other. They don't ask themselves any questions and they don't worry about it. They're not interested in each other, but it's completely innocent. They don't realize it.'
>
> 'That's true. It's only when you come back to the country after a long absence that you notice the obvious: people aren't interested in one another, it's normal.'
>
> 'Yes, it's normal.'

This story illustrates an experience that a lot of us share. We are accustomed to being around each other without really taking an interest in each other. It is, tragically, normal. There is something all too familiar about this in the lives of people who suffer from omission. Others simply aren't interested in seeking us out or hearing about our experience.

Kundera's story continues with Josef saying:

> 'But I had something else in mind. Not about you, or about your life—not you as a person. I was thinking about your experience. About what you'd seen, what had happened to you. Your French friends couldn't have any conception of that.'
>
> 'Oh the French, you know—they have no need for experience. With them, judgments precede experience. When we got there, they didn't need any information from us. They were already thoroughly informed that Stalinism is an evil and emigration is a tragedy. They weren't interested in what we thought, they were interested in us as living proof of what they thought. So they were generous to us and proud of it. When Communism collapsed all of a sudden, they looked hard at me, an investigator's look. And after that something soured. I didn't behave the way they expected.'
>
> She drinks a little wine, then: 'They had really done a lot for me. They saw me as the embodiment of an emigre's suffering. Then the time came for me to confirm that suffering by my joyous return to the homeland. And that confirmation didn't happen. They felt duped. And so did I, because up till then I'd thought they loved me not for my suffering but for myself.'[28]

---

[28] ibid., p. 167.

Indifferent, self-assured people don't need our help for them to comprehend us. They already comprehend us! 'They have no need for experience. With them, judgments precede experience.' There is no new information for them. They already have the information, and they already have it organised. But is it accurate? Do they actually have the information, or do they just think they have the information? How can there be love when the truth is so distorted? How can there be love when we aren't the source of the truth?

Passive interest is simply not enough to help us grow. Only in the context of 'active and constructive' relationships can we establish real intimacy and a sense of being valued by others. In these relationships, we get to tell our story, and to convey our experience. It is the safe and motivated curiosity of the other person that establishes a rapport of real substance. That sort of relationship is the birth of real love and the death of our loneliness. It is the gestation of a life well lived, and food for our hearts.

As I recall this Kundera story, I find myself wondering what I would say to Josef and Irena if they came to therapy. Of course I would want to connect with them and find a way to say that I regret that others haven't shown an interest in their personal story. At some point, though, after they felt heard and respected, I would want to say that whenever we feel lonely we have to take the initiative to be known. It is not their fault that others haven't shown an interest, but the solution will remain with them nonetheless.

Sometimes people are left with assumptions and there is no real closeness because we haven't taken the risk of sharing things about ourselves. It is true that some people aren't interested, but it is also true that others are only aloof because we haven't made ourselves properly known to them. We need to ask other people about their experiences, then we need to ask whether we can share our own experiences. Josef and Irena did just that. They found each other, they asked questions and they opened up. In the end, I would want to affirm them for doing the very thing they needed to do to overcome the isolation that they felt. They had to find an interested other and share what life had been like for them.

Who actually connects with you?

Do you have a variety of connections, or just one? How much time do you spend with them?

How frequently do you connect with them?

When you talk, do they listen? When you talk, do they keep eye contact? Or, when you talk, do they speak and not use eye contact?

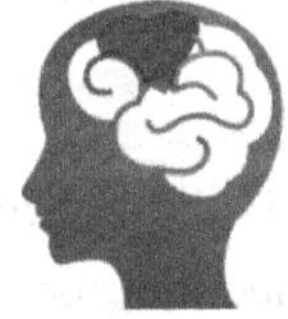

How would you rate the quality of your connections out of 10? Are they interested in you? Are they interested in connecting and understanding your lived experience?

Who in your life lets you establish the truth about yourself?

Do the people you are with let you establish what is true about you, or does their judgement seem established prior to them being told your experiences?

If in answering these questions it has occurred to you that you have strong connections, then be encouraged and thankful to the people around you who provide you with good quality relationships. Go and tell them that you really value them, and how much you appreciate your connection with them. Then go and be to others what others have been to you. Be a connector, put down your phone, look others in the eye and commit yourself to understanding the experience of other people by asking them questions. You will be a blessing to others.

However, if by answering these questions you have discovered that your connections are not that good, then there is something for you to do. First, you will need to determine the potential for the relationships to change. We will expand on this idea in Chapter 7 when we discuss matching 'safety' with 'proximity'. If there is the potential for change, I have outlined in that chapter a sequence of tasks that will help you to remedy those connections to make them beneficial for you. That section is entitled 'Increasing safety to match proximity'.

We have now sketched out the contours of what it is like when there is an absence of connection. The absence of connection, most commonly referred to as loneliness, is a terrible poverty and one that needs to be taken seriously when we suffer from it. But unfortunately, omission is not the only form of connection injury.

'Commission' refers to the intrusion of something bad into our lives. It too is terrible, and can affect us deeply at a heart level.

Commission: the presence of disconnection

Commission is the intrusion of something bad into the life of a person. While there is only one class of omission, there are two main types of commission: sexual and physical abuse. More subtle forms of commission can also occur such as verbal, emotional and mental abuse, though sexual and physical abuse are usually more easily detected by the sufferer and as a result they are more widely recognised as serious problems.

Commission is easier to track than omission in someone's history because the events are so horribly abrupt. Commission is the manifestation of a bad thing. Neglect, or omission, is the omitting of good things. Commission can be sudden, horrible and obvious. Omission is typically none of those things. As a result, when you ask someone who has suffered neglect, 'When did this omission happen?' they say something vague like, 'I don't know, it happened all the time, I thought it was normal, like it was just life.' However, when you ask someone who has been abused in the way we're now talking about, they can often, though not always because of the emotional intensity, tell you the date, their age, where they were and how they felt.

Childhood Sexual Abuse (CSA) is not uncommon. In fact, it is rife. A national survey involving both men and women revealed that one-third of women and one-sixth of men report a history of CSA.[29] A global meta-analysis of CSA prevalence found that between 164 and 197 (as high as 20%) of every thousand girls, and between 66 and 88 (as high as 9%) of every thousand boys report that they have endured this abuse.[30] The consequences of this can be, but are not always, devastating. CSA has been strongly linked with depression, drug and alcohol problems and eating disorders in women later in life, and anxiety-related disorders in men later in life.

---

[29] JM Najman, MP Dunne, DM Purdie, FM Boyle & PD Coxeter, 'Sexual abuse in childhood and sexual dysfunction in adulthood: an Australian population based study', *Archives of sexual behaviour*, vol. 34, 2005, pp. 517–526.

[30] M Stoltenborgh, MH van Ijzendoorn, EM Euser & MJ Bakermans-Kranenburg, 'A global perspective on child sexual abuse: meta-analysis of prevalence around the world', *Child maltreatment*, vol. 16, no. 2, 2011, pp. 79–101.

Its impact is wide-ranging, having 'adverse mental health, social, sexual, interpersonal and behavioural, as well as physical health consequences'.[31]

Physical abuse is less common than CSA. It occurs in the lives of approximately 20% of both boys and girls.[32] The consequences of abuse can be tremendous and lasting. In one study, the victims of childhood bullying showed increased use of mental health facilities over five decades.[33] As startling as this finding is, it is also revealing. CSA seems to contribute to mental health problems all by itself, whereas the contribution that physical abuse makes to mental health problems may depend on the broader context of the abuse. Researchers from the university of Otago found that once they controlled for 'social, family, and individual factors', the link between physical abuse and mental health consequences almost vanished.[34] This suggests that, while it is horrible, it may only have lasting consequences if it occurs in the broader context of bullying and or neglect.

Statistics show that both physical and sexual abuse can continue into adult years. Adult sexual abuse is reported by 22% of women

[31] J Cashmore & R Shackel, *The long-term effects of child sexual abuse* (CFCA Paper No. 11), Australian Institute of Family Studies, January 2013, available at <https://aifs.gov.au/cfca/publications/long-term-effects-child-sexual-abuse>.

[32] J Briere & DM Elliot, 'Prevalence and symptomatic sequelae of self reported childhood physical and sexual abuse in a general population sample of men and women', *Child abuse and neglect*, vol. 27, 2003, pp. 1205–1222.

[33] S Evans-Lacko, R Takizawa, N Brimblecombe, D King, M Knapp, B Maughan & L Arseneault, 'Childhood bullying victimization is associated with use of mental health services over five decades: a longitudinal nationally representative cohort study', *Psychological medicine*, vol. 47, no. 1, 2017, pp. 127–135.

[34] DM Fergusson, JM Boden & LJ Horwood, 'Exposure to childhood sexual and physical abuse and adjustment in early adulthood', *Child abuse and neglect*, vol. 32, no. 6, 2008, pp. 607–619.

and 3.8% of men[35], and in one large survey, 11.6% of respondents reported incidents of physical violence in their domestic situations.[36] Among those who are abused as adults, a history of childhood sexual and physical abuse is common. Sadly, abuse in younger years seems to place us at risk of abuse when we are older.

Sexual and physical abuse are the more obvious examples of nasty intrusive disconnections, but there are, as mentioned, less obvious abuses. Emotional abuse is understood to include verbal abuse, but is broader. It includes any controlling, undermining, manipulating, isolating, threatening or insulting behaviour. The Australian Bureau of Statistics reported that 'women were more likely to have experienced emotional abuse by a partner than men, with one in four (25%) women and one in seven (14%) men having experienced emotional abuse by a partner since the age of 15'.[37]

In other words, one-third of women and one-fifth of men in our communities, congregations, sporting clubs and workplaces have been exposed to events that can damage and traumatise. Every day we are meeting with someone who has gone through relational trauma. We just don't always know it.

The trouble is that both of these broad types of trauma—omission and commission—mingle. Too many who have suffered commission were already suffering from omission. This also works the other way. A lot of people who have been abused have also become neglected because they have been impacted in such a profound way that they have withdrawn from others. We render ourselves lonely

---

[35] DM Elliott, SM Doris & J Briere, 'Adult sexual assault: prevalence, symptomatology, and sex differences in the general population', *Journal of traumatic stress*, vol. 17, no. 3, 2004, pp. 203–211.

[36] MA Straus & RJ Gelles, *Physical violence in American families: risk factors and adaptation to violence in 8145 families*, Transaction, New Brunswick, 1990.

[37] Australian Bureau of Statistics, *Personal safety survey, 2012*, viewed November 2019, <http://www.abs.gov.au/ausstats/abs@.nsf/Lookup/4102.0main+features602014#DATA>.

because heart-level injuries, such as betrayal, worthlessness, shame or alienation, make us believe that others couldn't love us if they truly knew us. The heart has been broken, but we keep it a secret, and the quality of our relationships suffers because of it.

But try as we might, it is not as if we can sit in silence with a broken heart. It is not as if we can cordon off our hurts. Withdrawal and silence won't cut it as a remedy, because like it or not, the consequences of abuse radiate outwards from the heart into all areas of human functioning.

The effects of omission and commission on our functioning

Omission and commission cause heart-level injuries, as we will explore further shortly, but the damage that abuse causes isn't restricted to the heart. Just as connection has positive impacts, disconnection can have negative impacts in a variety of ways. It can impact minds, bodies, mood, behaviour, our relationships and our spiritual life:

- Abuse impacts on the mind, causing concentration and memory difficulties, increased vigilance, dissociation (ranging from a mild feeling of estrangement right up to the point of not knowing who or where we are), flashbacks during the day or nightmares during the night, and an inability to recall important aspects of the traumatic event.
- Abuse impacts on the physical body, resulting in an increased startle response, sleep disturbance, and physical reactivity including sweaty skin, racing heart rate and hyperventilation. Victims not only have to endure negative physical symptoms, but may be at risk of developing a range of medical problems. Exposure to relational abuse appears to be a risk factor for a variety of cardiovascular,

gastrointestinal, endocrinological and musculoskeletal system problems.[38]

- Abuse impacts on mood, causing anxiety, mood instability, a feeling of numbness or an inability to enjoy positive emotions like love. There is also an increased risk of developing additional psychiatric problems such as major depression.
- Abuse impacts on behaviour. We avoid people and places that act as reminders. When the abuse is severe, there is an increased risk of self-harm and addictions, particularly drug and alcohol abuse and/or dependence. Dissociative disorders might cause us to wander off in a so-called 'fugue state', and there can be an increased risk of suicide.
- Abuse impacts on our relationships. Feelings of estrangement from others can develop and a sense of estrangement can lead to isolation which increases the risk of being hurt again. Unfortunately, the abuse doesn't need to be particularly severe for this to occur. Shame stops us from telling people things about ourselves. We don't want to be with others because we don't want to be known, lest they judge us and make us feel worse.
- The same dynamic occurs spiritually. Relational abuse can undermine our belief that God is on our side. After all, how could a so-called 'good God' let horrible things happen? Belief in God proves to be difficult to sustain as symptoms of relational trauma often include a sense of meaninglessness, emotional numbness and a creeping belief that life is futile.

---

[38] MJ Friedman & B McEwen, 'PTSD, health and allostatic load?' in PP Schnurr & BL Green (eds), *Trauma and health: physical health consequences of exposure to extreme stress*, American Psychological Association, Washington, 2004, pp. 157-188.

Problems with our minds, bodies, moods, behaviour, and human and spiritual relationships all tell of a deeper hurt. They tell us that our hearts have been breaking.

Omission and commission impact all sectors of the heart

The significance of compromised connection can be devastating on all areas of the heart. It profoundly impacts the domain of connection, and we will devote the whole of the next chapter to the nature of this impact, but its impact is not restricted to just that domain. What I wish to do, briefly, is to 'zoom out' like a lens on a camera and capture a broader picture of the heart before we focus on connection injuries specifically. Omission and commission impact on all three domains of the heart depicted in Figure 1 in Chapter 1:

- **Connection injuries:** feeling betrayed, feeling worthless, feelings of shame or feelings of not belonging. Additionally, we notice the inability to connect with ourselves, inability to connect with others, and a sense of loneliness and being adrift.
- **Direction injuries (or identity injuries):** a sense of being lost, and a suite of labels that indicate an extremely negative self-image: 'I am a failure'; 'I am an idiot'; 'I am a dirty person'; 'I am a pathetic person'; 'I am a weak person'.
- **Choice injuries (or sensing that life is out of control):** despair and hopelessness, a sense of everything being beyond control, feeling powerless, ongoing stress, and having insufficient choices.

Once disconnection or lack of connection with others gets to the heart, typically all of these domains are impacted. Like an infection that spreads, the domains of the heart seen in Figure 1 are impacted by relational abuse. This is why relational abuse is heartbreaking, because when the foundation of the heart cracks, all domains of the heart crack as well.

We have now examined how relational trauma can impact on the mind, body, behaviour and relationships of the person who has suffered from it. We have also examined how relational abuse can be heartbreaking—impacting on each of the three domains of the heart. To be impacted in such a diffuse way is not unusual among those who have been through relational difficulties.

Cynthia was a lovely person to meet with. Rapport was easy to establish. She was very articulate and insightful. She had a very successful career in the corporate world, and had terrific creative talents. She was remarried and had two adult sons. Unfortunately for her, interactions with her current husband were making her feel quite unsafe, and this is what brought her to see me.

She reported that when she disagreed with her partner, she would have flashbacks of being hit in the head by her mother. Disagreements with her husband brought back the same feelings of being trapped and overwhelmed. She felt small, vulnerable and very unsafe.

When Cynthia was 13 she travelled with her stepfather and brother to another town for the holidays. They were going to drop her brother off at her cousin's home. It was a two-day drive through rural New South Wales. After dropping off her brother, her stepfather sexually molested her for the first time. For the next four years she endured this abuse. She hated it. She felt deeply shamed by it. In her late teenage years, Cynthia finally manifested the courage and told her mother what happened. One can only imagine how hard it is for a young girl to talk about this, especially to a mother who used to hit her with a brush while brushing her hair. Her mother replied, in a frank way,

'Yeah, I was worried that might happen.' Not only did Cynthia endure the commission of sexual abuse, but she also endured the neglect of her mother who failed to give love, understanding and protection. She, like many people who have been through sexual abuse, found the poor response of her mother harder to deal with than the abuse itself.

With tears rolling down her face, she spoke of terrifying and confusing emotions, of a sense of guilt and its antecedent—high levels of personal responsibility. Anxiety had been her constant companion for decades since. Even as a middle-aged lady, she had trouble showering if the bathroom door wasn't locked, as when she was showering was when her stepfather would molest her. Mostly, she spoke of shame, worthlessness and a lack of safety, but she also spoke of the many symptoms that we have mentioned above: difficulty concentrating, fear of relating to her partner, avoidance and mood instability.

For the past 30 years she hadn't spoken to anyone about what had happened, and was obviously relieved at being able to unburden herself. She was thankful to me for how I showed a patient interest in her and her story. (The gratitude often expressed by such patients always seems a little misplaced to me. My patience with them is invariably eclipsed by the courage it takes to talk about difficult times that they would prefer to bury.) Cynthia's trauma could only begin to heal when she took the courageous step of sharing her story with a safe person.

The long road to acknowledging trauma

This is a common understanding about research in the field of trauma: fifty years ago we believed that 'trauma' was a common reaction to an uncommon event. We would think of big, horrible events like war. These events are uncommon. Everyone gets traumatised by those incidents—at least that is what political activists after the Vietnam War would have had us believe.

Then we learned that traumatic events weren't uncommon at all. Trauma isn't just impersonal, it is personal. Trauma is the omission and commission experienced all too commonly. Many people experience the absence of love and/or the presence of nastiness.

Then there was a discovery with which many political agitators became disappointed: a traumatic reaction, such as reliving an event, is not as common as we thought.

So we went from thinking that trauma is a common reaction to an uncommon event (an example of this might be 'everyone who comes back from war is traumatised by it') to being forced to think differently and acknowledge, because of the research on omission and commission, that 'trauma is a common reaction to a common event' (because trauma includes not just war, but also physical abuse, sexual abuse and neglect). Now it has been concluded that 'trauma is an uncommon reaction to a common event' (because while vast numbers of people have been through it, not everyone suffers because of it).

Why would that be? How is it that so many people recover?

I hope that you already have your suspicions about what the answer might be. If you don't know by now, the answer will come to you. The thing that hurts us is also the thing that can heal us.

Pause and review

- Relational trauma is a commonly experienced event, much more common than, for example, natural disasters.
- There are two types of relational abuse: omission and commission. Acts of omission involve the poverty of care and connection. These are the good things that are omitted from our lives. Commission refers to physical, sexual and

emotional abuse. These are the bad things that intrude into our lives.

- It isn't just the heart that is impacted by relational abuse. The mind, behaviour, emotions and body are all impacted by abuse.

Have you endured abuse by omission of connection? Did it impact on your heart? If so, how?

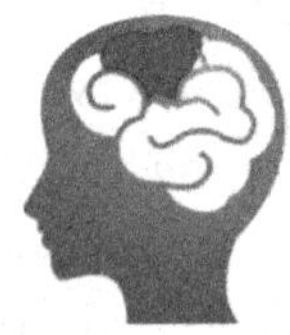

Have you endured abuse by commission? If so, when? Did it impact on your heart? If so, how?

What might be, or what have been, the pros and cons of sharing with others the impact that these experiences have had on you?

If you have not endured either form of abuse, how might you provide other people with safety to help them to share if they want to?

In this chapter we have examined the types of relational abuses: omission (neglect) and commission (physical and sexual). In the next chapter we will focus on the nature of the consequences for people who have been through such abuses. Specifically, the next chapter will focus on the injuries that belong to that foundational level of the heart.

It is to this area of the heart that we now turn our attention. I have called these injuries 'connection injuries' and there are four of them: betrayal, worthlessness, shame and alienation.

4

The four 'connection injuries'

When connection is established in positive ways through nurturing relationships, we see two essential consequences. They are:

- an ability to **trust**
- a steady, balanced sense of self-value or **self-esteem**.

Additionally, there are two further connection consequences that we see, but because these require something in addition to connection, I refer to them as 'connection-related'. They are:

- a sense of being **honoured** by others
- a sense of **belonging** with others.

All four consequences are the precious outcomes of being actively loved, cared for, supported and protected. But sadly, each of these positive functions has a flip side—a default injury that develops in the context of omission and/or commission.

In this chapter we will focus on all four of these connection benefits, but also on how each of these positive outcomes is reversed by disconnection. All four positive consequences and all four negative consequences share the same origin, often co-occur, and have a clear link with relational harmony or relational distress.

The four consequences of connection, together with their four associated 'connection injuries', are:

1. trust and **betrayal**
2. self-esteem and **worthlessness**
3. honour and **shame**
4. belonging and **alienation**.

1. Trust and betrayal

What is trust?

Trust is the faith that we put in people to do what we expect of them. It is the resignation of one's self to another person.

We all begin our lives in a place of total trust. I can't think of anyone who would contest that point. We are born unable to help ourselves and we have no choice but to depend on those around us to provide the care that we need.

Our dependence on caregivers when we are young may well be an uncontested point; however, not all of us consciously recognise that, for the rest of our lives, all of our meaningful relationships will also involve trust. Working relationships, friendships, and collaborations at church and in community groups are all underwritten by trust. Without trust, we cannot draw near to people.

This leaves us with a problem: we want to trust others, but trusting others can be difficult.

Maybe the problem is with others.

We cannot and should not trust just anyone. Not everyone is worthy of our trust. Loyalty is a virtue and not everyone exhibits it. Only those who can be relied upon to predictably deliver safe behaviours towards us are those to whom we should give our trust.

Given that not everyone is trustworthy, we put ourselves in the precarious position of being let down. The violation of trust looms as a possibility for us all. Sometimes betrayal feels like it could be around the corner, sometimes it feels remote, but the reality is that as soon as we trust, we take the risk of being betrayed in every relationship. When we think the problem is others we make sure we don't commit and always keep things to ourselves for fear that we will be betrayed. If we have been betrayed before, we remain vigilant for signs that it could happen again. 'Complex trauma survivors [that is, people who have suffered relational trauma early in their lives] have ample reason to mistrust other people', wrote Courtois and Ford.[1]

Maybe the problem is with us.

Trusting is what we want to do, but perhaps we have been too trusting. The closer we are to people, the more we want to invest in them and the more we suffer when they betray us. That is why violations of trust by those within our families or by close friends can affect us so deeply, even traumatise us. Close relationships need to be places of safety and nurture. When they aren't, the trust is broken and not only do we feel cheated by them, but we also consider ourselves stupid for trusting them in the first place. Trusting someone untrustworthy makes us cautious about future relationships. 'How could I have trusted him/her?' We admonish ourselves for reaching out. In a moment of insight we say to ourselves, 'Only those whom we trust can betray us' and we learn to tame the instinct to reach out. 'To thine own self be true,' we say. We remain aloof, and don't let others in. We swear to ourselves that we will never make ourselves vulnerable again, but we will. It is our nature.

---

[1] CA Courtois & JD Ford, *Treatment of complex trauma: a sequenced relationship-based approach*, The Guilford Press, New York, 2013 (quote from Chapter 2).

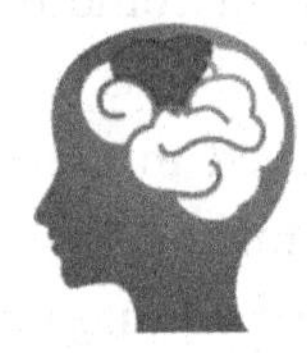

Think of some relationships that you have that you associate with feelings of trust. How would you describe those relationships?

Do you feel vulnerable or betrayed? Which relationships do you associate with these feelings?

Trusting relationships early in life shape the way we view the world later in life. Waters and Waters at State University, New York did an interesting experiment. Participants were given a list of words from which they had to develop a story. Words like 'mother', 'baby', 'play' and 'blanket' were used. The researchers found that the ways in which the participants used these words were determined by the pattern of the participants' early relationships. If their early relationships were safe and predictable, they created a story that was full of intimate interaction from a caregiver, and portrayed the baby as satisfied and happy. If their early relationships were unreliable, they told different stories. Those stories portrayed the mother as neglectful or easily distracted. They would use the word 'play' to portray what the baby did alone, independent of the mother.[2]

Connection is the preamble to trust. We can be connected with someone we meet, but that doesn't mean we trust them automatically. Connection happens automatically, and it comes with no expectations. Connection does not require us to be vulnerable to the other or ask anything that we are in need of from the other person. Connection is a binding but is also a synchrony and a spark … like being on the same wavelength. That is why people can say that they feel a connection with the ocean when they surf,

[2] HS Waters & E Waters, 'The attachment working models concept: among other things, we build script-like representations of secure base experiences', *Attachment and human development*, vol. 8, no. 3, 2006, pp. 185–197.

or the mountain when they ski. But it would be a stretch for surfers and skiers who have a connection to the outdoors to say they had an 'attachment' to the ocean and the mountain, though I concede that this is a real possibility.

What is attachment?

Attachment is the establishment of a trusting relationship with another human being. We don't readily attach to a chair even though we have been able to trust it to hold us up, but we do become attached to a caregiver because we have been able to trust them.

John Bowlby was a British psychoanalyst who conducted pioneering work with children after World War II. He made many observations of small children and noted that upon separation from their caregivers, they tended to cope in different ways depending on the nature of their attachment to their caregivers. When the child's attachment was positive, it appeared that the child felt safe to explore their surroundings. Children with good attachment were equipped with the pre-verbal understanding that a safe relationship was always within reach, and this gave them confidence to explore the world. Separation from their mums or dads was upsetting, but they were easily soothed when the mum or dad returned. After they calmed down they engaged their curiosity again and moved away from their caregivers to go and play, stretching themselves to be independent. How is it that a child is able to become secure like this?

A succinct contemporary definition of attachment is given to us by Daniel Siegel, Clinical Professor at the University of California, Los Angeles. He says, 'Human attachment can be understood as involving four S's. We need to be seen, safe, and soothed, in order to feel secure.'[3]

It is fascinating to learn what Siegel means by some of these

[3] DJ Siegel, *Brainstorm: the power and purpose of the teenage brain*, Scribe, Melbourne, 2014 (quote from Chapter 3).

words. As you would guess from our previous discussion of *wie Luft behandeln* ('looked at as though air'), being 'seen' is not merely a visual exercise, but it is a deep psychological process. It is more akin to being connected with and understood. 'Safe' is a straightforward word, meaning free from the threat of harm. 'Soothed' is also understandable—it is about the empathic reactions from an empathic caregiver. And when these three are combined, we develop a sense of security: 'I'm connected and understood, I am safe and loved; other people can be trusted.' This pattern underwrites the drive to become independent.

Professor Louis Cozolino from Pepperdine University says:

> These [secure] children ... seemed to expect their mothers would be attentive, helpful, and encouraging of their continued autonomy. It is believed that infants internalized their mother's sense of safety and comfort.[4]

Children appear to take into the world a gift from their caring mothers and/or fathers. The way they have been treated has become their own nature. It ends up creating the way they see themselves and the way they see the world. Their connection with parents leads them to put their faith in the people that they have a connection with. Pictorially, it might look like this:

[4] L Cozolino, op. cit., p. 203.

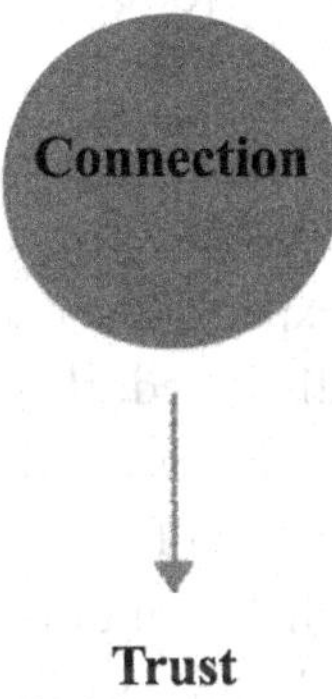

Figure 8. Connection leads to trust

How does attachment develop?

When a human being experiences repeated connection with another, they take the risk of trusting the other person. When we are younger and attachment is good, we generalise this to all people. The safe and loved child concludes that Mum and/or Dad are safe so most people are safe too. Their high dose of connection gives them the confidence to separate from their caregivers and move out into the world to live and work and play as independent adults.[5]

This is not everyone's experience. Those who had rejecting parents are more likely to internalise these experiences, and this leads to different expectations about whether or not others can be trusted.

---

[5] Some caregivers don't encourage this, so the child has a difficult time becoming independent because the caregiver has a difficult time letting go. Some caregivers give constant and good quality connection but the child has difficulty becoming independent because of other factors such as sensitivity and change of routines (caused by conditions such as Autism Spectrum Disorder). I wouldn't want to oversimplify the message: safe, warm and trusting relationships are essential elements for the growth of children who have to learn to trust their environments, but they aren't the only elements in play, and we need to be cautious when we make conclusions about why a child cannot trust their environment.

Fraley and Waller wrote in 1998:

> … the presence of a rejecting attachment figure may lead a child to develop an expectation that others are not available. This expectation may lead the child to avoid others when distressed, thereby reinforcing his or her negative expectations of others. Such a process could conceivably create a feedback loop and lead to a consolidation of beliefs that differ qualitatively from those of an individual who initially had a sensitive and responsive environment.[6]

The dynamic outlined in the quote above doesn't just apply to children when they have been 'rejected'. It applies to many forms of distorted attachment patterns.

Let's do an experiment: try changing the word 'rejecting' in the quote above to 'nasty', to 'indifferent', to 'inconsistent', or to any other representation of caregiver disconnectedness, and see if the quote above is still going to apply. Here it is again with added terms:

> … the presence of a [*nasty/indifferent/inconsistent*] attachment figure may lead a child to develop an expectation that others are not available [*in a connected way*]. This expectation may lead the child to avoid others when distressed, thereby reinforcing his or her negative expectations of others. Such a process could conceivably create a feedback loop and lead to a consolidation of beliefs that differ qualitatively from those of an individual who initially had a sensitive and responsive [*connected*] environment.

---

6 Cited in KA Brennan & JK Bosson, 'Attachment-style differences in attitudes toward and reactions to feedback from romantic partners: an exploration of the relational bases of self esteem', *Personality and social psychology bulletin*, vol. 24, no. 7, 1998, pp. 699–714 (p. 711).

It seems that whatever type of disconnected behaviour the caregiver gives, it is likely that trust will be eroded.

Did you notice the last sentence of the quote? It is crucial and worth repeating: 'Such a process creates a feedback loop and leads to a consolidation of beliefs that differ qualitatively from those of an individual who initially had a sensitive and responsive environment.' That is, people who have had negative experiences will think and act differently from those who have had positive and loving experiences.

These thoughts and actions spring from the hurt in our hearts, but they also *maintain* the hurt in our hearts. No-one has to wilfully draw out the thoughts, feelings, behaviours and physical reactions when they are hurting—they simply spring forth. The hurt person experiences physical symptoms such as an increase in heart rate and feels anxious. The person thinks, 'I need to go' and acts by withdrawing. In the short term, this may give relief, but the opportunity for support is cut off. Unfortunately, all of these experiences do not return empty-handed. They bend back and reinforce the hurt that they came from. The thoughts, feelings, actions and physical symptoms, while always understandable, are implicated in the maintenance of our suffering. The flower image seen in Figure 9 is what I use in therapy to illustrate how this works.[7] The image of the heart can be placed at the centre of the flower because it is the epicentre of psychological functioning.

---

[7] This flower is not my original creation. In Cognitive Behavioural Therapy it is often referred to as a 'vicious flower'. I have not given it that name here because my flower isn't particularly vicious. It is an understandable flower, not a vicious one. The key difference between my flower and the 'vicious flower' is that the latter often gets drawn up by other therapists with the centre of the flower containing a view or a belief. In my flower, the centre of it contains the heart. 'Everything you do flows from it', says Proverbs 4:23. The other key difference is that my flower has a stem that signifies that the flower has a past, and issues from the past can come up the stem of the flower to influence present-day functioning. The interested reader might consider reading S Moorey, 'The six cycles maintenance model: growing a "vicious flower" for depression', *Behavioural and cognitive psychotherapy*, vol. 38, 2010, pp. 173–184. Moorey is often cited for this sort of conceptualisation.

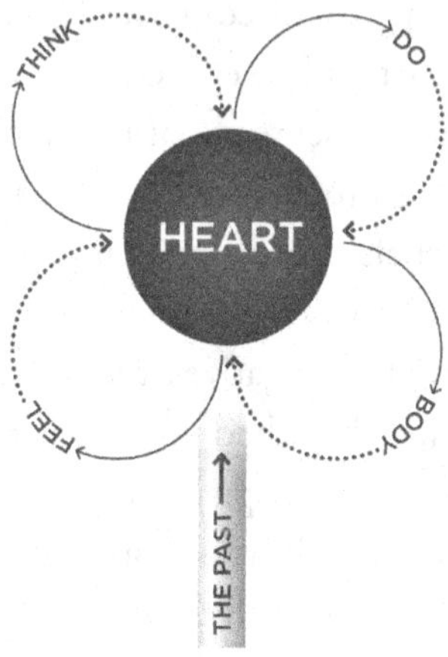

Figure 9. The 'Heart Flower'

The Heart Flower shows us that the heart has a past—a time when the flower was smaller— and what is in the past can rise up and impact the flower in the present. Changes in the heart lead to changes in mood, physical functioning, behaviour and thinking.

The Heart Flower is based on biblical wisdom. The writer of the Proverbs exhorted us to 'guard' the heart because 'everything you do flows from it'.[8] You can see that I've drawn unbroken lines that 'flow' straight out from the heart to depict that irresistible flow of energy out from it. The broken line is used to illustrate that there is always a feedback loop. Most therapies, such as Cognitive Behaviour Therapy and Mindfulness therapies, focus on trying to extinguish these feedback loops. In contrast, psychodynamic approaches focus on going down the stem of the flower into someone's history. The Heart Flower incorporates both approaches without neglecting one for the other, and it links the past with the present which is vital when we speak of trust and attachment.

People who have been blessed by connected parenting are able to trust and feel safe naturally. Those who have received disconnected parenting are consequently compromised in the 'trusting' and

[8] Proverbs 4:23.

'feeling safe with people' department. If that is you, you will have different ways of thinking and acting that stem from these injuries and you will need to learn to reverse the way you think and the way you act if you are to heal. It seems like a lot of work, and at times it is, but change is more than possible: it is probable—provided that we seek out connection with others.

Erik Erikson, the late German-born American psychologist who was famous for his outline of social development, asserted that it was during the first 18 months of life that infants come to trust others or perceive others as hostile or unreliable. This pre-verbal time is a time when the right hemisphere of the brain is in developmental 'overdrive'. This is the season of internalisation of relational patterns.

We're hardwired to trust. We reach out for others without thinking, before conscious thinking is possible. At this stage, connecting and trusting are not our choice. One investigation into unborn children found that even at 14 weeks' gestation, an unborn twin will move towards its co-twin in a way differentiated from the way it moves towards inanimate objects in the womb (such as the placenta).[9] Then, after we are born, we tune into who we can trust. We look desperately for the three S's (to be seen, safe and soothed) so that we can feel the fourth S, secure.

While we are desperate to be able to trust as newborns, our desire for this will remain with us for the rest of our lives. We require trusting relationships our whole lives, and we are impacted by them throughout our lives. We do not cease to have this need when we are 24 months old; nor does it cease when we are 42 years old. We reach out to others our whole lives and we benefit from trustworthy relationships throughout our lives, not just when we are young.

---

9 U Castiello, C Becchio, S Zoia, C Nelini, L Sartori, L Blason, G D'Ottavio, M Bulgheroni & V Gallese, 'Wired to be social: the ontogeny of human interaction', PLoS ONE, vol. 5, no. 10, 2010, e13199.

However, if you are starting to fret about the impact of your childhood, let me reassure you.

The early years are sensitive, but they are not critical. Human beings who go without trusting relationships early in their lives do not need to let that determine the rest of their lives. If you have missed out on trusting and loving early relationships, it means that you may need to work harder for longer in order to gain a sense of being able to trust others, but it does not set your attachment style in stone.

The beauty of a mother's voice, her sighs of empathy, the prosody of her voice as she wraps her child up in a blanket to be warm, the lullabies, the smile on her face—particularly in the muscles around her eyes—her proclivity towards fun, her eye contact[10] … all convey safety for the young child. She is a vessel for the child's distress. Without ever using the words, she says, 'I'm with you, I've got this … you're safe.' Unseen drives like hunger and sleep, and unseen feelings like loneliness or being too cold or hot, push a child into distress, but Mum understands it, and she knows what to do. All the child needs to do is trust. Connection like this is what is required for the development of safety, and where there is safety, good attachment develops. It is misleading, though, to suggest that we don't need this when we are older. Equally, it is misleading to suggest that if we didn't get this when we were young we can never achieve it. We can still receive this sort of safety, no matter what age we are.

---

[10] All of these connection behaviours are part of the social engagement system. We carry this system with us throughout all our lives. We need connection when we are young but we also need it as adults and into our senior years. When our social engagement system is active, the fear circuitry that is poised to mobilise us (fibres connecting heart and lungs) and the slower communicating fibres (linking the gut to the brain which immobilise us because we feel hopeless) are displaced by social connection. To be positively social is to be positively safe. When we are connected, there is no need for mobilisation or immobilisation. Connection, and its positive physical correlates, is what Stephen Porges called the 'preamble to attachment'. S Porges, Polyvagal theory: why this changes everything, NICABM trauma webinar series, 2012.

Connection sets in motion attachment patterns, and attachment patterns set in motion a range of feelings, physical reactions, behaviours and thinking styles. Disconnection will do the same thing. It sets in motion poor attachment patterns and a range of feelings, physical reactions, behaviours and thinking styles. If left unattended, these patterns can last for the rest of our lives. Retaining an unusual attachment pattern is not the *primary* problem, though. Lack of awareness is the primary problem. What we don't know, we can't understand, and what we can't understand, neither we nor others can respond to in a way that might restore trust to our hearts.

Understanding our own attachment styles

Personal understanding of your attachment pattern will serve you well. Research has shown that there are two dimensions to each person's attachment style.

One of the dimensions relates to how *anxious* we feel around others, and the other is the extent to which we *avoid* others. These dimensions are laid out in Figure 10.

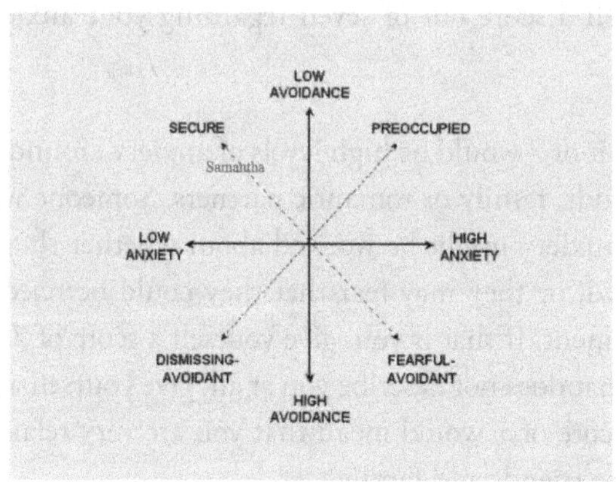

Figure 10. Attachment styles

Before I ask you to plot where you think you might fall on each of these continuums, I will take you through an example to get you into this mode of thinking.

Remember Samantha from Chapter 1? She had her trust broken by William when he physically abused her after her school reunion. But when I asked her about her friendships *prior* to getting married, she told me how she had often sought out friendships with others. To her, it didn't matter whether people were known or unknown. When she was at church as an adolescent, she would approach others freely (low avoidance) and would do so with only minimal apprehension (low anxiety). This placed her, at this time in her life, in the 'secure attachment' quadrant on the upper left side.

Now it is your turn.

Is your attachment style *anxious*?

Give yourself a score out of seven regarding your anxiety around others:

- 7 out of 7 would be high levels of anxiety around your close friends, family or romantic partners. Someone who is high in anxiety might be worried about whether they are really loved, or they may fear that they could be rejected at any moment. If that is you, give yourself a score of 7.
- If that does not describe you at all, give yourself a score of 1. A score of 1 would mean that you are very relaxed around close friends and family.

- If you are halfway between, neither extremely worried nor completely relaxed, give yourself a score of 4.
- You may consider that you are not in the middle either—upon further reflection, you might think you are slightly more anxious than that (so you could give yourself a score of 5), or slightly more relaxed (so you could give yourself a score of 3).

Whatever you decide, pick a score that best represents you.

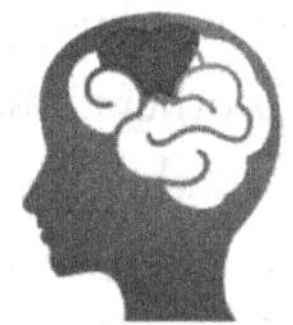

Is your attachment style *avoidant*?

Give yourself a score out of seven regarding the extent of your avoidance of others:

- If you are quite avoidant, you are not likely to feel comfortable around others and will cope with this by steering clear of relationships. You will not seek others out, nor will you find their company relaxing. If that is you, give yourself a low score on the 1–7 scale.
- If that does not describe you, you might give yourself a score at or near 7. If you gave yourself a high score you are likely to have low levels of avoidance—you are likely to seek people out for comfort. You would display 'approach' behaviours when you have something to share or something that you want to talk about.
- If you neither approach nor avoid people, you might give yourself a score in the middle range: a score of 4, for example.

If you scored yourself low on anxiety, and you tend to approach friends, family and romantic partners for connection like Samantha did in her youth, you are likely to have a '**secure**' attachment style. You are unlikely to be unsettled by closeness, but instead you are likely to report satisfaction from being in close contact with others. You don't mind depending on others, and neither do you mind people depending on you. If that describes you, then your score would place you in the top left region of the graph.

Alternatively, you might have scored yourself high on anxiety, but you still tend to approach others (i.e. you have low avoidance). If this is you, you might find yourself reaching out to others, but worried and concerned about whether they like you or whether they will reject you. In this circumstance, you might have placed yourself in the top right corner of the graph. People who place themselves in this area have a '**preoccupied**' attachment style.

If you are anxious and you avoid people, then your scores would put you in the bottom right corner. If that is where you located your own attachment pattern, then you are likely to be worried about friends and family, and you cope with this by withdrawing from them for safety. This type of attachment is called the '**fearful-avoidant**' attachment style.

Lastly, if you feel quite calm about your relationships but you have no need to reach out to others and you avoid them, then you are likely to have placed yourself in the bottom left area of the graph—the area titled '**dismissing-avoidant**'. You are likely to see yourself as self-sufficient and have no need for others.

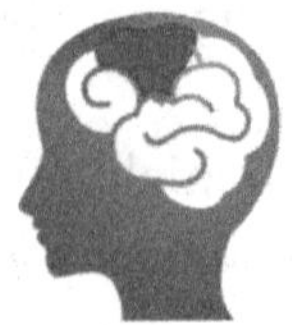

Where did you place yourself in Figure 10?

What is your attachment style?

Whatever your attachment style, you can see how your style is a kind of script for how you 'do' relationships. The script prompts expectations, beliefs, rules, thoughts and behaviours that spill out naturally from your heart. It operates like the image of the Heart Flower you saw previously. It is a script that will go looking for confirmation of itself.

If we have secure attachments like Samantha did, we are likely to expect others to be supportive and believe people to be decent, so our thoughts and behaviours follow naturally and we go out looking for satisfying relationships. Samantha would approach people freely, see that they responded well to her, and then conclude that people are usually nice and loving. On the other hand, if we are anxious about others, we are on the lookout for people who don't like us and we either approach others and obsess about how it will go, or we avoid others to protect ourselves.

Samantha suffered at the hands of her husband (emotionally and physically) and this left her distressed and confused. Samantha grew up in a family where trust was easy because people were safe and respectful, and that was part of the reason why William's behaviour was so shocking. It was not something that she had to look out for when she was growing up. It was not something that she had to manage. Her family environment was characterised by love and loyalty. William's behaviour was an abrupt intrusion of nastiness so foreign to her that it took several visits to me for her confusion to lift. Her story highlights that trust is important at any age, not just when you're young; it's important to all of us for ongoing peace in our hearts.

Every human brain has neural circuits that appear to be 'idling' as if all the time ready to assess others. These circuits are not few in number and they involve a whole collection of structures[11], and they become more active (are 'fired up') when we interact with or think about people.[12]

We enter into vigilant and sceptical modes of operation when we ask others to do something on our behalf, be it running the country or entering into friendship. This is appropriate functioning for any human being. When we come from a history of mistrust, we add extra vigilance and suspiciousness to this baseline functioning. It is no wonder that people who have not experienced trusting relationships early in their lives can spot a charlatan 20 miles away.

How to heal from broken trust

Jane is a mature lady and a friend of mine. She is a friendly but guarded person. When she was young she was sexually molested by a paedophile who was living just a block away from her house. She never told her mother out of fear of the reaction her mother might have. This sort of cautiousness about what other people might say or do has stayed with her all her life. She gathered together the motivation to talk to a professional about it. This is what she said:

> Trust is very hard to find when you have been betrayed. I had been sexually abused for quite a number of years and it was really eating at me because I didn't want to trust anyone. How could I go and get help when

[11] For those interested in neuroanatomy, the dorsal and ventral areas of the prefrontal cortex are implicated—which really is a fancy way of saying up the top of your head and at the front of your head, in that area of the brain above your eyes. If you make a 'C' shape with your index finger and your thumb and place your thumb in the little 'v' indentation in your skull above your eye and place your index finger on the top of your forehead— then just inside your skull from your thumb is the ventral area of your prefrontal cortex and just below your index finger is the dorsal region of your prefrontal cortex.

[12] J Arden & L Linford, *Brain-based therapy with adults: evidence-based treatments for everyday practice*, John Wiley and Sons, Hoboken, 2009.

> they might be the same and use me? I found someone who I shared my life with. That was very, very hard for me to do. I felt I had done wrong … I may have encouraged the abuse even though I was scared!

Her learned distrust of others led her to avoid on many levels: avoid others; avoid the topic of abusive relationships and all the feelings associated with it. There was a large part of her that didn't want to disclose things to others because she could be betrayed again. In the 'attachment styles' language that we have been using, she would be classed as 'anxious avoidant', placing her in the bottom right of Figure 10. Her anxiety and avoidance, while understandable, were prolonging a problem. There is more than a hint here about what kept her injury alive. The avoidance maintained her sense that she could not trust anyone. Avoidance didn't alleviate her sense of betrayal—it aggravated it, because she never provided herself with the opportunity to disprove her belief that 'others can't be trusted'.

For Jane to heal, she had to develop her relationships, but she needed to do this with wisdom, given what she had been through. She needed not only to connect with others in a safe way, but also to connect with herself to understand how her heart had been impacted. If we look carefully at her words above, we can see that her journey had already begun. Below are four of my reflections on her statement:

1. What hurts us is often not the incident, but how others react after the incident. Jane feared that others would blame her. This came from early experiences with her mother. Prior to being abused, what she had learned from her mother was that she could not trust her with sensitive information. When something went wrong, what was 'mirrored' back to Jane by her mother was that 'Jane is to blame'.
2. She internalised what she thought others would think. She believed that others thought that she was responsible, and because she felt responsible she also felt guilty.

3. The injury of betrayal had implications for other areas of her heart. Nasty disconnection injuries spilled over into other sectors of the heart, such as her identity ('I am guilty'), and this needed to be addressed in therapy.
4. Jane needed an environment characterised by safety. She needed to talk to people who were not going to blame or betray her.

Her story continued:

> I trusted that person [the psychologist] because I knew her to be confidential. My biggest fear was maybe someone else might find out or that the psychologist wouldn't understand how I could allow it to happen. That was not the case. When you have been betrayed you need someone you can trust. My life is so much better since I have been able to talk things out about what happened to me. You need someone who says they can't take away your pain you are feeling now but will listen and walk you through it. One thing that really stuck out to me was that the psychologist told me that she really appreciated me sharing these things with her as she knew it was hard for me.

From this additional comment, we can glean one further piece of wisdom about what is needed to help. Jane speaks of what is required for growth to occur:

5. Confidentiality and understanding are the qualities of the environment that nourish the regrowth of trust.

These five reflections spring from axioms that are vital for healing. Without them, conversations cease to be therapeutic. Confidentiality gave Jane control over her story and who was allowed to know it. This control increased her sense of safety in the situation. The understanding she received further bolstered the connection she had with the therapist because she became truly known. Being known and being safe led her to be able to trust again.

I asked her one time what she would want to say to others if they were starting out on their own journey of discovery. She said:

> You may feel you are dirty and in a gutter as I did. I felt I would be looked down on if I told anyone, but please go and talk to the right person and you will feel so much better.

The key words there are 'right person'. We will talk more about what that means in Chapter 7.

It is a great challenge that Jane presents, particularly when injuries of disconnection have led to low levels of trust and an anxious avoidant type of attachment.

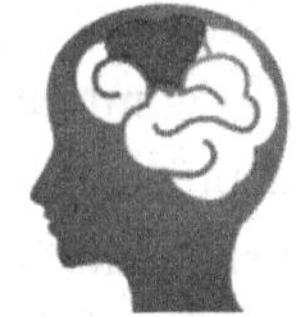

Before accepting the challenge to open up to others, perhaps pause to consider how you have coped with betrayal, and what type of attachment style you have. You may have suffered only a small amount of betrayal, or you may have suffered a lot. You may be quite anxious or not; you may be quite avoidant or not.

Whatever your individual experience is, there are parts of your reaction that, while being understandable, will maintain the sense of betrayal—for example, avoidance or difficulty with anxiety.

The important questions are: who is the 'right person' for you? What do you need to start trusting again?

2. Self-esteem and worthlessness

Self-esteem is the value that we think we have. This sense of value can be stable or unstable.

When self-esteem is stable, that is good if—but *only if*—self-esteem is adequate. Elevated levels of self-esteem are often linked to higher levels of energy and a sense of vitality and control. When we feel good about who we are, we become enthusiastic and open to new experiences. This has a way of setting us up for more positive interactions in the future.

When self-esteem is unstable, however, changes in our sense of value are more likely episodic and situational—that is, if things are going well, we think well of ourselves; but if things aren't going well, we don't.

When self-esteem is stable but low, we can be struck with a sense that we are without value or worth. When our self-esteem is low it is often associated with lower levels of energy and a tendency to withdraw from others. This, unfortunately, decreases the likelihood of positive interaction.

Low self-esteem is common for people who come for treatment for depression and is often used synonymously with 'worthlessness'. It still surprises me that poor self-esteem or feelings of worthlessness are not essential criteria for a diagnosis of depression. So common is the report of low self-esteem by people who suffer depression, it seems that such experiences are just part and parcel of the malady. They seem to be linked to each other, with both the mood and the sense of worthlessness influencing and supporting each other: when we hurt, we feel bad about who we are, and when we feel bad about who we are, we hurt.

Aaron Beck is widely recognised as one of the founding fathers (if not *the* founding father) of Cognitive Therapy. In the 1960s he began to build a theory of depression that has become known as the Cognitive Triad.[13] This theory established that when people become depressed, their thinking becomes dominated by three distinct themes. These themes maintain the depressed mood state. The themes that comprise the Cognitive Triad include:

- negative views of the self (e.g. 'I am worthless or inadequate')
- negative views of the world (e.g. 'There are too many obstacles for me to make changes')
- negative views of the future (e.g. 'Nothing will change').

For example, if someone loses his job, and his thinking is dominated by the Cognitive Triad, he might think to himself, 'I'm only worthwhile if I have work, and now I don't! I don't think other employers would be interested in me so there is no use in applying for work. My situation is hopeless.' If such thinking predominates, it would be no wonder that such a person would become depressed.

From Aaron Beck's perspective, a poor sense of self-esteem is one of three key issues linked to depression. It begins with poor connection early in life and then is maintained by the way a person thinks. Low levels of self-esteem are both a risk factor for developing depression and often a consequence of the depression.

Having a low level of self-esteem or no self-esteem is a problem. Low levels of self-esteem are by nature very distressing. This is linked to depression, as mentioned, but is also linked to a whole range of problems such as drug and alcohol abuse, Avoidant Personality Disorder, eating disorders, Social Phobia and a wide range of non-disordered problems of living such as poor academic performance, difficulties at work and relationship issues.

Injuries of disconnection put us on the trajectory towards low levels of self-esteem. Incidents of disconnection typically make us feel bad about who we are and this is not an injury that is sustainable. We cannot, nor should we, embrace or accept our lack of worth. Our

[13] AT Beck, 'Thinking and depression: idiosyncratic content and cognitive distortions', *Archives of General Psychiatry*, vol. 9, no. 4, 1963, pp. 324–333.

goal is to have it repaired and remedied. Our goal is not to accept or merely be mindful of it.

'Z' is the character voiced by Woody Allen in the animated film *Antz*. Z is an ant just like any other ant. At one stage, Z is on the therapist's couch. He pours out his soul to his therapist. He speaks about how he has problems in crowds, problems with spaces, feelings of being trapped, how when he was very young his mother had no time for him, how he felt abandoned by his father who was a drone, how as an ant he was only able to lift 'ten times his own body weight', and how the whole ant system just makes him feel 'insignificant'. Sensing that Z has just taken a great stride forward in his personal development, the therapist says to Z, 'Excellent, you've made a real breakthrough.'

'I have?' Z replies, sounding a little dumbfounded.

'Yes Z,' answers the therapist. 'You are insignificant!'

The therapist thinks that Z has made progress because he has come to accept his low self-esteem.

This is not progress. There is no 'coming to terms' with low self-esteem. Our distress will be relieved only if we learn that we are of value. From a biblical perspective, human beings are intrinsically worthwhile, and to have low self-esteem is to lose touch with that reality. We have an enduring need to know that our existence is of value, and we need to access and live in that knowledge if we are to know wholeness and health. Accepting a low level of self-esteem is not the goal of therapy.

However, a very high level of self-esteem is not the goal either. Extremely high levels of self-esteem can be symptomatic of disorders like mania and narcissism. Extremely high levels of self-esteem are not what we are looking for.

Adequate self-esteem is a goal that all human beings have and we are restless and discontent until we find it. When we don't get the connection with others that we need, it leads to lower levels of self-esteem and this is not sustainable. Self-esteem is a need that we have.

Of all the competing requirements that we have, to have a sense of value is the queen of them all. A recent study illustrates this well. Bushman, Moeller and Crocker found that college students valued self-esteem more than they valued eating a favourite food, having sex, drinking alcohol, receiving a pay cheque, and seeing a best friend.[14]

Feeling worthwhile is what we yearn for. Being without a sense of worth really hurts us, and it is a real problem for so many people. It is a problem to be addressed, not something to be overlooked. Our self-esteem is not a binary issue, though. It is not as if you either have it or you don't. Neither is it set in concrete, as if it is fixed across time. It changes according to our relationships, circumstances, cognitions and behaviours.

How does self-esteem develop?

The treatment we receive from those around us is responsible for the development of self-esteem. Lots of love from others will make it, and the absence of love will break it. As foundational as it is, I often read psychology texts with an eyebrow raised or a slight frown when it comes to the issue of self-esteem. It is a glaring omission in many recent self-esteem manuals that there is no mention of love. Instead of focusing on love, they focus on judgements, beliefs and behaviours. These factors are important in maintaining the level of self-esteem that we have, but they are not responsible for the formation of it.

The influential Russian psychologist Lev Vygotsky proffered

[14] BJ Bushman, SJ Moeller & J Crocker, 'Sweets, sex, or self-esteem? Comparing the value of self-esteem boosts with other pleasant rewards', *Journal of personality*, vol. 79, 2011, pp. 993–1012.

that an interpersonal process becomes an intrapersonal one.[15] Interpersonal processes are the ones that happen between us and other people. An intrapersonal process is the process that happens within us. It is the way we talk to ourselves, and the way we act towards ourselves. What Vygotsky points out is that the way we are treated by others becomes the way we treat ourselves. If we are loved and accepted, then we tend to love and accept ourselves. If we receive nastiness and it is conveyed to us that we aren't good enough, we tend to be nasty towards ourselves when we think we haven't made ourselves good enough.

The first deposit in the bank of self-esteem occurs during infancy. This initial deposit into our self-esteem account may well be the biggest in our lives. This is a time when our brain is working out how we fit in with those around us. The treatment we receive from caregivers is rapidly internalised. Deposits continue throughout our life, and we can build self-esteem or lose self-esteem, but this initial deposit, or lack of it, determines whether we begin life with an advantage (in the black) or with a disadvantage (in the red).

This first series of exchanges between us and our caregivers becomes the embedded relational motif, shaping what we expect from others and how we come to think of ourselves in relation to others. If the caregivers are good connectors, we think that is what everyone else will be like—that is, we expect that we will be treated well by others and are constantly surprised when others are unloving. If they are not good connectors (inconsistent, cold and/or nasty), that is what we think others are like, and indeed what God might

[15] This is actually a distillation of what Vygotsky said: 'The transformation of an interpersonal process into an intrapersonal one is the result of a long series of developmental events.' LS Vygotsky, *Mind in society: the development of higher psychological processes*, Harvard University Press, Cambridge, MA, 1978, p. 57, cited in J Wink & L Putney, *A vision of Vygotsky*, 2010, viewed October 2020, <http://www.joanwink.com/wp-content/uploads/2014/01/VoV-eBook.pdf>.

be like, and we come to expect that that is how others will treat us, and how God will treat us.

Joanna and Alister McGrath explained the establishment of self-esteem during infancy well:

> The optimal parental relationship is defined as warm, continuous, and intimate. It need not be limited to the child's biological mother. Within such a relationship the child learns to value himself or herself. He or she internalises the belief that 'because I am loved, because they are always there, because they accept me, I must be worth something'. Eventually the secure base provided by others can be carried around as part of the person's psychological baggage. This is self-esteem.[16]

Self-esteem is psychological 'luggage' that we take with us from the relational exchanges we have had. If our relationships have been positive, then we tend to have high self-esteem. If they have been negative—that is, abusive in terms of neglect or physical/sexual abuse—then self-esteem is likely to be lower. In many respects, self-esteem is the consequence of a litany of relational interactions that have led us to this point. In that sense, we are cajoled into a higher or lower sense of self-esteem by the sorts of relationships we have had.

Unfortunately, many of us fail to see that self-esteem is socially embedded. We move forward in life and try to remedy the solution ourselves. We strive and stretch, we achieve and we climb a career ladder. We think that these strategies will generate our sense of value. We try to please others, outperform others, improve our appearance, change this, do that, all in the hope that something deep within us might be restored.

However, when we are still, most of us know that self-esteem

---

[16] A McGrath & J McGrath, *Self-esteem: the cross and Christian confidence*, Crossway Books, Wheaton Illinois, 2002, p. 71.

is not about what we do. What we do, or what we achieve, is often a compensation for what we did not have. Self-esteem comes from our relationships, and achievement is merely the distracting promise of a false remedy. Achievement isn't the solution, nor is lack of achievement the problem. Self-esteem problems are the by-products of poor relationships, and only caring relationships will release us from their grip.

Many believe that people with low self-esteem just *think* they have poor relationships; that people with low self-esteem are just being sensitive, and actually do have good relationships but are misinterpreting the behaviours, verbal statements and intentions that people around them make. Misinterpretations regarding other people's behaviours, verbal statements and intentions may well maintain low self-esteem and may need to be reviewed. By and large, though, this way of thinking about people with low self-esteem is as pejorative as it is untrue.

Take, for example, a recent study from the *Journal of Personality*. Cortez and Wood from the University of Waterloo had independent coders rate how experiment participants were responded to after they had been excluded from a video game.[17] When the rejected participants were reunited with their partners, they were videoed without them knowing. The independent coders then assessed the degree to which each rejected person was supported and understood by their partner. What they found was that those 'rejected' participants who already had low self-esteem ('LSEs') also had partners who were less responsive to their distress. Conversely, they found that 'rejected' participants who already had higher levels of self-esteem tended

[17] K Cortez & JV Wood, 'Is it really "all in their heads"? How self-esteem predicts partner responsiveness, *Journal of personality*, vol. 8, no. 6, 2018, pp. 990–1002.

to have partners who were more supportive and understanding of their situation. The authors concluded: 'Although the common assumption has been that LSEs' negative partner perceptions are "all in their heads"—a reflection of their negative self-projection—we argue that LSEs' views of lower partner responsiveness are, in fact, warranted.'[18]

It is hard to know whether the chicken or the egg came first. It could well be that people who have low self-esteem choose partners who are less supportive because that is what they've grown up with. They've just come to have low expectations of others and they pick partners accordingly. Conversely, it could be that when people have partners who show low levels of support and understanding, their self-esteem suffers. It appears as though both are true, though there is good reason to think that the latter is more likely.

The conclusion that we can be confident about is that self-esteem is strongly linked to the quality of the connections we have with significant others. That is what self-esteem is. It is the conclusion that you make about your value in light of the sum total of your interpersonal experiences. We cope with this in a variety of ways. People will try to please others, achieve things, outperform others, always be right/pretty/skinny, and a whole range of other things, but these are counterfeit solutions to the real problem, which is not experiencing supportive, connective relationships.

Self-esteem set in motion

When I was young at primary school, I wanted what other kids had. I was jealous—not about everything that every other kid had, but about one particular toy. It was a little toy that you'd place at the top of a flight of stairs and tip over to the stair below. Once it was in motion, you could then watch as it hypnotically pitched and lunged its way down to the next stair below. Then when it made its

---

[18] ibid.

way to the stair below, it seemed to throw itself out like a high diver might over a cliff and descend onto the next stair all by itself. Then it would repeat and repeat and repeat without any input from anyone, all the way to be the bottom of the flight of stairs. These toys were called 'Slinkies'.

Self-esteem can operate a bit like a Slinky. Our genetic make-up combined with our relational environment can set psychological patterns in motion. The DNA lottery grants some of us a highly sensitive nature. If we grow up in a disconnected household where there is nastiness, neglect or both, and then endure rejection in our teenage years, we become soundly convinced that no-one likes us and we end up not liking ourselves. Disconnection imparts to us a pattern of insecure attachment and this pattern rolls down the years like a Slinky. Dysphoria, negative automatic thoughts and social withdrawal become almost inevitable. Genetic vulnerability, difficult relationships, thoughts then actions—this is how psychological processes can be set in motion.

When it comes to self-esteem, however, we do not have to be fatalistic. The progress of unhealthy psychological processes can be interrupted. Sensitivity does not need to be a curse, because when you are sensitive, you're not just sensitive to bad relationships—you are also sensitive to warm and caring relationships. Connection at any age promises respite from worthlessness, and ongoing loving relationships have the potential to unravel long-held hurts. If we get better connected we can be confident that we are setting ourselves up to feel better in the future.

Some argue that it is not the case that being social leads people to feel better. They argue the other way around. They say that when people feel better, *then* they tend to be social. To a small extent this is true, but this is not what has been found in the research. Investigators from the University of Queensland gathered together over 21,000 cases from the New Zealand Attitudes and Values Survey (NZAVS). They studied measures of social connectedness in one wave of data and measured this against how people responded to mental health questions in the next wave of data the following year. Their conclusion was that 'Social connectedness was found to be a stronger and more consistent predictor of mental health year-on-year than mental health was of social connectedness.'[19]

For clarity, I would say that connection leads to self-esteem and better mental health. But I want you to see what I am highlighting now. If we grow up with good connection, we are likely to have good self-esteem and better mental health. If we have good connection in the present, then we are likely to have good self-esteem and mental health further down the track, no matter what age we are. Pictorially, it looks like this:

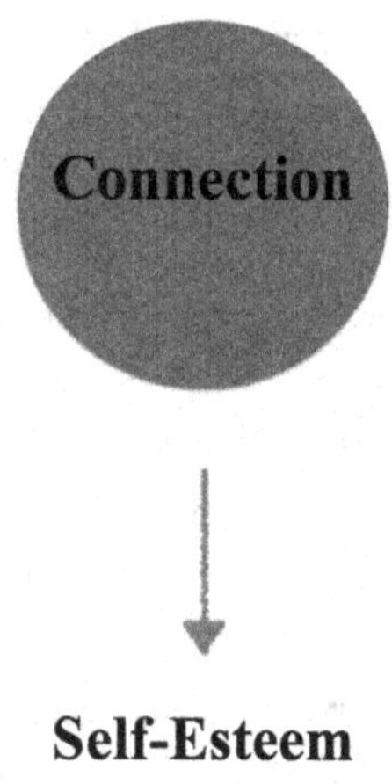

Figure 11. Connection leads to self-esteem

Remember Ben from Chapter 1? He lost his mother to cancer when he was 12. His mother was a warm person and provided him with considerable connection. When she died, this left him with an

[19] AK Saeri, T Cruwys, K Barlow, S Stronge & CG Sibley, 'Social connectedness improves public mental health: investigating bidirectional relationships in the New Zealand Attitudes and Values Survey', *Australian and New Zealand journal of psychiatry*, vol. 52, no. 4, 2018, pp. 365–374.

omission of connection and he filled that vacuum with pornographic images from the internet. The addiction made him feel powerless and the absence of Mum made him feel alone. He was left with no-one to talk to because his dad withdrew to the television, his eldest sister moved out and neither he nor his friends had the capacity to address his grief. The loneliness that was left by Mum's departure was never addressed. If his father, siblings and friends had connected with him, he may never have suffered from low self-esteem.

Through his simple gesture of reaching out to me, Ben took the first and biggest step towards addressing his low self-esteem. To be connected with and understood by others is what he needed when he was 12, and by doing that with me and his friends he began the journey of healing. He told me about the night his mother died. He told me about the night his sister left. He told me about how he wished his dad would cry with him, because they both suffered a terrible loss that year. By sharing with others who were connected, he began to see that he wasn't alone, and his heart began to open to a new possibility: 'Maybe I'm worth listening to.'

If 10 out of 10 equals healthy levels of self-esteem, what score would you give yourself out of 10?

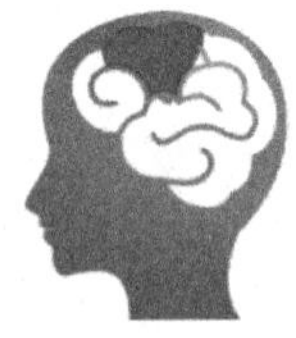

Has it previously been higher (peaks) or lower (troughs) than this current level in your life?

Are those peaks and troughs linked to connection levels at those times in your life?

Who connects with you so well that it gives a lift to your own self-esteem just by being around them?

We have examined those psychological developments that stem from connection: trust and self-esteem. Now we are going to turn our attention to two other connection-related outcomes: honour versus shame, and belonging versus alienation.

3. Honour and shame

What is honour?

When we are honoured, we are elevated and valued in the eyes of others; people look up to us and we sense that. Honour is the result of being brought near and held up. To receive the 'Medal of Honour', or to be on the 'Honour Roll', is to have shown excellence in a field of endeavour. Additionally, if a person has acted in honourable ways, that person is thought to have acted in right or morally appropriate ways and, as such, is deserving of the esteem of those around them.

When we have honour, then, we are thought of as being morally good. Shame, on the other hand, implies that we have done something morally wrong. Whether you feel honour or shame depends on whether your community connects with you or disconnects from you when you've done something that it thinks is worthy of comment.

Honour is different from respect. We can have respect for someone and not admire them. People we respect don't always act as a moral guide for us, but honourable people often do. Rugby teams frequently talk about respecting the opposition, but they don't actually like them or want to be like them. They just mean they are wary of them, and are giving them their attention.

One of the most famous stories in the Bible is about someone who was honoured by God.[20]

Elkanah had two wives. He and his wives belonged to the tribe

[20] You can find this story in the first chapter of the Old Testament book of 1 Samuel.

of Ephraim, a tribe that some believe was saturated in a culture of discontentment and jealousy.

Every year, Elkanah and his two wives, Hannah and Peninnah, went to worship and sacrifice at the temple. This was a good opportunity to connect with God, but one of them had another agenda.

'Whenever Hannah went up to the house of the LORD,' the Scripture says, 'her rival provoked her till she wept and would not eat.'[21]

When reading just this verse, it appears that the author of the book is tentative, as if he is reluctant to name the villain of the story; but we do get a hint of the motive that the villain might have in the word 'rival'.

The passage preceding this verse reads: 'But to Hannah [Elkanah] gave a double portion [of food] because he loved her, and the LORD had closed her womb.'[22] It seems safe to say that jealousy and narcissism were in the mix. Hannah was favoured by her husband. The jealous rival searched for a sore point to prod, and she found it. Hannah had no children. To shame, after all, is an act of social subjugation.

Peninnah was the rival, and she used Hannah's childless state to 'irritate' Hannah.[23] It was spiteful—she did it to bring Hannah to tears. It was relentless—it went on year after year. Hannah was being shamed and Peninnah was the jealous culprit. Hannah would live with this, unable to escape it, because Peninnah was also married to her husband. She would endure it and remain unprotected by Elkanah because he did nothing to address it directly. In her culture, children were a sign of God's favour and childlessness was a sign of God's judgement. Without a child, her social ranking would slip to be on par with the poor, the despised, the helpless, the widow. Without a child, the very security of her relationship with her husband was at risk as he might seek another wife or more attention from Peninnah in the hope that he could have

---

[21] 1 Samuel 1:7.

[22] 1 Samuel 1:5.

[23] 1 Samuel 1:6.

more children. Trapped in a nasty rivalry, feeling that she was defective, insecure in her marriage and walking in the shadow of possible spiritual judgement, she took her case to her Creator.

Hannah poured out her heart to God in prayer in the temple. Her pleading became remarkably emotional. So unusual were her pleadings that Eli, the priest at the time, accused her of being drunk. Hannah explained to Eli that she was not drunk but she was praying out of great anguish and grief. She wanted so badly to have a child of her own.[24]

The Scriptures record that 'the LORD remembered her' and blessed her with a son. Fittingly, Hannah gave her son the name 'Samuel', a name that sounds like the Hebrew for 'heard by God'.[25]

She was obviously thrilled to have a son. God had taken her pain seriously, and graciously intervened to grant her the desires of her heart. He had reached into her situation, connected with her and honoured her, and her heart was transformed by his personal and loving response to her situation. She was proved right by her actions and proved right by depending on God to resolve her situation. She was no longer the object of scorn or ridicule.

In a declaration that describes both what God had done for her and what God's character is like, she said: 'He raises the poor from the dust and lifts the needy from the ash heap; he seats them with princes and has them inherit a throne of honour.'[26]

It is quite clear that many women don't have their prayers answered in the same way. This can be painful. Many women and men would make great parents and, through no fault of their own, are unable to have children. Our culture still has an uneasiness about where these lovely people might fit. They too may have pleaded with God, but—unlike Hannah's—their hopes have been dashed. In the end, I don't know why some prayers are answered and some aren't.

---

[24] 1 Samuel 1:10–15.

[25] 1 Samuel 1:19–20.

[26] 1 Samuel 2:8.

To her own surprise, however, Hannah's prayers were answered. In her childless state, her heart was filled with pain and she was clearly worn down by her seemingly inescapable barrenness. However, her shame was transformed as she experienced firsthand the power of being heard and being taken seriously. Hannah had been honoured by God.

The changing of her situation is what ultimately honours Hannah. No doubt this was a relief to her, but I can't help but feel a touch of sadness for her. She felt like she had to 'do' something; she felt like she had to 'be' different. She, like so many people today, put herself under pressure to achieve honour by doing something or achieving something. Many of us strive to do something good. When the opportunity arises to be seen as a morally pure person in the eyes of others, we grab it. We want to show them our favourable side and hide our shortcomings. We stand tall in photos. We broadcast our achievements at a moment's notice. We work hard to prevent others from seeing that we are bad and bury secrets deep within us.

Why? Why do we do this?

Ultimately, the desire is not merely to do good or be good, but to be good in the eyes of others, and by so doing we can engineer a solution for our heart's deepest need—to be included and esteemed by our community.

It does not need to be this way. When we are known and loved, we will feel accepted. This can occur no matter what we have or have not achieved, and if it does occur we will know that we haven't done anything wrong and we are no longer defective.

Connection and understanding are the remedy; achieving is not. If we can be connected, the drive to be different or do something remarkable takes a dive, because we become satisfied with ourselves.

Focusing on being connected rather than focusing on doing or achieving leads us away from pride. When we are proud of ourselves, we stick out our chests and exhibit an image of ourselves as good and worthy. We wave flags that symbolise our identity, and we say 'I am a proud _____' as if the act of being proud represents having found the key to self-actualisation. We see ourselves as the agents of our transformation, self-made men or women, self-appointed people of honour. In an odd sort of way, pride leads to a detachment from others, a solipsism and a self-love where gratitude is shown to ourselves by ourselves.

Hannah is not proud of herself. She is made humble by the deep connection with, and the response from, her Creator. There is no boasting, only thankfulness. In pride, we are fully conscious of ourselves; in honour, there is almost a self-forgetfulness or a sense of only really existing in the state of love from another. Honour always comes with gratitude to others.

Pictorially, honour works like this:

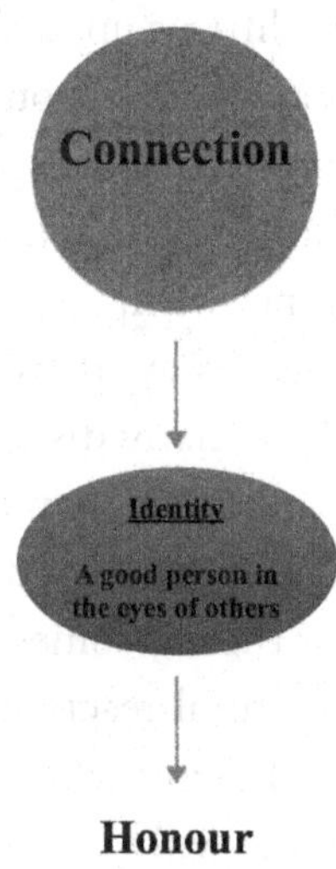

Figure 12. Connection leads to honour

If your history is one of being honoured by others, then you will know how positive this can be. Even if you don't feel honoured in the present moment, there may be times or circumstances in which you have been in the past.

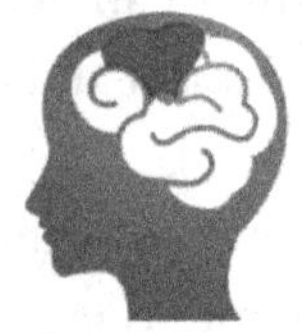

Is there someone you can thank who has honoured you?

Is there someone you have honoured or you could honour? How might you do that?

What is shame?

If honour is elevation in the eyes of others, shame is demotion in the eyes of others. Shame is the opposite of honour. If honour rinses us clean, brings us near and lifts us up, dishonour, or shame, is the thing that makes us dirty and casts us out and down. In its most pointed sense, to feel ashamed is to be a disgrace in the eyes of others.

A vast amount of the human brain is involved in getting on with others, and that sensitive inner wiring quickly detects when we are being treated in a substandard way. If we live in an environment where we are constantly or regularly dishonoured, we may end up living with a deep, pervading sense of shame that causes us to believe that for some reason we are substandard or deficient as human beings, as if we have done wrong or there is something wrong with us.

Embarrassment is the natural reaction we have when we have been exposed to people who disapprove of us. We can feel anxious at these times, sensing that others will scrutinise us and find us falling short of their standards. Shame, however, has more to do with the beliefs we have about ourselves as a result of social evaluation. Mario Jacoby explains this point:

> … what is unique about the feeling of shame is that it is not always a reaction to unethical behaviour. One may be ashamed of having red hair, having a slight or tall build, or of being overly stout. Criminal deeds or negligence are not all that are capable of bringing on the contempt of society. Membership in

> a certain race or family, for instance, can also provoke a sense of inferiority. Thus shame results from the manner in which my entire being or self is valued – or, more precisely, devalued – not only by others but by myself.[27]

While something that we have done (or have not done) can be the source of our shame, there are obviously many other sources. It can be a permanent feature about ourselves that has become stigmatised by others and causes us to feel inferior. It can be a shocking incident in which we were involved, one that we cannot bear to think of or admit to, or we may have no idea as to exactly why or when shame came to live in our hearts.

The renowned author Philip Roth illustrates what shame is like in his novel, *The Human Stain*. The protagonist in this story is Professor Coleman Silk. Silk notes that two of his students continually fail to turn up, so he asks the class, 'Do they exist or are they spooks?' and his life unravels thereafter. It seems like an innocent, albeit clumsy, question—it was not a reference to their African heritage, but a reference to their ghost-like manner. The respected academic is accused of being a racist nonetheless. Crushed by the charge, he resigns in shame from his position. After leaving academia, the real story unfolds and the secret that he has hidden even from his now dead wife and his own children is incrementally revealed. He gradually loses his grip on the story he has spun for decades and he finds himself unable to maintain the masquerade.

Professor Silk has a secret. It may well be possible that he is a racist, but it doesn't seem like a clear-cut case of racism. It is possible that he has discriminated against those students, that he has been bigoted towards them, that he has disliked them because of who or what they represent to him. However, if he has discriminated against them, he can only have done it if he dislikes himself. The

[27] M Jacoby, *Shame and the origins of self-esteem: a Jungian approach*, Routledge, London, 2016, p. 2.

accusation reveals the possibility of his own self-loathing—because *he is* African-American.

The Human Stain is a story about a deep sense of shame that one man carries. Coleman Silk has learned early in life that his racial identity devalued him as a person. Being powerless to change something so deeply unacceptable to the world in which he lives, he has chosen to live a lie rather than reveal his true identity.

For many of us, shame may not be associated with something as specific as the colour of our skin or the colour of our hair. Indeed, there are many people who have different skin colours or different coloured hair from those around us and never feel shame. It all depends on the community in which we live. It is not whether we have these things, but whether we are mistreated by others for having these things, that causes shame. This is why Hannah in the Bible felt shame—not because she didn't have a child, but because year after year, her rival had provoked her.

Mistreatment for any reason carries with it personal implications. Our minds look for an explanation: 'What would make this mistreatment reasonable?' We grasp at the things we can control, because if we control these variables, we can prevent the hurt that we have been feeling. It is an easy step after being mistreated to assume that the problem lies within us, and that in some way we must be faulty human beings. We think, 'If I hadn't done that, hadn't said that, hadn't been like that,' then the bad thing wouldn't have happened, but none of this is likely to be true—it is just our minds grasping for solutions.

The injury of shame gathers around it negative feelings including anger, anxiety, sadness, humiliation and contempt. Everyone instinctively wants to run away from such painful feelings, but this is where things get complicated. We have already seen that to keep feelings hidden from others means there will be no disarming of their disruptive power. How can shame be corrected if we withdraw from people who might love and accept us?

Our psychological destiny is sealed by our own willingness to protect ourselves. The desire for safety from others cuts off the remedy and we are left with the onerous task of resolving the distress on our own. When we are unable to, we avoid the feelings and our inevitable fate becomes a state of being disconnected from ourselves and awash with emotion. Avoiding others means we cheat ourselves of the opportunity to be soothed by them, and wilful avoidance of thoughts, feelings and memories ensures that we fail to understand ourselves.

At these times, we place ourselves at the mercy of the emotions that come from our hearts. The residual emotions, at once suppressed and unknown, gather strength and push us around. We grasp at control of them in a variety of troubling methods. Addictions that we never really thought about become potential antidotes. The toxic mix of perceived inferiority and defectiveness leads many, for example, to look to ways of eating to remedy shame. We punish ourselves by not eating; we soothe ourselves by eating too much. We think we are not deserving of compassion but only deserving of poor treatment. We used to hate the way we were treated, but now we treat ourselves the same way. Perpetrators whom we haven't seen in years live on in our hearts and our heads.

We cope with shame, just like we can cope with any of the connection injuries, in a variety of ways.

We can **fake** that we're okay and that we are upstanding, respectable, balanced and happy people, even though we do not feel this way.

We can **fight** against shame by pushing others down, or trying to control people by blaming them. We focus on what other people are doing or not doing and tell them so. We don't just fight them, but we fight ourselves. We tell ourselves not to think of what hurt us and wrestle with the feelings, or curse ourselves for being the sort of person to allow ourselves to be in the position we have been in.

We can **flee** from shame by avoiding people and topics that in any way have a link to the injury. All of these strategies are exhausting, unhealthy and ineffective.

Only when we **face** ourselves, and then **face** safe people in the context of truth and love, will shame properly heal.

Organising our relationships to include those who genuinely care about us is like putting in 'scaffolding' around ourselves for recovery. Like a beautiful, old, weathered building, once magnificent but now beaten down by the elements, we need to put structures around us so healing can take place. Once we have safe and loving relationships, we are able to start the restoration. Our thinking needs to change; our behaviour needs to change; the way we respond to ourselves needs to change; but mostly what needs to change is to find a way to safely face others and tell them what is on our hearts.

Remember Sally from Chapter 1? She was the professional lady who told me she felt 'dirty' because of what she had been through. Of all the four examples (Ben, Tony, Samantha and Sally), she is the one whose experience most closely resembles having Post Traumatic Stress Disorder, because she felt she would 'relive' her memories and feelings when she spoke of them. She felt ashamed of herself because of the commission she had been through when she was younger. The traumatic incidents left her feeling 'dirty', like she was stained by them. She thought that being sullied in this way ruled her out of having a relationship with a man. She felt scared of having a partner, not just because of the physical affection, but because she feared the partner finding out and thinking less of her.

The fact that we have the capacity to feel shame is evidence that people impact on us deeply, and it is a clear indication that we derive our value from those around us. It is both healthy and wise for us to be deliberate about the relationships with which we surround ourselves.

This brings up some very significant questions.

Are there people in your life who shame you? Do you spend too much time with these people? Do you reveal too much to such people?

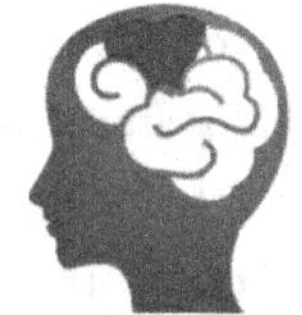

From whom do you get a sense of being 'lifted up'? How frequently do you meet with such people? How frequently do you need to meet with people who lift you up?

How much have you revealed of yourself to your safe friends? Do you need to reveal more to get the full benefit of these friendships?

As you read this book, you may sense shame rising up in you and want to know what you can do about it. If you have been living with shame, it is extremely helpful to establish a relationship where you specifically experience honour. Seek out people who are able to treat you in a way that conveys that you are loved and accepted. Find people who understand your behaviour. Surround yourself with people who do not point the finger at you. Professor Silk in *The Human Stain* hid even from his own family, and because he hid his secret shame, he never found the healing experience of love that he needed to feel better about himself.

When we are shamed, we are disendorsed by our community and thought of as bad. As we have discussed, shame equals disconnection and disgrace in the eyes of others, as if there is something morally impure about us, or something defective about us.

Belonging and alienation are different from honour and shame. They are primarily about connection, and whether we feel like we belong or are alienated by a group is determined by whether or not we have a role within that group.

4. Belonging and alienation

What does it mean to belong?

In its oldest form, 'belonging' means 'to go along with, to properly relate to'. It can mean 'to be the property of', as in the statement 'those are my belongings'. Sometimes, belonging means that when a person has characteristics that they share with other people, then that person belongs with people who share those characteristics. This would be obvious in the statement, 'You are a boy: you belong with those boys over there.'

The person most widely recognised for bringing belonging to the attention of psychologists was Abraham Maslow (1908-1970). Maslow was a pioneering psychologist in the Humanistic tradition. He developed a Hierarchy of Needs that many people know about. According to Maslow, after the physiological needs are addressed, and after the needs of security/order/stability have been addressed, the next most important primary psychological need is belonging. Like Bowlby before him, he maintained that this is a need not a desire, and if we are to ever become self-actualised (what you and I might describe as 'whole'), we will have to have the need for belonging satisfied.

It is interesting to note two things about the literature on belonging.

First, discussion about belonging has been steadily declining since a peak in the early 1800s. There is a brief plateau in the decline from the mid to late 1950s, but the decline continues after Maslow. It reaches a bottom point in the 1990s and there is a modest increase in the literature after that.[28]

Secondly, Abraham Maslow provided no scientific data for the assertion that belonging is a primary psychological need.

How is it that a psychological assertion can become so widely known without scientific support? Perhaps the reason is that we sense

[28] From Google Ngram, 1800–2008 using the word 'belonging'. Smoothing of 3, English corpus, not case sensitive.

this to be true about what it means to be human and we don't feel a need to investigate further.

Professor Roy Baumeister, not content with the absence of empirical support, sought to put some evidence behind Maslow's original assertion. Having gathered the evidence, he wrote, 'Existing evidence supports the hypothesis that the need to belong is a powerful, fundamental, and extremely pervasive motivation.'[29] Like Maslow before him, when Baumeister stated this he wasn't so much providing a new revelation, or even confirmation of a recent revelation, as providing confirmation of an ancient one.

When Paul wrote to the church in ancient Corinth, he acknowledged the great diversity of the people in the church. He used the metaphor of a body. Some of us are feet, some of us are eyes, some of us are ears. This all sounds very Greek—the 'unity in the diversity' business—but I think Paul's point is more than this. Real belonging, Paul says, occurs when all parts are seen as indispensable and valuable, because they all play their separate roles that help in the overall functioning of the group. The body is served by the different parts that have different roles; those roles, though they are different, are aligned to the overall functioning of the body. That is real belonging: feeling connected but having different roles.

The issue of belonging has been an important one in the history of the church. Diversity in racial groups, age groups and educational backgrounds are all important. Homogeneity is not something to be sought; diversity is something to be valued.[30] Refugees, people on the fringe of society, the widow, the marginalised, and the powerless all

---

[29] RF Baumeister & MR Leary, 'The need to belong: desire for interpersonal attachments as a fundamental human motivation', *Psychological bulletin*, vol. 117, no. 3, 1995, pp. 497–529 (p. 497).

[30] Right in the midst of the 1 Corinthians verses that we have been referring to, it reads 'For we were all baptized by one Spirit so as to form one body—whether Jews or Gentiles, slave or free—and we were all given the one Spirit to drink. Even so the body is not made up of one part but of many.' (1 Corinthians 12:13–14)

have a special place of importance in the Christian faith. They have had a special place in the past and ought to in the future, because it is only when all parts contribute that the body will be fully functional.

Belonging is embedded in and comes from connection. However, just like honour, a sense of belonging requires something more than connection. A sense of belonging is achieved when we have a role that is distinct from others but contributes to and is valued by those around us. Belonging is 'role plus connection'.

In my son's soccer team, we have a ritual. All the boys gather around arm in arm in a circle at a practice session and onc person starts. They each take a turn at going around the circle saying what they think is the special thing that each other player brings to the team. It may be their tenacity, it may be courage, it may be the great passing of the midfielders, or the big clearing kicks from the backs. Whatever it is, they affirm each other for the distinct thing each of them brings that serves the overall function of the team. It is a terrific exercise and one that revitalises the team.

Pictorially, belonging looks like this.

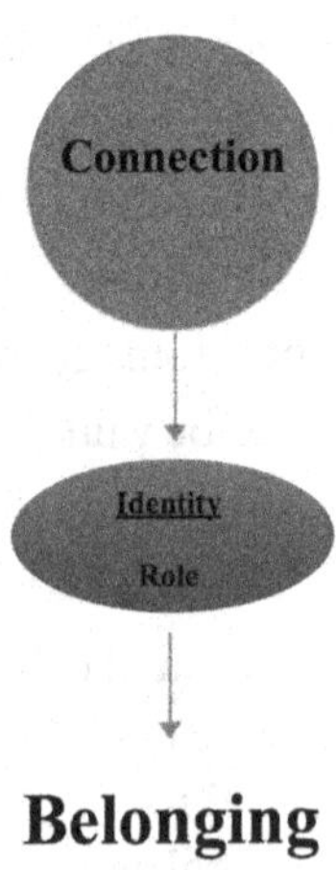

Figure 13. Connection leads to belonging

Safeguarding ourselves from feelings of not belonging is helpful to our functioning. Researchers at Stanford University have found that when African-American students are able to do this, they reduce the 'minority achievement' gap. [31] Through group work, minority students were taught to interpret social adversity as 'common and transient'. If they were discriminated against they taught themselves to think, 'This happens to lots of people … it will pass.' By using their heads, they were able to protect their hearts, and by so doing they were able to prevent a sense that they didn't belong at university. Having done the skills training, the group participants were able to halve the minority achievement gap, but they were also able to improve the participants' perceived health and reduce their need to see a doctor, three years post-intervention!

This finding confirms for us two things.

Firstly, it confirms that relationships can hurt. At any time, in any human organisation, being disconnected from the group is difficult.

Secondly, it doesn't have to get to our hearts. We can involve ourselves in relationships that help us to think differently, heal, grow and keep us whole.

Experiencing alienation

When the Psalmist wrote Psalms 42 and 43, he knew what it was like to no longer belong.

The impact of the exile on the Psalmist is acute. His soul 'pants' and 'thirsts' to be with God.[32] His tears have become his 'food day and night'.[33] He doesn't understand his own reaction: 'Why,

---

[31] GM Walton & GL Cohen, 'A brief social-belonging intervention improves academic and health outcomes of minority students', *Science*, vol. 331, 2011, pp. 1447–1451.

[32] Psalm 42:1–2

[33] Psalm 42:3

my soul, are you downcast?' he asks himself in both psalms.[34] He remembers the role he used to have: 'These things I remember as I pour out my soul: how I used to go to the house of God under the protection of the Mighty One with shouts of joy and praise among the festive throng.'[35] Part of the reason for his profound sense of isolation is not the mocking of people around him, but the loss of his role as a worship leader. The social isolation and loss of role have relegated him into a crippling sense of alienation, and his nostalgia weighs him down to the point of depression.

The loss of belonging is a painful experience for anyone. In our society, it is seen clearly in retirees. Take retiring athletes as an example. Having had a prized role, enjoying a sense of purpose and the support of an encouraging community, they have become used to a profound sense of belonging, but this belonging decomposes and alienation sets in when they are forced into retirement. The cruel hand of age or unexpected injury forces athletes out of the community that gave them support, and they are cruelly expelled into a world in which they may have no role and no support.

'When an athlete's sense of value, significance and belonging are enmeshed to their sporting commitments and achievements, then their sense of self will be threatened incredibly upon retirement,' says Dr Clive Jones, a Sports Psychologist.[36] Athletes go from being valued and driven to feeling unknown and alien, pariahs in a world where everyone except them seems to be on a clear trajectory, and everyone else seems to have a place to go.

Dan Vickerman's life ended shortly after his retirement from a career as one of Australia's best rugby union players. He was a much-loved player, father and husband. After he passed away, his friend, Brendan Cannon, noted that 'You go from being the king of your

---

[34] Psalm 42:5 and Psalm 43:5

[35] Psalm 42:4.

[36] J Willoughby, *Raw* Four Corners *episode shines light on post-retirement struggles*, The New Daily, 1 May 2017, viewed May 2017, <http://thenewdaily.com.au/sport/sport-focus/2017/05/01/athletes-after-retirement/>.

domain, where you know exactly what your job is, the influence you can have on your teammates … then all of a sudden, you are standing on your own in a room full of strangers, which are your new work friends.'[37]

The contrast is extreme. People go from belonging to not belonging; from being connected and having a purpose that others around you value to having no purpose and feeling alienated from people. You don't have to be a retired sports person to know that. Anyone who retires from work, moves cities to find work or even changes their living situation will know that a change of connection and roles will lead to a sense of being an alien. It is no wonder that one of the things that will safeguard us after a traumatic event is having a safe sense of belonging and being supported after we have been traumatised.[38]

Remember Tony from Chapter 1? He had worked as an accountant for thirty years. He was greatly appreciated at work and was quite touched by all the lovely things that were said to him by his colleagues when he left. He was keen to start his retirement and threw himself into travel, gardening and church. When his energy dropped, he began to wonder what was going on for him. As much as he loved his own father, he remembered that work was the only topic that his father spoke to him about; or more accurately, that work was the only topic that his father was *interested* in talking to Tony about. Tony learned early in his life that having a role made him a legitimate

---

[37] Original quote taken from ABC *Four Corners* ABC program entitled 'After the game' (<http://www.abc.net.au/4corners/stories/2017/05/01/4659870.htm>). Video no longer available, but you can find this quote in News Corp Australia Network, *Retired athletes reveal their struggles out of limelight*, The Chronicle, 2 May 2017, viewed May 2019, <https://www.thechronicle.com.au/news/retired-athletes-reveal-their-struggles-out-of-lim/3173019/>.

[38] CR Brewin, B Andrews & JD Valentine, op. cit.

and interesting person. When he retired, he felt alienated from his community.

Tony grew up believing that he only had a legitimate connection with others if he had a significant role in society. He thought, 'If I tell people what I do, they will like me and look up to me.' Previously, when he told them he was an accountant, people would ask him about it, and he interpreted that to mean he was accepted; however, without this role he felt anxious and was prone to avoiding others.

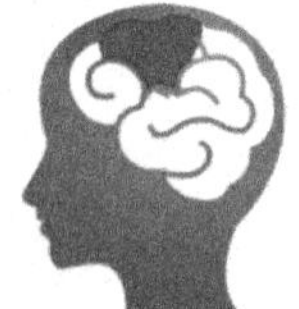

What is your primary role?

What would it be like for you to go without it?

Where or with whom do you belong?

Have you ever felt alienated from a group?

How did that impact on you?

How did you deal with it?

Pause and review

- Disconnection can be forceful in the damage that it delivers to our hearts. It inflicts the wounds of:
  - betrayal
  - worthlessness (low self-esteem)
  - shame
  - alienation.

  Sadly, all four of these wounds are indicators of the poor treatment we have received from others. They will all cause us pain and compromise our lives to varying degrees, but there is hope.

- Connection is a positively powerful phenomenon. Genuine, caring relationships can bring about healing and also:
    - o stimulate the growth of the ability to trust
    - o provide a sure knowledge that we are of value
    - o give us honour
    - o satisfy our need for belonging.

  This is how God meant our lives to be.

From the word 'Go', we require connection. Our need for love and connection is, as we have discussed, the deepest, most basic and primary of human psychological requirements. This need places us in a vulnerable situation. The need for love puts us at risk because we require something from someone else. We are designed for relating and we depend on others to provide us with what we need. We need to receive connection and we need to provide connection. We are connection creatures. To be without connection is to endure the abuse of omission, and this is, as we have discussed, very troublesome. 'You can't be numb for love,' Bono from U2 sings, 'the only pain is to feel nothing at all.' Even if we pretend we don't need it; even if we try to keep people at a distance either by passively avoiding commitments or by actively being nasty, we live horribly impoverished lives if we can't love and be loved.

Love and connection. They set in motion a life filled with trust, self-esteem, honour and belonging.

Whether you are two, twenty-two or sixty-two, you can set yourself up for a future of flourishing by being in connected relationships.

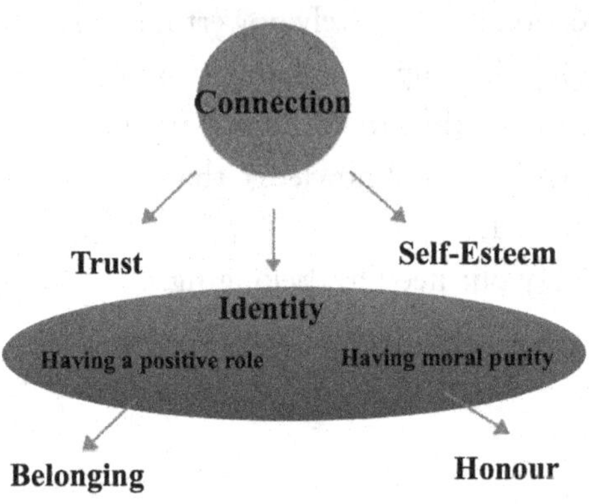

Figure 14. Connection leads to trust, self-esteem, honour and belonging

So far in this book, we have sketched out the contours and consequences of connection and disconnection. Before we discuss how we might deal with the negative consequences of disconnection, we are going to get a little more personal by turning our attention to how the heart might reveal its brokenness and its fullness to us. I am going to focus more on your personal experiences in Chapter 8, but for now we are going to consider how the heart speaks to us.

5

The four languages of the heart

To respond well to what is on our hearts, we need to know what is there. To know what is on our hearts, we must listen to ourselves. We need to carefully consider our experience. We need to wonder how our hearts may be communicating distress. To listen properly, we need to learn the language.

As we saw in Figure 9 in the previous chapter (the 'Heart Flower'), our hearts can speak a few different languages: behavioural, cognitive, physical and emotional.

There are times when what is on our hearts comes out through our **behaviour**. This is most commonly seen in young children. We know when they are upset, not because they have come to us and told us, but because of what they do.

'Why did you hit your sister?' we ask.

'Because I was angry.'

Behavioural expression of what is on our hearts is not the exclusive domain of children, though. What we do as adults indicates what is on our hearts. When our hearts are settled, we tend to treat others with respect and care. That is the positive outworking of what is on our hearts; but it also works negatively. When we are scared or feeling down, we react quickly or withdraw to avoid others.

We can also tell what is on our hearts because of the **thinking patterns** we have. One person I know caught himself often preparing for an argument that he hardly ever actually had. Before meetings, he would rehearse scenarios in his mind. 'If that person says this, I'll say that.' These pre-mortems, as opposed to post-mortems, would sensitise him and put him on high alert. His thought life revealed his heart-level concern about being subjugated and devalued by others.

Our **bodies** testify to what is on our hearts as well. Changing energy levels can speak to us if we listen. What excites us speaks of what we are attached to and what we value, and what we find draining testifies to what we find difficult. On many occasions, the body 'speaks out' our distress for us in soft ways, but there are times when it speaks out our distress in quite dramatic ways.

Some people will see a neurologist because they might have difficulty walking, experience paralysis, or have changes in their sensory systems, even though they actually have nothing wrong with them in a physical sense. For most people, such symptoms have a physical cause such as a stroke or a tumour. Not these people. They're told by clinicians, 'You have a "software" problem, not a "hardware" problem', which means there is nothing wrong with them physically, but there is obviously some sort of distress that they are expressing.

Such patients are diagnosed with Functional Neurological Disorder, but this, like many diagnoses, I find unhelpful. It would be more accurate to say, 'Your heart is communicating something through your body. There is nothing wrong with your body, but there is something going on for you in your heart.'

The most common physical expressions of distress are the garden-variety mobilisation symptoms that we spoke of in Chapter 3. These include the symptoms that typically occur in the region of your chest: heart rate increases, shortness of breath and sweaty hands. At these times, the body tells the story that something bad will happen or is happening to us.

Mobilisation symptoms, commonly experienced as anxiety, aren't the only variety of bodily expression of heart-related distress. Many people experience 'immobilisation' symptoms. These symptoms display themselves in the area of your torso below your chest. At these times, energy and appetite drop and we involuntarily slow down or even stop. This sort of response is common when people experience shame.

Of all the ways that our hearts can express distress or delight, it is most likely that it will be through our **emotions**. To put it succinctly, our hearts primarily speak an emotional language. They can speak a physical language, they can speak a cognitive or a behavioural language, but the default way for the heart to express itself is via the emotions. Emotions are the common language of distress, the *lingua franca* that we share.[1] Sometimes, our hearts speak softly in faint whispers of anxiety or excitement. At other times, our hearts will scream with depression or anger, demanding to be heard.

On most occasions, how you feel is the most reliable indication of how you are going at a heart level. This is why the question, 'How do you feel?' is such a productive question. The answer that the respondent gives provides a prism though which other people can see into his or her heart. 'What have you been doing?' is good; 'What are you thinking?' is also good; but neither of them is as good as the question, 'How are you feeling?' because the feelings reveal best what is in our hearts.

[1] There are many conditions that are associated with an inability to know the feelings we have. Depression, anxiety and especially PTSD are known to be linked to this difficulty. The difficulty is often referred to as alexithymia. It is seen in autism, but is seen also in people who have had frontal lobe injuries (brain injuries to the front of the brain above the eyes), or in people who have consumed excessive amounts of alcohol. It may not be a surprise to many women, but it occurs almost twice as much in men than it does in women. See JK Salminen, S Saarijärvi, E Äärelä, T Toikka & J Kauhanen, 'Prevalence of alexithymia and its association with sociodemographic variables in the general population of Finland', *Journal of psychosomatic research*, vol. 46, no. 1, 1999, pp. 75–82.

Humans as centrifugal beings

Our thoughts, our actions, our bodily symptoms and our feelings all reveal something about the hidden reality of what is on our hearts. When we are upset, sometimes we will act differently, sometimes we will feel differently, sometimes our bodies will respond differently and sometimes we will think differently. Sometimes we will do all four. These responses are involuntary and we have only limited control over them. This is because human beings primarily operate centrifugally. That is, what is in our hearts flows out swiftly and without conscious volition from our hearts and into our behaviour, our emotions, our thinking and our bodies. Note how in the 'Heart Flower' (Figure 9) all the unbroken arrows swing outward, because that is the centrifugal trajectory: we think, feel and act naturally. It is only on rare occasions that we have to force out a feeling or a thought. Normally, it is effortless and sometimes without our awareness. The energy comes from the inside out.

For better or for worse, this is what happens—what is happening in our hearts comes out in our system. No-one has to put effort into being defensive when they feel that they are under attack. No-one has to put effort into withdrawing when they are depressed. No-one has to try hard to raise their voice when they are angry. What happens in our hearts comes out naturally into our behaviour, our thinking, our bodies and our emotions. The energy simply flows out centrifugally.

That is the breathtaking psychological insight of King Solomon. When he wrote the proverb, 'Above all else, guard your heart'[2] in the Bible, he knew that the heart was the source or the seat of all psychological functioning. But why do we have to guard it? The proverb continues, 'for everything you do flows from it'. Over 2500 years later, we are still benefiting from his wisdom. At the centre of each human being is a heart that is profound and deeply personal. From that centre, our distress or delight finds its outward expression in our thinking, our behaviour, our feelings and our bodies. We are centrifugal beings.

---

[2] See Proverbs 4:23–27.

Understanding that this is the way human beings are helps us to recognise that all these domains of functioning (the behavioural, the cognitive, the physical and the emotional) are vantage points from which we can see what is on our hearts. Our mood is usually the best way in. All the other domains can also inform us about how we are going at a heart level, but feelings are our best bet.

When I am starting out with clients, I often ask them to integrate their experiences by helping them to connect with themselves across the different domains of their functioning. Remaining curious outside of therapy time, observing experiences and linking them together helps each person to grow in personal insight, but more than that: it sets them up for the next step, which is to use all this information to see what is happening at a heart level.

'SMART' is an acronym I use in therapy. It stands for:

- Situation
- Mood
- Action
- Reaction
- Thoughts.

I have included a SMART handout in Appendix B so that you can use it as you need to, but I will discuss it briefly now.

Like the heart contained within the Magic Eye image in Figure 5 at the beginning of Chapter 3, using the SMART process allows you to look through your situations, moods, actions, reactions and thoughts to see what is on your heart.

The task is to wait for a situation that you sense distresses you. After the situation settles, document the following:

Situation: What were you doing and who were you with when you became troubled?

Mood: What feelings did you experience at the time? Think of as many different emotions as you can and identify which emotions you felt. Give them an intensity rating (mild, moderate or severe).

Actions: What did you do or say at the time? How did you cope?

Reaction: How did your body react? (Consider heart rate, breathing, dizziness, pain, fatigue, etc.)

Thinking: List any thoughts, pictures, memories or images that came into your mind at the time.

Remember Sally from Chapter 1? She was the professional lady in her thirties who was suffering from shame. She did the SMART exercise for me after her first visit. This is what she wrote down:

Situation: 'I was talking to a friend about how I was feeling.'

Mood: 'I felt scared (moderately).'

Actions: 'I froze, but I really wanted to distract her away from what we were talking about, but I couldn't find the words!'

Reaction: 'My heart started racing. My legs felt heavy.'

Thinking: 'I'm trapped, but why? She is one of my best friends! You're being ridiculous. Later that night I dreamt of hiding from her.'

I'll show you how Sally and I worked through the SMART exercise, so that you might be able to do the same for yourself.

When Sally came to her next appointment, the challenge was to see through each of these domains of functioning. Each of these reactions (sensitivity to the type of situation, and reactions in our mood, body and thinking) represents a vantage point from which we might be able to discern what is happening at a deeper level, and because we know that each of these responses comes from the heart, they can each tell us something about what is on the heart.

Let's start with mood, because this is the most common way in which the heart speaks.

For Sally, her anxiety suggested that she understood something bad would happen to her. Her physical reaction also suggested that this was the case. When I asked her what the worst thing she thought could happen was if she were to answer her friend's question, she replied, 'I'd tell the truth.'

I felt dissatisfied with this, but knew we were getting somewhere, so I asked, 'What would be the worst thing that could happen if you told the truth?'

Sally responded, 'My emotions would overwhelm me. I'd lose control of them. That is why I don't like talking about them.'

She was scared of her emotions, and although I was full of empathy and concern for Sally, I wanted to be sure that I didn't focus on that too quickly. There can be things that I miss if I rush and move too quickly, so I cast the net more widely before we focused on her fear of losing control.

'Okay. Anything else you were scared could happen?' I queried.

Her response was really important, and I was so glad I didn't rush.

'Yes. My friend. My dear friend … she already does so much for me. If she found out how I felt about myself, and I became overwhelmed, I got scared she would reject me for it.'

Sally had looked through her mood, through the scared feeling, to her heart. She saw in her heart a fear of rejection. She also had fear about her emotions. She feared that her feelings would overcome her, which explained why she occasionally disconnected from how she felt. We will talk about this sort of avoidance shortly, but Sally's core concern was about being a burden and that then leading to rejection. Her concern about rejection explained her physical reaction (heart rate increase), her action (freezing), and her thinking (that she was trapped, because she wanted to share but didn't want sharing about herself to lead to a deterioration in the relationship).

Now you might take the opportunity to try the same process. Pick any situation in which you became distressed. It doesn't have to be dramatic. It may be productive to pick a situation that you frequently find a little upsetting. First we will touch on the situation, the precipitating circumstance, and then mood because it is the most common way that your heart communicates.

Think of a time lately that you found distressing. What was the **situation**? In that situation, how would you describe your **mood**? What might that say about what is on your heart?

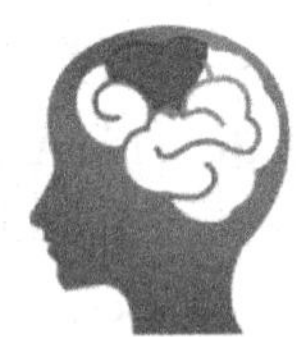

As I have stated, the heart also communicates in the other domains, and they are useful to consider too. You've done the first two letters of SMART; now examine your **actions**, **reactions** and **thinking**.

In that situation, how did you cope/act at the time? How did your body react? Did any thoughts or images go through your mind at the time or shortly afterwards? How might your action/bodily reaction/thinking inform you about what is happening in your heart? Is that similar to what you suspected when you considered your mood?

We are going to examine what to do with what you find in your heart in Chapter 9. For now, we just want to capture the dynamic we've just examined. We have established a way to connect with our hearts by remaining curious about the different domains of human functioning: thoughts, actions, feelings and physical changes that 'flow from' our hearts. We want to see each of them, but we also want to see through them. We want to see what might explain them and what has given rise to them.

The heart of the matter, meaning the substance of the matter, is also the heart of the person, the substance of ourselves. All these areas of functioning (our sensitivity to the situation, moods, actions, reactions and thoughts) are symptoms of the heart. They flow centrifugally out of it, and while they aren't a part of the heart, they all speak of what is in it. This is a fundamentally different way of approaching people and life. It is where a 'heart in mind' approach differs from a lot of mainstream approaches.

Symptoms of the heart

Many people think that symptoms are things to be reduced. This is understandable, because symptoms are distressing by nature, but it is not the goal of therapy. To be sure, we want to reduce symptoms, but we want to do more than that. People who talk about 'symptom reduction' are usually the same people who forget that symptoms are always symptoms *of* something. For example, a high temperature is a symptom *of* having a virus. It is helpful to take medication like paracetamol to help reduce the symptom (the high temperature) because in itself this symptom is distressing, but the real task is to address the real cause that the symptom emanates from—the virus. Temperature, aches and pains are 'symptoms of' something and warrant attention, but the primary challenge for the physician is to understand what the symptoms can tell us about what is really going on.

It is just the same way with changes in behaviour, cognition, mood and our bodies. They're all symptoms of changes in the heart, not merely distressing experiences that need to be reduced. Reducing these symptoms will help us to tolerate and endure our distress, but if we really want to restore what has been damaged, we need to go to the cause.

Feelings, just like behaviours, thoughts and energy levels, aren't there to be dismissed or tolerated by being mindful of them. They're there to be understood and reckoned with. Symptoms such as anger, anxiety and depression do make their own contribution to ongoing distress as we have acknowledged (see how in Figure 9 the petal loops back in a broken line to secure what is in the heart), but symptom reduction is only part of the solution.

We can do so much better than that. We can uncover the cause! Curiosity is the key because there will be nothing uncovered without it. The way we cope in a situation (faking, fighting, fleeing or facing), images that come into our minds, memories that suddenly leap into our consciousness, and even our dreams are hints for us about what could be happening to us at a deeper level. What is happening in our bodies, in that 'theatre of the emotions', also needs to be considered, because that too will inform us of what is happening.

As I wrote that last sentence I remembered something. Well over twenty years ago now, my physical heart skipped a beat when I first gazed at my wife at a Christian conference outside Sydney. It skipped a beat because I was deeply moved by her beauty and manner. My body spoke of what was in my heart.

When you connect with yourself, personal growth isn't far away; but personal growth is preceded by understanding, and understanding is preceded by curiosity. We don't need to stop at the symptoms and see only the symptoms. What a waste that would be. We need to see through the symptoms. To see only the symptoms would be just as bad as seeing through the symptoms to nothing at all. C. S. Lewis once wrote, 'The whole point of seeing through something is to see something through it.'[3] He is right. We don't want to only see through the symptoms but see the symptoms as symptoms *of* something … symptoms of the heart. We want to see through the thoughts, the images, the behaviours, the feelings and our bodily reactions to get a sense of what is on our hearts, because what is on our hearts is the substantial part of us.

For this reason, therapists will spend considerable time trying to understand the emotional, behavioural, cognitive and physiological expression of distress. When I am with someone, I always ask myself, 'What do these symptoms say about what is really going on for them?'

For me and for you, that is how we come to understand what is on our hearts. We find a caring person and, with them, we become curious about what the symptoms say to us about what is happening to us at a deeper level. Curiosity is key. Seeing the symptoms, and understanding what the symptoms mean, how the symptoms overlap and when they started, will inform us about what troubles us. It is not always a smooth process, as we will see.

Speed bumps on the way

Two potential speed bumps are looming which may slow down your journey of recognising what is on your heart.

The first speed bump has written on it the word 'alexithymia'. Alexithymia literally means 'no word for emotion'. It is a state in which we simply don't know what it is that we feel. People can experience this for a variety of reasons. It could be because of 'cloudy mirrors' and uninterested, volatile and/or emotionally illiterate caregivers, for example. You may have a little of this, or you may have a lot.

If you experience a little alexithymia, don't be put off. Let the struggle to name the emotions inform you of the need to be patient

---

[3] CS Lewis, *The abolition of man*, Oxford University Press, Oxford, 1943.

with yourself. Don't insist on being accurate, just insist on maintaining a gentle curiosity. Collect information that will help, like physical symptoms, things you do or say, and thoughts and memories that come to you. Share these with friends or write them down in a journal, but all the while, entertain the idea of what you *might* feel. Sometimes, people can achieve clarity about their feelings by looking at a list of feelings and nominating which ones they have. I have included a list of feelings in Appendix C. You might try looking through them if you are struggling in this way.

The second speed bump may be that you actually dislike the process. Sally didn't like to go too near her emotions. She had a 'hot-stove' experience in that when she verbalised her feelings, they threatened to overwhelm her. She learned not to connect with herself in the hope that she might keep herself emotionally composed.

This 'affect avoidance' led her to shut herself off from herself. Unfortunately for her, and for all of us when we do the same, by doing so she robbed herself of the opportunity to understand herself and turned her emotions into enemies to be feared.

It is all well and good talking about connecting with others, but connecting with ourselves can be difficult. The message is the same. Speed bumps are there to go over—we just need to go slowly. I encouraged Sally to use her difficulty with emotions as a starting point for her journey. I encouraged her to not let her reluctance take her out of the self-connection process, but to use it as part of the same process. I asked her, 'What is that feeling that tempts you to run away from self-connection? When have you felt this way before? Who were you with? How did they react?'

When we go to connect with another person, we turn towards them, focus on them and consider what their experiences are like for them. When we connect with ourselves, we do the same. We turn towards ourselves, focus on ourselves and consider what our experiences have been like for us. Considering that process now, what was it like when you turned towards yourself, focused on you and considered your own experiences?

- What was it like to approach yourself?
- Was it difficult?
- Was it easy?
- When you tried to connect with yourself, did you feel disgust?
- Did you feel anger?
- Did you feel hatred or loathing?
- Did you feel satisfaction or contentment?
- Importantly, how did the way you feel suggest an attachment style that you have towards yourself—insecure or secure? Anxious? Avoidant?

Use the experience of reflecting on these questions to gather information that will help improve your understanding of yourself.

You may have one, both or neither of these speed bumps. Alternatively, there may be none now, then one or two later. Your challenge is to remain in the quest, and you can only do this when you have gentle and flexible expectations. No matter what happens, we can be confident that connecting with ourselves leads to understanding, and understanding leads to a response to ourselves that benefits us and those around us. This process is the same as the interpersonal process: connection with others leads to better understanding of them and more appropriate responses to them, but we have to go at a speed that they are comfortable with. Pacing is a key issue. If we want to connect with ourselves, we have to find a pace that we are comfortable with, and this pace will change over time.

Pause and review

- Human beings are centrifugal beings. That means that our thoughts, actions, physical reactions and feelings flow out from a deep part of us. For thousands of years, that deeper place has been referred to as the 'heart'.

- The way we feel, act, react and think are all symptoms of what is in our hearts. We can get an idea of what is in our hearts by remembering that all these symptoms are symptoms of a heart-level disturbance. By looking through these symptoms, a bit like a prism, we can come to better understand ourselves.
- There are some potential speed bumps that might slow us down as we try to connect with ourselves. They include alexithymia, not having the words, or the 'hot-stove' experience where we have learned to avoid feelings because they are difficult to deal with. But speed bumps are there not to stop us, but just to remind us to go slowly.

Have there been any times in your life when you felt depressed, anxious or angry in excessive ways? What might those emotions say about what was going on for you at a heart level at those times?

Do you find yourself becoming controlling of situations? Do you fight or flee or fake your way through some relationships? Why is that?

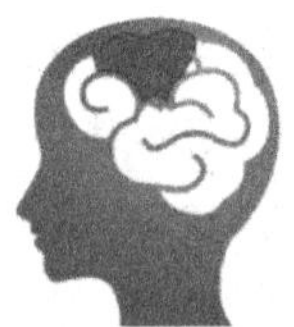

Are there images or memories that seem to preoccupy you? What might these say about your history of connection?

Have there been times when your body reacts unnecessarily? What was happening at the time?

On those occasions, when you felt/acted/reacted/thought that way, what was that like for you? What did it say about you at a deep level?

Have you hit one or both of the speed bumps of not being able to identify your feelings or being unwilling to examine how you are feeling?

In Part One of this book, we spoke about the heart and the importance of connection. In Part Two, we have covered the nature of poor connection (omission and commission) and how poor connection leads to deep psychological injuries: betrayal, worthlessness, shame and alienation. We have just closed out Part Two with an outline of what it means to be a centrifugal being, how we might consider our symptoms to help us understand what is on our hearts, and what problems we might encounter in the process.

We will revisit connecting with ourselves in Chapter 8. In that chapter, we are going to build on and consolidate what we have learned in this chapter about symptoms by linking what is in our hearts with what is in the past.

First, though, having outlined how relationships hurt, we now turn our attention towards how we might begin to heal from those injuries. This is what Part Three is all about. To start this process, we are going to establish a three-point connection framework. By so doing, we are taking the first step towards recovering and flourishing.

PART THREE

HOW RELATIONSHIPS HEAL

6

Connection with God (God heals people)

A woman in her home town walked to a well in the midday sun. Her intention was to get water. She had no needs other than to quench her thirst—at least, that's what she thought.

There was a man sitting at the well. The journey was familiar to her but the person she saw at the well was not. He looked like a foreigner. Relationships with men hadn't been easy for her, and her stomach signalled an alarm. She was right to be concerned: the man at the well was from a race of people known to hate her own.

She hesitated as she approached. The ground radiated heat up through her fragile sandals and her ankles negotiated the rubble beneath her feet. She looked up and anxiety crashed into and through her body. Men often scared her.

She noticed that the man looked tired. He had no way of getting a drink. The heat was oppressive, and the woman's partner at home was waiting for her to return. She didn't want to upset him by going back with nothing, so in spite of the threat that the stranger represented, she approached the well.

Suddenly, there was a misalignment. The foreigner committed a social blasphemy. He asked her a question: '*Will you give me a drink?*'

She was not expecting this; she was expecting to be ignored. She was used to being overlooked or looked through by men whom she met.

'*How can you ask me for a drink?*' she replied.

'*If you knew … who it is that asks you for a drink, you would have asked him* [for water],' he responded.

Confusion was added to her apprehension. His comments seemed laced with arrogance. Arrogance from these people was what she had previously experienced. Now she was on familiar ground. Yet, he still talked to her, almost as if he was interested in her—as if, somehow, she was worthy of his conversation. She wanted out of the interaction because it was too awkward to bear.

'It is time to distract him,' she thought, so she tried to call the traveller's bluff. 'Is he seriously going to offer me any more than what any of his ancestors have?' she wondered. She pointed out to him that it was one of his own great ancestors who had built the well.

'*Are you greater than our father Jacob?*' she asked.

He didn't take the bait. Rather, he responded with his own enigmatic statement: '*Everyone who drinks this water will be thirsty again, but whoever drinks the water I give them will never thirst.*'

There seemed to be a generosity about the stranger: not only did he talk to her in spite of her race; not only did he talk in spite of her gender; he seemed to be offering something to her, as if he was using water as a metaphor. He placed himself above the ancestor who had built the well, but seemed to be offering her something that would quench her thirst, and she was thirsty … so very thirsty.

'*Give me this water so that I won't get thirsty,*' she replied.

Then he called *her* bluff. '*Go, call your husband and come back.*'

'*I have no husband,*' she replied.

'*You are right when you say you have no husband. The fact is, you have had five husbands, and the man you now have is not your husband. What you have just said is quite true.*'

'Who is this man?' she thought. 'What on earth is this conversation about? How could he know these things? What I wanted was water—that is my need, and my intention is to drink—but is he saying that I don't really want that? I thought he was in need; is he saying that I'm the one who is in need? Is my need really what I thought it was?' A swirl of mental activity tormented her.

'*Sir,*' the woman said, '*I can see that you are a prophet. Our ancestors worshiped on this mountain, but you Jews claim that the place where we must worship is in Jerusalem.*'

The traveller broke so many social and religious norms in his interaction with this woman. She had thought he required her help with drawing water from the well, but what became clear was that she was in greater need. She thirsted for what she had been unable to get, as a woman, as a Samaritan, and as a human.

'*Woman,*' he replied, '*believe me, a time is coming when you will worship the Father neither on this mountain nor in Jerusalem.*'

She heard his words, and it touched on one of the deep longings of her heart. He was answering a question that she hadn't asked him. She hadn't found the explanation she needed, but she looked forward to a time in the future when she would find peace in her heart. Her deepest hope flowed centrifugally out of her heart, took shape in the form of words and came out her mouth.

'*I know that Messiah (called Christ) is coming. When he comes, he will explain everything to us.*'

'*I, the one speaking to you—I am he,*' the traveller replied.[1]

The traveller's name was Jesus. In that ancient interaction, he completely reconfigured how we can have our heart-level needs met in God.

---

[1] You can find this beautiful story in John 4:4–26. The key to understanding this passage is to remember that Samaritans were a hated group of people. (This is also what makes the story of the 'good Samaritan' one of the most commonly misunderstood teachings of Jesus.) Jesus makes heroes of the hated people. The marginalised or the maligned are the ones he loves. In Chapter 4 of the Gospel of John, Jesus here takes time to talk to someone hated, a Samaritan and an outcast—and a woman with a chequered relational history. The direct quotes from the story in the Bible are in italics. I have added the thoughts of the woman; they are not part of the original story.

All the mistakes that she had made were not the issue. Becoming a different sort of person was not the solution. She needed to repent, but no more than any other person. There would be no pilgrimages for salvation hereafter. There would be no race to belong to, nor would there be a more righteous gender. What she had done was not the focus—the focus was on what Jesus had done and who he was. She did not need to go to him; he came to her. She did not have to be somewhere or be someone different. She needed only to tell the truth about herself and look to Jesus, then she would be saved.

What beautiful news it is, to be thirsty and have someone offer you water. For a woman with a history of unstable relationships, her hopes became realised in that conversation. She could never have known what was going to happen when she set out for the well in the heat of that day. With an enemy in front of her and an impatient partner behind her, she approached Jesus and prepared herself to be reproached. Yet Jesus spoke to her, connected with her and responded to her as a genuine person.

This nameless woman walked the earth roughly 2000 years ago. She reminds me of a lot of people who I sit with—people who have had a difficult journey negotiating their way through troubling and transient relationships; decent people who thirst for more than what they've had.

Learning to live with the 'heart in mind' means learning to live with an awareness of how relationships are a foundational requirement of living well. While connection with safe and relationally warm people is required to meet the needs of our hearts, this is not the only powerful source of positive connection. For many of us, our spiritual connection proves to be a great source of strength. It is to this vertical connection that our attention now turns. We will explore why and how connecting with an unseen God can be so helpful in our journey.

What benefits does a spiritual relationship hold?

The benefits of having a close spiritual connection are compelling.

In a comprehensive review of the research on spirituality and mental and physical health, Duke University researcher Harold Koenig noted that:

> A large volume of research shows that people who are more R/S [Religious/Spiritual] have better mental health and adapt more quickly to health problems compared to those who are less R/S.[2]

Take depression as an example. Koenig examined 444 studies that investigated the relationship between depression and spirituality. He found that, of the 178 studies that had the highest scientific standards:

- 67% of the studies documented that the more religious someone was, the less depressed they were.
- 7% of the studies found that the more religious someone was, the more depressed they were.

Presumably, because the author did not explicitly say this, 26% of the 178 studies indicated that there was no relationship between religiosity and depression.

The conclusion is clear: religiosity appears to be, in most cases, good for you; sometimes neither good nor bad for you; and in a very small number of cases, bad for you.

I am not expecting you as the reader to have a thriving spiritual life. Nor am I expecting you to be an expert in this area. My own spiritual life is sometimes neither thriving nor marked out by expertise. Neither of these attributes is required for you to benefit

---

[2] HG Koenig, 'Religion, spirituality and health: the research and clinical implications', *ISRN psychiatry*, vol. 2012, 2012, pp. 1–33 (p. 15).

from a spiritual relationship—only positive motivation is necessary (intrinsic motivation, not extrinsic motivation[3]).

If you would like your faith to be an area of your life that serves as another connection point, then read on. If, however, this is not an important area of functioning to you, and you have no desire to explore the possibilities, you are welcome to skip this chapter. I will not prescribe nor proscribe anything for you in this regard. You are free, as you should be, to do your spirituality your own way.

You might ask, 'If we can skip this chapter altogether, why introduce this topic?'

We could bypass the spiritual connection, and if we did, we would all still benefit from discussing human connection. Building safe relationships with others would remain an important and strategic proposal for all people, whether you are heartbroken or not, and whether you have a faith or not.

The dilemma we face is whether or not we would even want to discard such a helpful resource. Take, as an analogy, exercise. We know that exercise is good for our mental and cognitive health. It isn't the perfect answer, but it is moderately good for an extensive number of problems: stress, depression, anxiety, fatigue, hormonal changes,

---

[3] In the late 1960s, Allport and Ross constructed the Religious Orientation Scale (ROS). Since that time it has been used to delineate between mature or intrinsically-motivated spirituality and immature or extrinsically-motivated spirituality. The latter is characterised by the attitude that church and faith are just means to an end, whereas the former is characterised by the attitude that church and faith are ends in themselves. It is ironic that people who want something out of their faith typically don't get much, and people who want little from their faith typically benefit more. In their review of the literature on motivation and spirituality, Hunter and Merrill note that 'in nearly all of these studies [that were reviewed], intrinsic religion has been shown to act as a protective factor against mental illness, whereas extrinsic religion is generally found to act as a risk factor for mental illness.' BD Hunter & RM Merrill, 'Religious orientation and health among active older adults in the United States', *Journal of religion and health*, vol. 52, no. 3, 2013, pp. 851–63 (quote from p. 852).

ageing, and learning and attention deficit problems.[4] Why would we not consider using exercise when we help people with their emotions?

So it is with our spiritual life. Why would we want to ignore what has already been established as a constructive resource for the heart? Besides, if we do overlook a divine solution, we may depend on others or ourselves for the solution to heartbreak, and that is not without its challenges.

A world without God: a world of pressure on ourselves and others

The non-negotiable need to give and receive good connection demands to be met. If we decide to leave God out of the picture, we need to be aware that we have only two real options: either we depend on someone else to help us, or we depend on ourselves. To find trust, self-esteem, honour and belonging, we will either have to outsource the solution to others, or we will have to do it in-house.

Thunder clouds appear on the horizon when we rely on others to deliver what our hearts desire. If we depend on someone else, we become sensitive to what they do or don't do for us. We become brittle and easily upset. When others sense that, they start to become cautious. They try not stepping out of line for fear of upsetting us; spontaneity goes; fun suffers. Freedom becomes restricted by the weight of our quiet coercion. Our offence is never far away. Our distress becomes externalised ('They made me upset'); we forget that people aren't deliberately offensive; and we forget that we are the ones who 'take' offence.

When freedom goes, so does shared connection. Rules arise that limit the freedom that others have and they make our connection with others brittle: 'My son should always value my wisdom'; 'My step-daughter should be affectionate to me'; 'My boyfriend should never find another woman interesting'; 'My girlfriend should always listen

[4] JJ Ratey, *Spark: the revolutionary new science of exercise and the brain*, Little, Brown and Company, New York, 2008.

and value what I say'; 'My boss should promote me.' In order for our value and identity to be maintained, the rules we have for others must be obeyed by them; but the people on whom we depend don't always know the rules, never agreed to the rules, and are often shocked by the strength of our emotional reactions. When they break the rules, we become terribly upset, but the problem isn't the behaviour of others so much as the silent rules we have and how we expected others, albeit unofficially, to be the solution to our need for value.

What a horrible burden we can place on others. Close relationships offer the opportunity to love and be loved. Family provides us with the opportunity to serve people other than ourselves and many of us find meaning in that. There is a terrible loss that looms large for those of us who separate from our families, especially in those of us who have neglected our relationships outside of our marriages. Divorce and separation take a heavy toll. Yet it is not the loss of the marriage so much as the heart-related injuries that hurt most.

Many of us recognise this, but we can miss the point. The investment in our partner to be the making of our identity and value can lead to controlling behaviour and coercion, expecting partners to abide by the unspoken rules that we have for them. These rules bind our partners to the union, but their autonomy is slowly strangled. When the control goes up, the connection goes down. For many, the fate of the relationship is sealed long before a breakup or divorce proceedings, and it all starts with the outsourcing of our value to someone else.

Ultimately, we need to ask someone else to heal our hearts. If we can't count on someone else, then maybe we should count on ourselves.

Those thunder clouds disappear, but a new weather front develops on the horizon. If we depend on ourselves then we are solely responsible for our own hearts, and the stakes are high. We have to *do* something, and it had better be good. Many are excited by this challenge and welcome it. However, life is full of struggles and obstacles, and the challenge can be too great, the burden too heavy, the resources and opportunities too scarce. The new weather front holds back a storm. There is rain in the clouds, and the heavy clouds bring darkness.

When we appoint ourselves to give us trust, self-esteem, honour and belonging, we undertake a huge responsibility. Responsibility is all well and good, but we may not have as much control over our lives as we think. Lots of responsibility and little control is the recipe for 'learned helplessness'. Some people find a way out of this by bolstering their personal sense of control. Advocates such as life coach Tony Robbins give plenty of encouragement. He and others like him remind us that 'the power is within us', but they offer no fall-back position.

Their encouragement ironically exacerbates the problem. If the power really is within us and we don't achieve everything we want, a personalised sense of failure is our fate, because we have no-one else to blame but ourselves for not using the power that we have. It is an all-or-nothing, high-risk strategy.

Popular music applies the pressure by reminding us that we have nothing more than the present life, so we'd better do it now and get it right. Bruno Mars sings triumphantly in 'Today My Life Begins':

> Life's too short to have regrets
> So I'm learning now to leave it in the past and try to
> forget
> We only have one life to live
> So you better make the best of it.

The problem is, especially when you're my age, we do have regrets. Being human involves making mistakes and it is not always possible to leave the past behind. Progress is not assured, but what is sure is that set-backs and struggle are part of everyone's life.

Tantalised by the thought that 'we can have it all', because 'we have the power within us', we push on regardless. We hold on believing that it is possible to engineer our own value, significance and fulfilment by achieving, actualising, earning and acquiring. Yet, when well-meaning pop singers remind us that 'we have only one life' as a way of encouraging us to break free from the shackles of fear, we ironically become haunted by the final implication that being solely responsible for our own hearts might leave us with poor self-esteem and guilt that we haven't made something more of ourselves.

The message is clear. It is not enough to exist. You have to produce or do something remarkable, and it is on the basis of what you do that you'll be evaluated. The stakes are high and the ambient air feels urgent. 'Do it, do it now, you've got 40 adult years to be remarkable.'

If there is no God who can make us worthy, if others won't obey our rules to make us worthy, and if we can't release the power we have within us, despair looms on the horizon. The longings of the heart remain indifferent to our incapacity to satisfy them. Many people are aware of living under this pressure, a pressure that is almost too much. The atheist philosopher Alain De Botton expresses it better than most:

> … when a belief in a next world is interpreted as a childish and scientifically impossible opiate, the pressure to succeed and fulfil oneself will inevitably be inflamed by the awareness that there is only a single and frighteningly brief opportunity to do so. Earthly achievements … are the sum total of all one will ever be.[5]

What a horrible burden we place on ourselves. Is it any wonder that 45–59 year old men are the group most at risk of suicide?[6] It is as

[5] A De Botton, *Status anxiety*, Vintage Books, New York, 2005, p. 56.

[6] The Office for National Statistics in the United Kingdom and the Centres for Disease Control and Prevention in the United States confirm this trend, though the latter uses a wider age bracket when it defines 'middle age'. The Australian Bureau of Statistics states, 'The highest proportion of suicide deaths occurs in the 45–49 year age group among both males and females … While the number of males who die by suicide exceeds the number of females for every age group …' Australian Bureau of Statistics, *Causes of death, Australia, 2017*, viewed November 2019, <https://www.abs.gov.au/ausstats/abs@.nsf/Lookup/by%20Subject/3303.0~2017~Main%20Features~Intentional%20self-harm,%20key%20characteristics~3>.

if, at that age, they are driving along and they drive up and over the crest of a hill. At this time, at that age, they can, for the first time in their careers, see the finish line. As retirement looms on the horizon, their destiny becomes clearer. It is at this time that men get a sense of what their ceiling level success will look like. Only a select few of them will attain the vocational prestige, position, power and remuneration level they dreamt of in their twenties. It was easy to excuse lack of success when the men were in their youth. At that time of their lives, they were not expected to be successful. At that time of their lives there was always a future in which they could hope. By the time they reach their middle years, though, they can see where they might end up; they can see how they are going to measure up. Retirement will be their ultimate reckoning. Will they meet their own expectations? Time is running out and their value, their belonging, their sense of honour hangs in the balance. With the diminishing years come diminishing hopes.[7]

There is good news, though—a potential reprieve from the inclement weather. Neither you, nor the people around you, need to be the ultimate solution.

There is a stunning resignation that Christian people make. They confess their own inability to complete the task of healing their own hearts, and they confess that they shouldn't rely on another person to do that either. They recognise it as being inefficacious; they see it as a foolish endeavour. For them, it has been an empirical question: they tried to do it, and they failed at it. They regret appointing themselves or others as the ones to give them trust/self-esteem/honour/belonging. It is a foundational moment of living with a

[7] Women at this age are also dealing with their own disappointments and responsibilities, but suicide rates are much lower in the female age-matched population.

faith when we turn our backs on others and on ourselves as the chief architects of our own psychological salvation.

Personal merit is nullified. Being 'lost' evaporates like the morning dew. Pride floats away like chalk in the wind. God becomes the agent and the destination. Grace is poured into the vacuum in our hearts. Our Creator sits on the seat recently vacated by us and vacated by the people we previously appointed. We don't worship them. We don't worship ourselves. We stop grasping. The 'shoulds' we have for ourselves and others are discarded. Opportunities are interesting, but aren't urgent. We no longer consume the world out of our own need—we seek to serve and lift up others who are in need. We give out because we are filled up.

God is an 'opt-in' relationship. We don't have to have God in our hearts, but if we want to, there are real opportunities available to us. For hundreds of millions of people, the Christian God provides nourishment for our hearts in profound ways. It is a relationship that provides a perpetual resource for our deepest needs. For this reason, faith isn't something that we grow out of, because none of us grows out of a need for love, value, belonging and honour. Dependence on God, in this view, looks healthy, because to depend on ourselves or others seems so unhealthy. It is an oddity, a discordant suggestion; it is the sound of fingernails being dragged down the chalkboard, the suggestion that maturity should involve moving on from the very source of love itself. Echoing the Apostle's words to Jesus, 'Where else have we to go,' wrote Nicky Chiswell in her song that carries the same title, 'when you alone have words of eternal life?'

Our vertical connection: the perfect love for our hearts

From the beginning of the Bible, it is obvious that words are important to God. The very fact that he chose to 'speak' but not be seen tells us that the best way to get to know him is to listen. So if we listen, what has he got to say? What he says is that he is best understood as a father. He invites us to see him that way: 'I thought you would call me "Father",' he says in Jeremiah 3:19.

At the time when this verse was written, this way of describing a deity was revolutionary. The contrast with other creation stories and religious views is stark. Jeremiah and the prophets before him tell us that humans weren't created out of fear of other warring gods, as the Babylonians told us—they were the deliberate creation of a loving father. Over and over again, the Bible tells us that God is first and foremost a God of love. As a father, he created us and knows us intimately. His intentions for us are good. Driven by compassion, he seeks to connect with his children in a loving, nurturing relationship that goes to the depth of our hearts. While the very best treatment we can receive from those around us will always be to some degree less than perfect, the relationship offered to us by God through this vertical connection is unchanging and complete, because he himself is unchanging and a completely loving father.

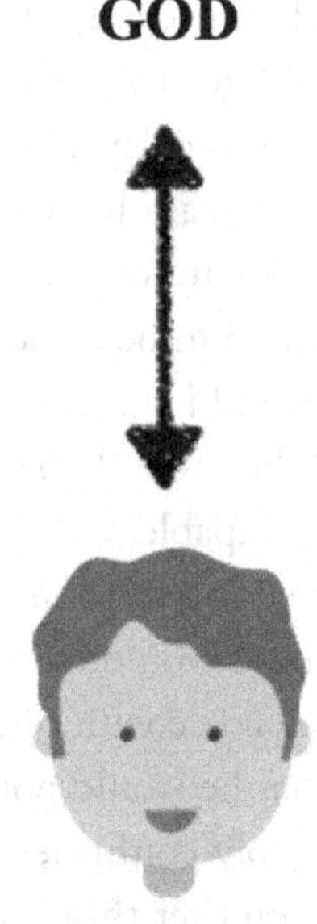

Figure 15. Vertical connection

The gospel story is about the initiative taken by a loving father to rescue his children. This is water for thirsty people. However, while it seems like an inherently beautiful message, for many the notion of a God who knows and cares for us can seem very remote. In our limited and fractured humanity, it can be a slow process to fathom then internalise the gospel story, but every now and then we catch a glimpse of how deeply God might feel about us, how he yearns to be with us, and how he really is interested in everything about us.

I had such an experience when God spoke to me through a wise and godly friend. It was a transformational moment in my spiritual journey and one I will never forget. I think it resonated so deeply because it was true to form … it captured the way God wants me to see him.

Like all allied health workers and psychiatrists, psychologists are required to undertake ongoing learning to maintain their registration to practise. On one occasion, I was in Sydney for a weekend to attend a conference with a good friend, John. As we walked through the city, I told him I'd had an excited call from my eight-year-old daughter to report that she'd got full marks for both her 'number facts' and her spelling on the same day. I said to my friend John, 'All I want to do is celebrate her—to ask her what it was like for her and what it felt like for her to work hard to achieve those results, and how she felt about herself.' I wanted to be in her presence and to live in her joy and show her how proud I was of her. I knew it wasn't about her marks—it was about a heart-level change. She had discovered that she was competent and capable.

It was only as I was speaking to John that I realised that what I was actually saying was that I would have preferred to be at home with her and not at the conference with him. I also knew that John was a robust person, and that he would not take any of what I was saying personally, and his reply confirmed it. He asked me a very unexpected question: 'Do you ever think that that is the way your Father in heaven thinks of you?'

I was stumped. There was a long pause. Well, at least it felt like a long pause, but it probably wasn't. It was early in the morning. The morning sun was still hiding behind tall buildings. We had walked up empty city streets. The air was cool; the coffee cup felt hot in my hand. Then I realised something that hadn't occurred to me. Sadly, I had never thought that this is the way God thinks of me. Never once had I thought that God would delight in me simply for my sake, the way I delight in my daughter for her sake.

One of the distinct advantages of the Christian walk is that God establishes so clearly who we are to him from the outset. We are each a child of God. We are his children and he is our Father, the sort of father who is itching to celebrate us and lift us up, just like I wanted to do for my child. The book of Galatians tells us:

> God sent the Spirit of his Son into our hearts, the Spirit who calls out, 'Abba, Father.' So you are no longer a slave, but God's child; and since you are his child, God has made you also an heir.[8]

My conversation with John highlighted God's closeness to me and the intensely personal way in which he sees me as his own child in whom he delights. The costly gift of Jesus' life was not a random gift to a faceless humanity: it was a personal gift to everyone ever created. It reveals what is on God's own heart—a deep desire to seek connection with each of us, and for us to be honoured by him, be valued by him, belong to him and trust him. The Bible contains so many invitations to seek and find him, to turn to him, to come to him, abide with him and walk with him. He sent Jesus to be our 'way' back to him because he longs for us to live in connection with him in an ongoing, close and personal way—the same way a loved child connects with a loving father.

God's choice of the father–child relationship to describe the connection he desires to have with us is powerful. It pulls us into a style of relating that is characterised by intimacy and privilege. We

---

[8] Galatians 4:6–7.

relate to a King who is also our father, the sort of King and father who is predisposed and motivated to make us an heir.

Several years ago, I gave a talk to about 150 Bible college students. They were a motivated, responsive and delightful group of people and I felt very honoured to be with them. However, I told them, 'Don't turn up out of the blue at my house at 6pm and sit down at the table to eat. You don't have that sort of privilege. You are all fine people, but only my children have that privilege. They can walk into my house at any time. They can sit down and eat at the table if they want to. And when they do, I'll join them.'

This captures something of the extraordinary quality of the father–child relationship. It is a day-in, day-out relationship involving provision, protection and belonging. It is trusting, close and safe. Being 'a child of God' is meant to inspire confidence. 'And Can It Be That I Should Gain?' is a hymn that Charles Wesley wrote shortly after his conversion in the 1730s. In the fifth stanza, he writes about how there is no condemnation, only a freedom of access to God: 'Bold I approach the eternal throne …'

He approaches God on his throne *boldly*. Only the child of the King has such an extraordinary sense of entitlement to be near, to be safe and to belong. 'Bold I approach the eternal throne *and* claim the crown through Christ my own.' God wants us to live our lives knowing we are deeply loved by him and knowing that our permanent place of belonging is with him as his child. A heart that is able to receive and experience such robust love and audacious freedom will be profoundly nourished by it.

It is precisely the purity of this sort of love that leads to the washing away of shame, the building of belonging, trust and hope, and the restoration of a sense of value. The four big injuries of the connection domain can be undermined by a Creator Father. We sense a safety in the relationship that invites us to trust him. We feel valued because of the empathy. We are washed clean by the purity. We belong. It is not a cure, but it is a tremendous start and a great asset on our journey.

In the same way that connection injuries spill over into other domains of the heart, the benefits of our spiritual connection aren't restricted to the remedy of connection injuries. The benefits flow into other areas of our hearts also. Identity and direction are formed by love, wonder and gratitude. Hope comes to us like a visitor we weren't quite expecting. Like a cup being filled up and over the brim, we become invigorated to be something bigger than what we are.

To be filled up with trust, self-esteem, honour and belonging is satisfaction itself. Once achieved, our task is to keep our hearts in our minds and let our minds guide or set our hearts on loves that nourish it, lest we become duped by false promises, worship counterfeit gods and be led to assume that other things and activities will satisfy us. We have an inordinate capacity to lie to ourselves saying this or that alternate option is all we need. We feign contentment, but we aren't content—we are just distracted. C. S. Lewis put it well:

> It would seem that Our Lord finds our desires not too strong, but too weak. We are half-hearted creatures, fooling about with drink and sex and ambition when infinite joy is offered us, like an ignorant child who wants to go on making mud pies in a slum because he cannot imagine what is meant by the offer of a holiday at the sea. We are far too easily pleased.[9]

With God, we have the ultimate relationship in which we are intimately known and loved. In him we have a permanent base of belonging, an orientation for our lives and a reason for being. He gives us a place of significance in this universe and equips us to live with purpose, as well as the promise of an eternity that is not marred by the struggles of this life. Our appetite for love, purpose and hope speak of what we were made for. Our thirst speaks of our need for water. This is how God is glorified, when we realise that he is the answer to what our hearts long for and nothing else will do. When

[9] CS Lewis, *The weight of glory*, Harper Collins, New York, 1949.

John Piper wrote that 'God is most glorified in us when we are most satisfied in Him,'[10] he spoke not just of God being the answer but about how it is possible to have deep longings properly met: how we can have heart-level satisfaction.

Physical, mental and social satisfaction are all significant in their own ways, but being filled up with love, having a sense of identity and hope that transcends suffering, is satisfaction beyond measure. Satisfaction is available for us in part now, and more fully later, and God is most glorified when we realise that such satisfaction can be found only in Him. Our desires are extravagant, but they're extravagantly satisfied in a God who loves us more than we know.

Pause and review

- The appetite of the heart is always there. We will seek the solution within us, or outside us. If we rely on ourselves or on others, the pressure builds.
- Asking God to fill our hearts takes the pressure off us and others to do that job (we are going to talk more about how to do this in Chapter 9).
- The God of the Bible is best understood in the way that he describes himself. He has the role of a 'loving father'. We are his children, intrinsically valuable, in the hands of a Father to whom we belong. This is deeply nourishing for the heart, and is extravagant in its potential to help us at a heart level. Outsourcing the solution to our heart problems to the God of the Bible presents a real opportunity to have our heart-level needs met.

[10] J Piper, *Desiring God: meditations of a Christian hedonist*, Multnomah Books, Colorado, 1996.

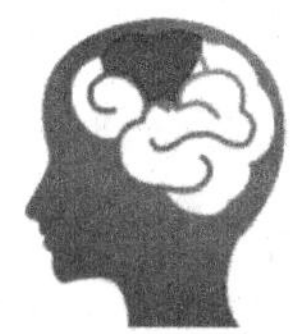

Do you feel that God delights in you and your growth like a father does in his own child?

A relationship with a safe and loving Creator will no doubt help us on our journey, but a connected community of people is also what is needed to help us to grow—not one that neglects our spiritual life, but one that incorporates and adds something to it. As discussed in Chapter 2, positive relationships are crucial, so we will want to incorporate them into our lives in carefully considered ways. In the next chapter we will turn our attention to how we might do this.

7

Connection with others (people heal people)

As we saw in the last chapter, a positive vertical connection with a safe and loving Creator is helpful; but our connections with people—positive horizontal relationships—also help us to grow in crucial ways.

Figure 16. Horizontal connection

Positive connection plays an important part in the healing and healthy functioning of your heart. It will benefit you greatly to engage with the sorts of relationships that are good for you, and to understand and potentially disengage from those relationships that are not. There is one essential principle in play here which I have called 'matching'. The two descriptors that we have to match are the levels of *safety* and *proximity*.

Safety

Positive connection is what we want to create, but we want to illuminate more clearly what that looks like. For a relationship to deliver positive benefits, it must be safe. In terms of relationships, safety requires three conditions to be met:

- connection (and understanding)
- confidentiality
- choices

These are the three Cs of safety.

Safety can be compromised in horrible and obvious ways where choices are taken from us (physical and sexual violence), but it can be compromised in many subtle ways also. Common examples include when others:

- use a raised voice to intimidate
- never show warmth
- demand that you apologise
- laugh at you or find pleasure in your misfortune
- gossip about you behind your back
- have secret agendas or ulterior motives
- withhold affection or refuse to talk to you
- tease or demean you
- judge or evaluate you
- stop you from fully explaining yourself
- use manipulative language such as 'You would do this if you loved me'
- restrict your choices
- tell you that you are wrong and never right
- put labels on you like 'You are a failure', 'You are pathetic', 'You are ____'
- imply that you aren't capable (of acting on your own behalf).

This list is not exhaustive, but I hope that you can get from it a feel for those behaviours that aren't safe. You may see some of them in other people. Indeed, you may see some of them in yourself. If we are to grow at a heart level, safe relationships are a must. They are the foundation for heart-level development.

Are you in safe relationships?

Closeness with anyone requires safety and it is vital that we highlight this. Safety is what underwrites all successful close relationships. Safety requires rapport, it requires trust, and it requires understanding, freedom and care. Warm, trustworthy, understanding people who give others the freedom to think and act differently from them are wonderfully safe people.

Safety is seen when someone is connected and understanding, keeps confidentiality, and always gives choices to other people. When we are close to someone who is warm, thinks well of us, tries to understand, keeps our secrets, cares, listens, encourages freedom, hugs, helps and never hinders, we feel an internal benefit. You don't have to have high levels of safety with everyone, but you will need it if you want to remain close to someone.

The longevity of our relationships will be determined by whether or not there is a match between the proximity shared with that person and the level of safety. So what is meant by proximity?

Proximity

Proximity is the nearness we have to something else. Close proximity to someone else, from a behavioural perspective, is characterised by **frequent** contact, involving **intense** (or deep) relating, for a long **duration**.

These are the three markers of proximity: frequency, intensity and duration (FID markers). If you are close to someone, the FID markers are all high. Examples of relationships with close proximity are marriage, best friends or a close working relationship. You see these people often, you regularly end up having deep and meaningful conversations with them about topics dear to your heart, and you meet with them, or have known them, for extended periods of time.

Matching safety with proximity

Safety we have already defined. We know that a relationship is safe when there is a high amount of connection, high levels of confidentiality, and choice (CCC). Proximity needs to occur in conjunction with safety if a relationship is to work. Specifically, a relationship is positive and most beneficial when proximity is high and safety is also high. That is, FID matches CCC.

If the safety level is low, only a relationship with low proximity will work. When behavioural markers of a relationship (frequency of contact, intensity of the relationship and duration of contact) are low, it does not matter as much that the safety level (connection, confidentiality and choice) is low also. Unsafe people will have no impact on you, because you'll have little contact with them. For example, if you work with someone who likes to spread lies about people and feels they have to win every argument, you can have a functional relationship with that person if the proximity is maintained at a low level—that is, infrequent contact, superficial conversations and brief encounters for the purpose of business. As long as there is a match between proximity and safety (in this case, low levels of safety matching low levels of proximity), the relationship will function.

If the safety level is high, you can have all the proximity that you and the other person want. When someone you are with provides connection and confidentiality and always gives you choices, it makes it possible to trust and to share. The longevity of a relationship, marriage or otherwise, is underwritten by these qualities.

The problem arises when we have a mismatch between safety and proximity.

One experience that is very common among lonely people is that they have low proximity to people who are loving. This sort of mismatch is not sustainable because our hearts require intimacy. This isn't a volatile situation, but it is an impoverished one.

The situation becomes more dramatic when we have too much proximity to those who are unsafe.

In a close relationship, proximity to another skyrockets. Unfortunately, many of us enter into close relationships without assessing the safety level. When a relationship partner neither connects nor keeps confidentiality, and becomes controlling, the relationship is doomed. One lovely person I met told me about his sister's boyfriend. He described this boyfriend as 'unkind'. I asked him what he thought was going to happen, and he replied, 'I'll just wait it out.' When people are in close relationships with people who aren't safe, you can almost set a timer and watch it count down to zero.

Safety is essential if we are to remain in close proximity to someone. The consequence of staying close to someone who is not safe is that we will end up injured. This is true of friendships, marriage relationships and close working relationships.

The high-proximity–low-safety mismatch can also occur in the parent–child relationship. Because a child is completely dependent on their parent, proximity is extremely high. A child must have frequent contact with a caregiver if they are to survive. If safety is low, the child will inevitably be hurt in the process. As adults, we can make changes to the relationships we pursue, but children do not have the choice to stay or go. That is one of the reasons why children suffer so badly: they have no power or control; they can't reduce proximity to match the low levels of safety; and, as a result, they have to endure disconnection. The hand that feeds them is often the hand that hurts them and there is nothing to be done. This is the foundation for trauma: to be in close proximity to an unsafe person and have no ability to change it. Abused children can be left flooded with terrible emotions, at once overwhelmed by a carer's omission and/or commission and having no power over the situation.

As adults, we can do better. To ensure safety, we must match our proximity with the level of safety the person offers. If they offer a lot of safety, then we are free to match that with high levels of proximity. If they offer only a little, then we are free to—in fact we ought to—match that with low levels of proximity. This is tremendous news to adult survivors of childhood trauma—you *do* have a choice. You didn't then, but you do now.

Building relationships that are both safe and close is like building scaffolding so that recovery and flourishing can take place. We have to get this right, otherwise growth and recovery are undermined. Here are some questions that might help you to determine whether the safety and proximity levels are matched in your relationships.

If safe people are those who are connected and understanding, are confidential and give choices to you, are there enough people in your life like that?

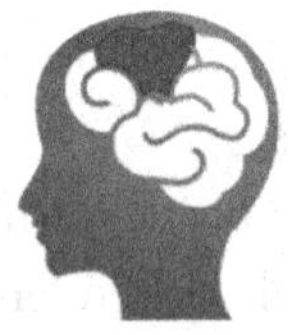

Are the people you frequently see respectful to you?

Are the people whom you share deeply with good at understanding?

Are the people close to you controlling? Do they tell you what to think or what to do?

If the answer is 'yes' to the first three questions and 'no' to the fourth, then your relationships are safe and this is something to be thankful for. Your social environment is set for recovery or continued growth. The only task is to enjoy and maintain the relationships and, if you begin to flourish, find a way of giving back to them and others.

If your answers don't follow this pattern, then later in this chapter we are going to address how you might be able to change your relationships so that you can benefit from a better balance.

I have emphasised safety as the essential requirement, or a missing piece in the narrative of those whose relationships have impacted them in negative ways. It is the capstone that holds the whole connection archway in place. Without it, connection collapses.

In reality, though, it is only one of the factors that are required for connection to occur. In bold below you will see a list of qualities that are required if we are to enjoy positive relationships, each with a short explanation of why that ingredient is important. Connection requires that we are '**FRIENDS**':

Fun and facing

Rapport is vital for connection and the best conduit for it is having fun together.

Moreover, as previously emphasised, we can't fight, we can't fake, we can't flee … we need to face each other. Honesty with each other maintains trust and we can only be that way when we face each other.

Respectful

Respect is essential. Without a positive attitude towards others, and the acknowledgement that they have rights and are worthy of consideration, connection will wither.

Individual *and* ***interested***

Even though you may be close to others, ongoing closeness requires that you are known as someone who has their own thoughts and feelings.

We also need others around us to show an 'active and constructive' interest in our internal worlds if we are to find good connection.

Empathetic

Empathy is vital. We have to be in synch with the hurts, but also with the excitement. We need to experience what others do, to feel what they do—to experience life as they have, if we are to be connected.

Not neglected

We don't need to be connected all the time, nor do we need our connections to be perfect. We just need a sense that people will be available to us when we need them.

Determined *(by ourselves)*

Freedom is essential for connection. In fact, control destroys connection. Each person requires a sense that they can decide what they want.

Safe

Yes, safe—protected from harm in all its possible nefarious forms; protected from physical harm, sexual harm and emotional manipulation.

We are now moving from social awareness to social architecture. We are attempting to create for ourselves an environment that will be safe and enriching. People sometimes say that 'time heals all wounds', but that is not true. It is always time *plus* something else that heals all wounds, and what I am proposing is that it is *time plus positive relationships* that heal all wounds. It is the disparity that we are looking for—a difference between then and now:

- Then we were scared; now we are safe.
- Then there was no fun; now there is.
- Then there was no respect; now there is.
- Then we were overlooked; now we are seen.
- Then we were overcome with emotion and left to solve and resolve our emotions in isolation; now we are seen and soothed.

That takes time, but it is not time that is essential for healing; indeed, there are many people who have been upset for very long periods of time. No—it is time plus safety and connection. Those are the active ingredients of recovery.

We create positive environments for plants when we want them to grow. We pick a good place in the garden. We clear out weeds. We make sure there is enough access to sunlight. We give them nutrient rich soil and water them regularly.

For human beings, similar rules apply. We bring close those who are safe, and let go of those who aren't. If we can do this, we will set the stage for heart-level recovery and growth well into the future. Our goal is to build a new social structure and make sure we get enough of it.

The pyramid of support

Having looked at the power of connection and the trauma that disconnection can cause to our hearts, it is logical to conclude that when it comes to relationships, the safer the better. We need to be surrounded by a loving God and loving people. To recover from injury and flourish as human beings, we will need to build a pyramid of safe and supportive relationships around us.

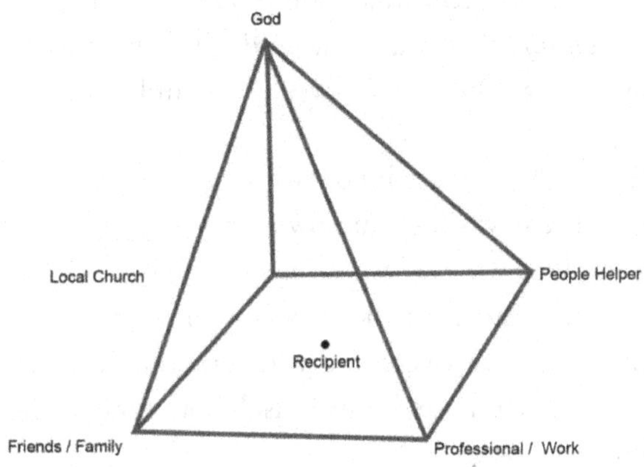

Figure 17. The pyramid of support

The pyramid is an immediately recognisable structure. Like the actual pyramids in Egypt, there are four corners at the base and a point at the top. We place ourselves (the 'recipients') in the middle of the base. The four corners represent the different types of close relationships in our life. These might include friends and family at one corner, professional connections and workmates at another, local church or club associates at another, and perhaps professional 'people helpers' like counsellors at the fourth corner. The peak of the pyramid represents our connection to God.

The concept of the relationship pyramid was developed by Dr John Warlow, psychiatrist and Director of Living Wholeness. It illustrates the types of positive connections we can have, and also where they might be lacking. Ideally, we will have at least four categories of genuinely engaged, safe people or people groups in our life. When we aren't doing well, we can turn to family, our local church or God to help us in the healing process. When things become particularly difficult we can turn to people who are designated 'helpers' and professional people (doctors, psychologists, counsellors or psychiatrists). The relationships in our pyramids will need to be close, open and honest for us to heal. The people in our pyramids *must* be safe. People who are not safe cannot be in our pyramids, so move them out and seek others who are safe to replace them. Do not make exceptions. Each of us must build our pyramids wisely. The inclusion criteria (that people are loving, are connected, are confidential and provide choices) are also the exclusion criteria (people can't be in the pyramid if they are unloving, disconnected, controlling and lacking in confidentiality). This principle should also apply to God. If God is, as the Bible reports him to be, patient and loving, then add him in. If you have somehow formed the idea that God is mean and spiteful, that sort of God—a nasty, disconnected God—will need to be replaced with the God of the Bible. The old misconceptions will need to be corrected.

Having established who our safe vertical and horizontal connections are, we need to 'dose up' on them. We have done a bit of social engineering, insofar as we have been trying to surround ourselves with loving relationships, but if we don't engage properly with those relationships we may not benefit from them. Here, the illustration of an antibiotic is helpful. All too often, people who are depressed or anxious hang around with either unsafe or merely passively interested people. When we are upset we need to slowly and safely put in boundaries between ourselves and unsafe people (decrease the proximity). This is the first task. The second task is to ensure that we get a high enough 'dose' of contact with safe people (increase the proximity). The frequency, intensity and duration of contact with these people all need to be high.

Suppose you are sick and you take yourself off to the doctor. The doctor checks you out then prescribes antibiotics for your maladies. You take the medication home and try one tablet, even though the doctor told you to take two each time. It doesn't rid you of your symptoms, so you conclude that the medication doesn't work. A week later, still suffering from the symptoms, you decide to give the doctor the benefit of the doubt and take one tablet one more time. Again the drug comes into your system, your liver cleans it out, and … nothing.

In graph form we would draw it like this:

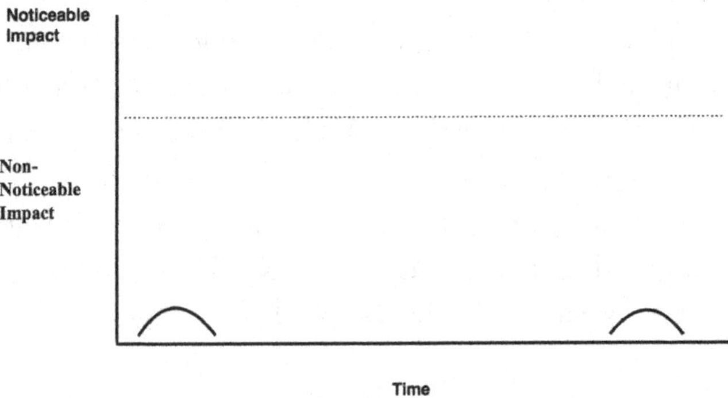

Figure 18. Connection dosage

The vertical axis represents the impact of the antibiotic. Above the dotted line is 'noticeable impact' and below the dotted line there is a non-noticeable impact and the symptoms remain. Across the bottom, on the horizontal axis, we have time. There has been one dose on day one, and another dose at a later time. On each occasion there was a very small, almost undetectable impact, which quickly disappeared. Neither dose came close to the 'noticeable impact' line.

After a week you return to your doctor and tell him it doesn't work. The doctor enquires about how you took it and you tell him, 'I took one tablet on the first day. It didn't do anything, so I gave it another try seven days later, and again it didn't work.'

The doctor explains, 'That isn't the way it works. What I said was, "Take two tablets every day and after a while you'll notice the benefit"— it has to build up in your system to work. The dose you have been taking was not *frequent* enough, nor was it *intense* enough, nor were you taking the medication for *long* enough for you to get the full benefit.'

If our doses of positive connection are too infrequent and too small, and not experienced consistently over a longer period of time, there will be no lasting benefit. However, if the frequency, intensity and duration (FID) of contact are elevated, we will be ready for recovery. The characteristics of this pattern, one that will take us beyond the positive impact line, might look like this:

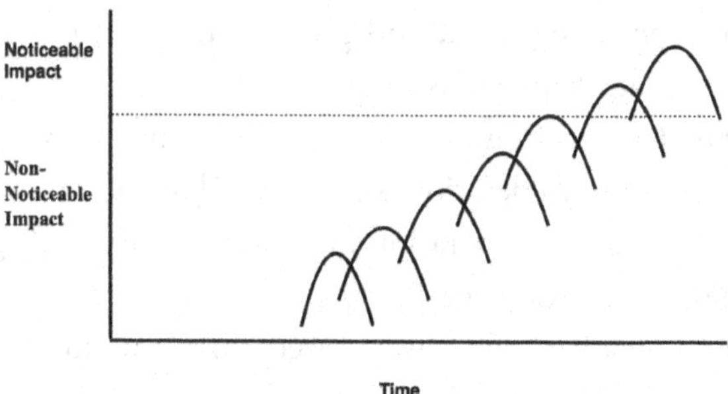

Figure 19. Accumulation of connection dosage

Time is fundamental for connection. If there is no time, there can be no connection between you and God, no connection between you and others and no connection between you and yourself. For example, I have no connection with Bruce Springsteen, because he has no time for me. In fact, because the FID of our contact equals zero, there is no relationship at all. It has actually reached the point where I'm not even sure he knows I exist.

No time for someone equals no connection. This appears to be logical, but are we truly aware of our need to give relationships the time they need? One of the saddest and most ominous risk factors for Western society is that we are all so busy that we simply have no time. The need to give time to close relationships appears to be off our psychological radar. We are busy, and proud of it.

I went to Subway for lunch the other day, and the friendly guy who served me asked, 'How are you, busy?' as if busyness were a virtue. I said, 'No, I just came from a swim at the pool.' My response seemed to jar with him. It was obviously not the expected answer and he grimaced as if to say, 'Why are you not busy?' As a society, we place great value on working hard but we do not stop to question how detrimental it might be to cram every day full from dawn till well after dusk. We are defiantly proud of our busyness. We seem to be proud of looking tired, of exhausting ourselves. We give the bulk of our energy to work, and give the dregs of our energy to relationships that are precious to us.

I once had a conversation with an older man who was speaking to me about how my generation isn't prepared to commit to the long hours at work that his generation did. I immediately felt guilt and awkwardness ('How does he know I am so lazy?' I thought). But my guilt and awkwardness disappeared three minutes later when we were talking about all those hard-working people in the older generation who spent so much of their time and energy on work.

'How are their marriages?' I asked.

There was an awkward silence, and no answer was given.

Don't let busyness put the squeeze on time, because lack of time will put the squeeze on connection. And you know your heart really can't survive without that.

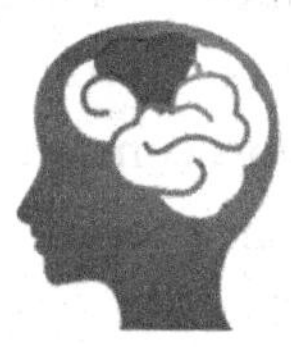

How much time is available to relate to the people who are in your pyramid of support?

Pause and review

We have sketched out how important it is to have people in our lives who are safe and genuinely interested in us. The difficulties that we experience when we are deprived of loving connection testify to what we might be made for—we were made to love and be loved.

More specifically, in this chapter we've considered the following:

- Safety is defined by three factors: connection, confidentiality and choice (CCC).
- Our proximity or closeness to someone can be determined by the following three factors: frequency, intensity and duration (FID).
- Our task is to match safety with closeness. If someone is safe, then the FID markers can all increase. If a person is not so safe to be with, then we should, in careful ways, lower the frequency, intensity and duration of our contact.
- The positive effects of connection with others will occur only if we use our time well.

If, having read this section, you are feeling positive and know the direction you need to take in your close relationships, or know the relationships that you want to bring closer, you can put this chapter down, or go to the next chapter.

If you are still feeling a little concerned about a mismatching in your life, we are about to get a little more focused. If safety and proximity are incompatible in some of your relationships, you may find your scenario in one of the following sections. I am going to focus on one variation in particular because it is the most common. (I'm not assuming that this is the problem for everyone, nor am I going to assume that this is a 'cookie-cutter solution'.)

I will focus primarily on the sort of relationship where proximity is high and difficult to change, and the safety level is not high enough, yet positive change and growth is possible. If this is not something that you relate to, you can turn to the next section titled 'Addressing further mismatches in safety and proximity' later in this chapter, where I have included other mismatch combinations (including when proximity can be reduced to match low safety, when the proximity is high but there is little or no insight into the need to increase safety, and when you need to reduce the proximity but it may be unsafe to do so).

Increasing safety to match proximity

It is important to match up proximity with safety, but it is not always simple. In some of our not-so-safe relationships, we *can't* easily decrease proximity or we don't *desire* to decrease the proximity. This is the predicament of so many people caught in harmful relationships. It could be a relationship with a partner at home or family member that has gone sour, or at work with a colleague. We are often contractually organised into relationships that we either did not expect, such as when a marriage becomes difficult, or did not want, such as being told to work with someone combative at work.

What can we do at such times? The only real option when proximity is hard to change is to set about increasing the safety levels.

The starting point with changing the safety is honesty with yourself. After that, the task is to be honest with others about how safe you actually feel and how you would like things to change.

We are dealing here with mild to moderate levels of disconnected behaviour. (Let me be clear: this is *not* a situation where there is the threat of violence.) An example of this might be having a partner who says to you, 'You're being too oversensitive.' If your partner can cope with honestly facing this behaviour without escalating the problem, then there is a good chance that growth can occur.

Many years ago, I was working in a Brain Injury Ward. I went to a colleague's office and after I knocked at the door, he yelled and swore at me. I was completely shocked and avoided him for the rest of the day. When I was at home, I decided that I couldn't let this go, so I resolved to speak to him because he was usually a decent guy. I told him the following day 'Hey, I'm not sure if I deserved that. I was only returning a file.' He went quiet, then apologised, and I forgave him without hesitation. We were friends thereafter.

Facing and forgiving others, examining our own choices, embracing new freedom, looking to the future and having fun are all essential parts of this growth pattern, and we are now going to move through each of these steps. They are not one-off boxes to tick, but behaviours to develop because even good relationships require maintenance.

Face

In this section we are focusing on relationships that have mild to moderate levels of disconnection.

Given that the focus is now on the mild to moderate range, facing the other person directly holds great potential for change. But when friends, family and colleagues face each other, it must be invitational by nature. We must ask whether they would like to talk about the way the relationship is going.

The reason for this is because there is always a relationship between choice and connection. When the capacity to make choices goes up, connection with the person who gives you choices goes up.

When the ability to make choices goes down, then your connection with the person who denies you choices goes down with it.

An invitational gesture thus offers a choice so that we can retain the connection with the person we want to talk to. When we go to face someone, it will be vital to give the other person choices at the beginning of the conversation. Emphasise to the other person that they don't have to talk if they don't want to, or perhaps emphasise that they can talk at another time, if they are not ready. You might help them to make an informed choice about whether or not they decide to talk by declaring to them the goal of the conversation.

Framing the goal in constructive ways will help. For example, 'I want us to understand each other' is a way of ensuring that all parties become honoured in discussion; or, 'I'm keen for us both to talk about how we might be able to improve our relationship' will also be a way of ensuring that no-one will feel attacked.

The actual conversation then needs to become a sharing of ideas. In effect, it should look like a casual game of tennis: one person serves and the receiver lobs the ball back over the net. Returning the ball is a bit like paraphrasing, revealing that you have heard the other person and clarifying your understanding of what you have been told. So, for example, if my wife says to me, 'The way we spoke to each other last night had me concerned about what the kids might think about the example we are setting,' I might say back to her, 'You're concerned that we aren't modelling good behaviour?' No top spin, no back spin, no rushing to the net and definitely no John McEnroe impersonations. Then, once the 'server' feels understood, which may take several serves of the ball, and may use different balls (topics), the server decides that the other person can have a service set.

The tennis metaphor, invented by Dr John Warlow of Living Wholeness, provides a useful structure for considering the flow of conversation with basic rules of listening, understanding and speaking. The desirable game is a peaceful one, where there is a server who keeps on serving the ball gently and a receiver who just lobs the ball back, with both players staying behind the base line.

There are times when some people find this sort of conversational tennis game really difficult. They either storm off the court, rush the net, throw their racquets, serve the ball too hard, or tell the other person how to hold the racquet. It is at these times that the individual has to reflect on and examine why they are finding it difficult to play the game. Perhaps there is a time for individual 'tennis coaching' (that is, professional counselling). That will be for your partner, work colleague or family member to decide. You can ask them whether they need it, but let them decide whether or not they do. No matter what, we have to stick to the rules, particularly when it gets difficult. The rules are there for the enjoyment of the game, and without the rules, anarchy follows. Yet it is not just the rules of the game—it is the spirit of the game that we need. It is not a game of tennis that you play to win—it is a game of tennis that you play to connect with and understand each other.

(For those of you who find the tennis metaphor a bit tricky to visualise, I have put more information on my website, www.heartinmind.com.au. Type the word 'tennis' into the search section and you will find a link.)

One of the most common reasons that our own tennis game can come unglued is because we have been unable to let go of what has happened in the relationship in the days, months or even years preceding the discussion. Just like the US Open winner Pat Rafter, we fire away a serve and sprint to the net to volley it back as quickly as we can to overwhelm the 'opposition'. The style of play at this point has very little to do with the game and more to do with what is in our hearts and the negative things that we are holding on to.

Forgive

A favourite political cartoon in our family was stuck on our fridge for quite a while. It depicts a recent Australian Prime Minister cajoling a crowd of people to 'move forward', a phrase that this leader became famous for. Behind the Prime Minister is the previous leader from the same party, lying face-down on the ground with a knife sticking out of his back. In another corner, also in the background, are a couple of previous Prime Ministers wrestling each other. All of them are from the same side of politics. Despite the encouragement from the current Prime Minister, the observant crowd is not convinced that they need to move forward. They seem to be static; they look past her and through her. The drama of the backdrop holds their attention.

This is the tension that many of us find ourselves in. We want to move forward, but the reality is that many of us are unable to. We don't seem to have the capacity to move ahead, because the past holds us back. Others may recommend that we 'move forward', but those who do typically have a light load and they project that light load onto us. They think others are like them and that we should be able to cope as they are coping. They say things like, 'You've just got to get on with your life' or 'You need to let that go.' A lot of us are not like that. A lot of us can't be like that. And to be honest, sometimes when people *are* like that, it just looks like avoidance of the big things that have been left unspoken.

The bottom line is that we can't move forward with a heavy heart. Heavy or broken hearts weigh us down, and at times, we become overwhelmed by emotion because of what has happened in the past. We simply can't 'move forward' without our hearts being healed first, and for others to suggest so is insensitive and shows a lack of insight into the seriousness of what we have been through.

Many of us know that we will have to forgive so that we can let go of what we have been through. Yet, despite this, we find ourselves resistant. We don't want to let go, and at times we are simply unable to. Resentment or rumination overwhelm us. We think that what others did, or what we did, was unforgivable.

We hold on to the hurt in the hope that there might be justice, but this strategy is far from efficacious. Withholding forgiveness never miraculously delivers peace, but instead leaves us only with an acrid taste of emotional toxicity. Nelson Mandela said, 'Resentment is like drinking poison and then hoping it will kill your enemies.'[1] Sadly, we only end up drinking the poison. We don't realise that when we are angry with others for long periods of time, time has rolled on, and our hearts have shrivelled. We really have become the victims because we are no longer at peace.

From a secular perspective, when we forgive, we let go. Letting go is difficult at the best of times, but it is nearly impossible to forgive when we feel betrayal, worthlessness, shame and/or alienation. Forgiveness is made possible by the absence of significant heart-level injuries. That is why it is important to connect with ourselves prior to forgiving others. When we are no longer injured, we will let go and forgive others, sometimes without even being prompted to do so.

Christian forgiveness is something much grander, much more challenging and much more liberating than the sort of forgiveness that we speak of when we think of 'letting go'. It comprises not just the forgiving of another, but seeking God's forgiveness even when we have been transgressed against. It recognises that we can be not just broken, but broken *and* sinful. This is put well by Dietrich Bonhoeffer, the Lutheran pastor who took a stand against Hitler's control of Germany. He wrote:

> The most experienced psychologist or observer of human nature knows infinitely less of the human heart than the simplest Christian who lives beneath

---

[1] D Horsey, *Nelson Mandela transformed himself and then his nation*, 2013, viewed October 2020, <https://www.latimes.com/opinion/topoftheticket/la-xpm-2013-dec-06-la-na-tt-nelson-mandela-20131206-story.html>.

> the Cross of Jesus. The greatest psychological insight, ability, and experience cannot grasp this one thing: what sin is. Worldly wisdom knows what distress and weakness and failure are, but it does not know the godlessness of man. And so it also does not know that man is destroyed only by his sin and can be healed only by forgiveness. Only the Christian knows this. In the presence of a psychiatrist I can only be a sick man; in the presence of a Christian brother I can dare to be a sinner. The psychiatrist must first search my heart and yet he never plumbs its ultimate depth. The Christian brother knows when I come to him: here is a sinner like myself, a godless man who wants to confess and yearns for God's forgiveness. The psychiatrist views me as if there were no God. The brother views me as I am before the judging and merciful God in the Cross of Jesus Christ.[2]

Repent

Seeking God's forgiveness at times when we are hurting is courageous. It requires that we face what has happened, we face what is on our hearts, and we face God. The task requires a galvanising of the will. The process of forgiving others and seeking forgiveness for ourselves is far more challenging than merely 'letting go', as we have mentioned, because it involves examining ourselves and determining where we have been getting our value and identity from. Resistance is often rife as it feels outrageous to repent and redirect our lives away from what has happened when we have been hurt. It is as if the head must drag an unwilling heart repeatedly to the cross to remind us that real forgiveness is costly but possible.

---

[2] D Bonhoeffer, *Life together: the classic exploration of Christian community*, HarperOne, San Francisco, 2009.

Admittedly, it seems obstructive, almost provocative, to introduce the idea that we may need to repent when we're upset. Repenting is a distinctly Christian idea. It involves turning away from what we thought was worthy of pursuing and turning towards a new love, and a new value system.

Charles Spurgeon wrote that:

> Repentance is a discovery of the evil of sin, a mourning that we have committed it, a resolution to forsake it. It is, in fact, a change of mind of a very deep and practical character, which makes the man love what once he hated, and hate what once he loved.[3]

We contemplate repenting not necessarily because we have been bad—on many occasions we haven't done anything wrong at all, and great wrong has been done against us. But repentance is deeper than that.

We repent because we have given someone else the power to decide our value and identity. It's not their job.

We repent because we gave ourselves the job to heal our own hearts and we feel bad about ourselves for failing to overcome our brokenness alone. It's not our job either.

So whose responsibility is it?

For the Christian, the challenge is to have God satisfy our heart requirements. When we feel bad, disgusting, stupid or dirty, we have let events and people into our hearts. These reckless and even at times evil people now have the power to define us. The violation is theirs, but we gave them a role that we should never have given them. They have been given God's own task. They are the ones that have determined our value; they have ensured our shame and changed

---

[3] C Spurgeon, quoted at *Theologue: a reformed theology blog*, 2014, viewed October 2020, <https://theologue.wordpress.com/2014/12/02/charles-spurgeon-on-repentance/>.

our identity. How could we ever forgive such people for the damage that they have done?

Recovery from relational trauma is, and always has been, a spiritual process. True forgiveness is filled with spiritual activity, because it takes us way beyond just letting go or moving forward, but into our hearts to let new things give us value. The bottom line is that our forgiveness of others requires our repentance as well. By forgiving others, we remove from our hearts the bad people and bad events, and by repenting we put God at the centre of our being and have him determine our trust, self-esteem, honour and belonging.

People can't let go of what has defined them until they turn their backs on what has defined them and find a better way to fill their hearts. This is why it is stupid when people say, 'You've just got to get on with your life.' We just can't, until our hearts are changed. Forgiveness requires repentance and forgiveness won't work without repentance.

This sort of activity, forgiveness plus repentance, is typically not on offer with the local psychologist, nor is it on offer from practitioners of Buddhist mindfulness. It is the sort of forgiveness that delivers freedom from terrible psychological injuries and the opportunity to live in synchronised harmony with a divine melody. It gives us a new focus and a new direction, one separate from the tyranny of bitterness. It brings light into the dark shadows—the shadows cast by the bad things that have been done to us.

Only the other day I sat with Kelly whose husband had been unfaithful to her. She was heartbroken. It is no wonder. Love leads to real investments of the heart. She trusted him, and he broke that trust. Kelly and her husband have one child together, and upon hearing the news about his affair she was distraught. She was full of what I considered to be righteous anger.

Her sense of betrayal was visceral. Her honest desire was to leave the marriage and never go back, but she was trapped between this and what she desired for herself and for her child: a loving family home with a mum and a dad. She thought herself to be a 'failure' and 'unattractive'. She was ashamed of herself, and because of that she told no-one what was happening in case she was judged. Isolated, ashamed, and sensing that she was a failure, her direction was bending towards leaving.

I affirmed that she was free, and that no-one would blame her for leaving. When I asked whether there was a place for repenting at this time, she wondered whether I was expecting her to repent of her inclination to leave her husband. I definitely wasn't.

We talked a little, and because of her graciousness to me she was willing to let me share how we have to repent of letting someone else give us the labels that we feel we have. In Kelly's case, she was accepting labels put on her by her husband's actions and attitudes. I encouraged her to ask herself, 'Ought that to be God's job? Why do you let your partner's behaviour define you? Can you let Jesus' action on the cross define you?'

In what is a typical phenomenon for people in her situation, her head was in the conversation but her heart was yet to follow. This became her new pursuit. C. S. Lewis once said, 'The heart never takes the place of the head: but it can, and should, obey it.'[4] Kelly's heart is under clear instruction now: to find a way to transition out of hurt and into heart-level remorse; to let God define her and let him value her; to push her husband's actions out of her heart, and let Jesus' actions on the cross into her heart.

Maybe she will leave her husband and maybe she will stay … that decision is hers and she is free to make it, but whatever she decides her challenge will be to forgive and repent of letting her husband's actions write what is on her heart. She is more than that.

This is conscious living in a deeply challenging way. If Kelly can

---

[4] CS Lewis, *The abolition of man.*

do it, then so can we. The challenge is great, but the freedom we attain is far greater.

Set you and the other person free

When we spiritually forgive and repent at a heart level, we become free to undertake a new direction. The weight of rumination, the toxic edginess of anger and the relational touchiness all recede and create space for new curiosities.

Christian forgiveness and repentance puts us on the cusp of a new adventure. No longer tied to the past and with a heart that is lighter, we taste psychological freedom. This adventure will not be complete without a destination, though. A genuinely Christian destination for your relationship has its own definable contours. Positive relationships will be characterised by goodness, righteousness, holiness and purity. Forgiveness brings us great freedom, but it is a freedom 'for' something. This is where freedom lives with direction, values and priorities. Freedom allows us to pursue commonly held, cherished ideals. The forgiveness that we have received and given invites us to create a destination with people we love, surrounded by safe connection.

Kelly can now forgive her partner and set him and herself free. If Kelly's partner uses his freedom to value faithfulness—if he is really motivated to change, and repents of his hurtful actions—then she may think that he is using his freedom as a freedom for loving her. Only when she sees him commit to this new direction will she sense that she can trust him again.

Freedom has an appetite all of its own, but it craves something other than itself. It desires something to reach for. For the Christian, freedom is to be united with Christ. We are set free *for* him, to be loved and labelled *by* him—and when we are freed from sin by his grace and our repentance, we are free to follow him. This action is most beautifully captured by Charles Wesley in the old hymn, 'And Can it Be That I Should Gain?':

> Long my imprisoned spirit lay,
> Fast bound in sin and nature's night;
> Thine eye diffused a quickening ray—
> I woke, the dungeon flamed with light;
> My chains fell off, my heart was free,
> I rose, went forth, and followed Thee.[5]

'I rose, went forth, and *followed* Thee.' When the chains fell off, the direction soon developed.

With a lighter heart, having forgiven others and repented, we can reconnect. This is where it gets exciting, because now we really can 'move forward' to a new goal. The goal is Christlikeness for both parties, but one also tailored to our circumstances.

Focus on the future

In the stress, storm and fun of family life we often fall out of touch with our family aspirations. Technology, lethargy, commitments and busyness rise up and strangle motivation.

One particularly busy Saturday morning in my household, I happened upon a note written by my son. It is charming, and to the point. It begins with 'Dear Dad', with the words 'Dear' and 'Dad' vertically stacked and sharing the same large capital 'D'; and then it says, 'I would like a family that is kind, physical, fun, generous.'

I had forgotten until I read it, but I had asked my kids to tell me the sort of family they would like to have. When I initially asked my kids this question over dinner, we struck a bit of a misunderstanding. What my son thought I had asked was not 'What sort of family

---

[5] C Wesley, 'And Can it Be That I Should Gain?', 1738, viewed October 2020, <https://hymnary.org/text/and_can_it_be_that_i_should_gain>.

would you like to have?' but 'Whose family would you like to have?' So when it was his turn to respond to the question 'What sort of family would you like?', he nominated another family from church with three sons.

I had to raise the same question again with him in person because, as you can tell, the first conversation didn't go as well as planned. The note that he wrote in response contained his naturally boyish desire to be 'physical', but it also revealed that he wanted a kind, fun and generous household. His response was incorporated with his older sisters' responses and we came up with six Hs for our family direction. We wanted to be:

- Happy
- Humorous
- Hallelujah (our alliterative attempt at the spiritual focus of our family)
- Hearing
- Healthy
- Helpful.

Now we have a point of reference, an orientation and a sense of forward motion. We have created a yardstick against which to measure how we are going with our family goals.

All effective therapies revolve around the presence of three key features in a relationship: collaboration, transparency and feedback.[6] These three factors are thought to be the active ingredients that underpin the success of all treatments: Cognitive Therapy, Cognitive Behaviour Therapy, Narrative Therapy, Psychodynamic Therapy, and so on. Relationships outside of therapy are much the same.

[6] BE Wampold, *The great psychotherapy debate: models, methods, and findings*, Routledge, New York, 2001.

It will not help my kids if I tell them what we are doing without them agreeing to it. It won't help them if, worse still, I have an agenda but I'm not transparent about it. Nor will it help them to grow in insight if I keep telling them how they are going or how we are going as a family: I must encourage each one to be the judge of that. If they don't, there is no way they will get what they want, their direction will flail, and they will use their freedom for things other than what they truly want.

I must admit, having found this note, that I have fallen short of what he desired for our family. I've become too busy trying to work, write reports, maintain connection with friends and family and lose some weight by going to the gym. I too need to forgive myself and refocus on the future for his sake and for my sake. My family needs to keep going back to its six Hs so my son can reach his goal.

Bruce Feiler wrote a book entitled *The Secrets of Happy Families*. It became a *New York Times* bestseller. When Feiler was asked what he would recommend if he could give only one piece of advice for families, he replied, 'Set aside time to talk about what it means to be a part of your family.' He encourages families to construct a mission statement:

> Initiate a conversation about what it means to be a part of your family. Sit down with them and say 'Okay, these are our ten central values. This is the family we want to be. We want to be a family that doesn't fight all the time' or 'We want to be a family that goes camping or sailing' or whatever it might be. When my family did it, it was literally a transforming experience. We ended up printing it and it hangs now in our dining room.[7]

[7] Bruce Feiler's book is titled *The Secrets of Happy Families*. This quote was taken from E Barker, '6 things the happiest families all have in common', *The Week*, 3 September 2014, viewed June 2017, <http://theweek.com/articles/444395/6-things-happiest-families-all-have-common>.

We have been discussing families but we're also discussing reconciling partners as well as people in partnership at work or in friendship outside of work. Committing to goals will give a couple or a family an identity, but we will need connection in order to make that direction sustainable.

Have fun

Looking back, I think those conversations with my family about our own mission statement were only possible because there was good connection between us prior to those conversations. (I didn't know it at the time. It seems odd that I know how important connection is, I teach people about these things, I write about these things, yet every now and again I forget.) Rapport makes it possible to have more serious conversations about how relationships are going and where we want them to go. Rapport gives people a sense that it is safe enough to face each other.

Several hours prior to that conversation with my son, I saw him carrying out some mock combat by himself on the trampoline. I saw him through the windows punching the air, then falling onto his back. All of his sisters were out with their mum, and my son and I had just finished reading together.

For him (and all other children), connection is an 'F' word—it is spelt 'F-U-N'. I knew that if I really wanted to connect with him I had to get onto the trampoline and participate in the combat. Knowing this, I stopped myself from doing any more writing, walked out into the backyard and climbed onto the trampoline.

A smile splashed across his face as I climbed onto the mat. I did some karate kicks, but he corrected the narrative.

'Dad, I'm not doing that, I'm doing wrestling.'

'OK,' I said, and I threw myself against the side of the tramp as if bouncing off the ropes.

'Who are you?' I asked.

'I'm John Cena,' the boy declared, rushing towards me.

He got me into a headlock. There was grunting and heavy breathing. We disentangled … and I prepared to scare the living daylights out of him.

'John Cena! He's weak!' I said.

We began a bobbing dance, circling around each other the way wrestlers do.

'Who are *you*, then?' asked the little guy.

'I'm The Junk Yard Dog!' I declared, pulling my arms back and up, flexing my middle-aged biceps—expecting him to run off the tramp screaming.

He dropped his guard and stopped bouncing around me, and a perplexed gaze washed over his face. 'Who is that?'[8]

It suddenly occurred to me how old I had become. The Junk Yard Dog was a wrestler when I was nine, not when he was nine.

Well, that backfired.

'Don't you know who that is? You'll just have to find out the hard way,' I replied.

Shrieks, complaints, laughter, and—for me—exhaustion ensued.

It's important to emphasise that connection is spelt F-U-N. When we are young, connection is built on it. Kids learn to love each other by having fun with each other. They do things for fun. Fun is the goal, not the by-product of another goal. To have fun with friends and family is the foundation of the attachment process.

I have fun with my son because I enjoy his company. I do it for me, really. It isn't an act of altruism—I'm not doing him a favour. He is honestly a likeable kid. But I do it also knowing that time spent having fun with him at this time of his life will be like investing in the future of our relationship. Like all blue chip investments, having fun with our children will pay dividends for many years to come.

---

[8] The Junk Yard Dog is a wrestler from the late 1980s and is still, to this day, one of the best wrestlers in the World Wrestling Federation. At least in my mind. No matter what my son says.

Children have fun in different ways, though. As adults, we need to tune into their ways of having fun and ask permission to join in with them to give them a sense of control. For some children, fun is about tackling an adult; for others it is about looking for beetles or cooking together. Whatever their way of having fun is, our challenge is to connect with them on their own terms and see having fun with them as an end in itself.

As adults, we don't always do things for fun like we did as kids, but fun comes in different forms and is essential for any successful relationship, no matter what age we are. One of the most common ways to connect as we get older is to have adventures and laugh together. Without humour, without adventure, without fun activities, we all wilt in the relationships that we try to maintain. It is not only what sets us up for a good future—it is what sustains us as we pursue our relationship goals.

Have you faced and forgiven your friend or partner?

Have you laid out a set of priorities like a destination?

Are you having fun in your relationships?

If you have faced and forgiven each other, and mapped out your priorities and values, then the fun you have will feel clean and pure because of the good work you've done before it. If you have done all of these things, then you may well be on the road to flourishing.

Flourishing. What a beautiful word. It suggests an explosion in beauty—like when a flower opens and pitches itself outward, seeming to become more of a flower. The colours are more vibrant, the scent more remarkable. We show them to neighbours, we pick them for lovers. They were always flowers prior to flourishing; it is just that their beauty has not been fully realised until this point.

Love for another person is what underpins the inclination to see those around us flourish. When we have no love we simply do not care whether friends or family flourish. When we love people, we long for their prosperity: financially, physically, athletically, relationally, spiritually and vocationally … in extravagant ways beyond the success that we ourselves have enjoyed.

Unfortunately, there are many who are not afforded the opportunity to flourish because love was not in the air. Many of us have been around others who simply don't love enough, or, worse still, around nasty, difficult, narcissistic people. If we have regained a positive human connection, we are setting ourselves up to flourish even if we did grow up around such people. And if we haven't regained a positive human connection with others and there is limited potential for change, we may need to reduce the proximity to unloving people if we are ever going to flourish.

In the remaining sections of this chapter we are going to look at how we might reduce our proximity to others. Sometimes it can be easy to do this, and we are going to look at that shortly. There are times when we may not even be fully aware that we need to do it, so there will also be a section on that. Finally, there are situations in which the safety level is so low that it is difficult, if not dangerous, to reduce the proximity. To change our social environment in such cases we will need to move cautiously and with wisdom.

Addressing further mismatches in safety and proximity

In this chapter we have emphasised the need to match proximity with safety.

In the body of this chapter so far we have proposed ways in which you might increase the safety level if the proximity is high and fixed (such as in a marriage). In that section, we presumed that the people we would talk to would be responsive to our plea for more safety and connection.

In this section, however, we will address other mismatch combinations—ones in which the reduction of proximity seems like a more appropriate response.

What to do if you can easily reduce the proximity

When the safety level is low, reducing the proximity to the unsafe people around you will help. On some occasions, like the ones that we have discussed so far in this chapter, you can't change the proximity easily, but there are many occasions when you can. For example, you can decide whether to start a romantic relationship with someone, or whether to spend time with people at lunch, or with people at school, university or work. These are times for us to become aware, make judgements about levels of connection—not quickly, but in considered ways over time—and actively decide whether or not it will be helpful to us to have close proximity. Sadly, for many of us, such considerations are not on our psychological radar.

I once met with a lovely, gentle lady who worked in the health industry. She was newly married and had no children. At one stage, I was talking to her about the need to match up proximity with people and safety levels. She became teary and began to disengage a little from our conversation, and I had to stop my explanation when I was halfway through a sentence. (I began silently reprimanding myself for talking so much in therapy. I hate it when I do that.) Was she being reminded of a previous trauma, I wondered?

'Jess, are you okay? What is going on?' I asked.

'Sorry,' she replied. 'I didn't know.'

'Didn't know what?' I asked.

'That I was allowed,' she said.

She wasn't being reminded of a trauma at all. She wasn't reliving; she was relieved. She was even astounded. She never knew that she was even allowed to have a say in who she would like to have close. Even to this day, many years after this conversation, a lump forms in my throat and a tingle begins in my nostrils when I write about this beautiful person. How sad it is for a young woman not to know that she has choices.

For every traumatised child, there are moments in that person's adult years when new insights are born. Like a bubble in a New Zealand mud pool, they just seem to rise up and appear in our minds—not intellectually, or more aptly not 'merely' intellectually, but in a more primitive way, a way that resonates for us and orientates us towards or away from something. We reframe the experience we had and see it in a new light, and the sense of agency, the power that comes with choice, galvanises our motivation to change things and do relationships differently.

You can choose whom to be close to and whom not to be close to. If you forget that you have a choice, you will fail to fashion your social environment in a way that will help you to recover.

In many respects, a challenge of this sort of social engineering is a tacit acknowledgement that our psychological functioning is to a large extent contingent on others. As we have already discussed, who we are, our happiness and our sense of being loved is to a large extent determined by the nature of the relationships that are around us. If they are loving and safe, we will, over the long term, be well. If they are not, we are going to be constantly challenged by the tangle of anxiety, conflict and misunderstandings that unsafe relationships are likely to bring. If we are to be well, we will have to cultivate better relationships.

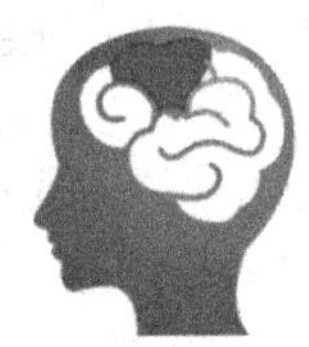

Is there anyone who you think is unsafe in your life, whose proximity to you could be easily decreased?

Would it be helpful for you to reduce the frequency of contact, to share less of yourself with them, and, if you do see them, to spend shorter periods of time with them?

Acquaintances that you have, friends of friends that you sometimes run into, a neighbour three doors down or someone that you run into at a soccer game or the dog park—these are the sorts of relationships that we can fashion so that we have the amount of proximity we feel is healthy.

When unsafe people want to increase their proximity to you, the most important word for you is 'No'.

'Would you like to go out for coffee?' the unsafe person asks.

'No thanks,' is your reply.

'Would you like me to walk you home?'

'No thanks.'

'Can I get your number?'

'No.'

'Give me a hug.'

'No.

'Would you like to ...?'

Whatever the invitation, the proximity to that person can be regulated by the word 'No'.

The flip side, of course, is that some people we meet at soccer games and dog parks may be quite safe. They are warm, interested in you, let you speak and give you choices. You may choose to increase the proximity to these people by saying 'Yes'.

'Would you like to have coffee?'

'Yes—thanks.'

Choosing whom to be close to and whom not to be close to is freedom and safety entwined. Choice feeds connection because when we have choices we always tend to feel safer. The key here is that we are not waiting for other people to give us choices. *We* make the choice. Nor do we think choice is a one-off activity. Choosing to be close or not be close with most people is an everyday activity. Even with the same person, it is an ongoing consideration for all of us, because people can at one time be safe and at another time not be safe. The bottom line is that we don't have to live like unsafe children … we can decide whom to be close to.

For some of us, the idea of choosing is elusive or perhaps even foreign to us, like it was for my friend Jess. She has had to learn to live her life in an awareness of her choices. This is going to make her a little more anxious, but the anxiety that she will feel in the moments when she says 'No' will be a lot less than the overall anxiety that she will carry day in, day out if she never says 'No'. She cannot go back. She cannot put herself in neutral. When we operate without choosing or judging our safety levels, we are on autopilot and the old patterns of thoughts, feelings and behaviours simply reiterate themselves. This leaves us open to being oblivious to dangers.

What to do if you're unsure whether you need to change the proximity

Why do some people choose to be around people who are not safe?

It seems complex, but it appears to have a lot to do with our past experiences. The experiences that we have had in the past are always considered 'normal' until a point in our development when we realise that that isn't the case. In this chapter, we have explored how we might 'match' safety with proximity to people, but being able to do this depends on having insight into ourselves and others. If we have insight, then it is easy to see that what we have experienced was not normal, and motivation to change this will come easily.

However, not all of us have this insight.

We dance in a pattern of familiar steps. We choose harmful

relationships even though we have suffered because of them. We choose the people who treat us the way we are used to being treated. We feel bad about who we are and we yearn for someone to love us properly, but somehow we can find ourselves attracted to people who treat us according to the way we may feel about ourselves. In some perverse way, we are 'at home' with such people. There is a fit between the way we get treated and the way we see ourselves. This can at times take a dramatic form. There are times when we almost 're-enact' previous trauma by being attracted to disconnected people.

Some researchers[9] have thought that we choose unsafe friends or partners to anaesthetise us against deeper feelings of shame. When we are threatened, we feel nothing else but this threat, and this, they say, puts the shame beyond our reach. At these times, we can feel fearful and not ashamed, scared and not heartbroken. I'm not too sure about that theory.

The opposite appears to be the case. When we have been abused, sometimes we feel nothing. We can't experience the small things, like the pleasure of holding hands, or the beauty of hearing rain on the roof. Having gone through so much, we go numb. Our systems shut us down as a way of coping. Unfortunately, this shuts down not just the painful feelings, but *all* feelings. It shuts down not just our emotions but also our insights into the pattern of abuse.

I remember being quite perplexed at university on learning that one of the most common risk factors for adult abuse was the history of having been abused. I understood that there was an increased risk for girls more than guys, because a lot of abuse is carried out by men. I understood that socio-economic hardship could be a factor that might lead some to be at risk of abuse as adults. But previous trauma? In my youthful naïvety, I thought

---

[9] For example, DB Benveniste, *The repetition compulsion all over again*, 2016, viewed October 2020, <https://benvenistephd.com/wp-content/uploads/2019/01/repetition.pdf>.

that if you went through something so bad, you'd be more alert to the possibility of it occurring and better at avoiding it. I was reading the words but failing to understand what they were saying.

Sigmund Freud referred to this pattern of self-abuse as 'repetition compulsion'.[10] In its broadest sense, people do this when they expose themselves to the same sorts of people and the same sorts of situations that hurt them. It seems a bit like a subconscious script that people play out in the unspoken hope that they might feel something—might feel anything at all—and somehow gain mastery over their relationships. It is a sad reality that this sort of script never really delivers on the hope that the victim has invested in it.

Confusion is the cardinal experience of people in this predicament, so wonder and curiosity are the starting points for change. Reflecting on patterns in our relationships in our history is a good start. Then, our heads must overrule our hearts yet again and we need to seek out new people who we know are good for us. There are times when we might find it boring to establish these friendships. New friends don't 'party' like the old ones. A new partner just doesn't seem exciting or have any spark.

Many years ago, my wife and I went out to dinner with a friend of hers and her new partner. Liz was a funny person and her partner was a lovely guy. At one stage over dinner, the topic of conversation turned to how their relationship had started.

Even though it was many years ago now, I can still remember her exact words. Liz said, 'Oh, I didn't really like him until we

[10] S Freud, *Beyond the pleasure principle*, 1920, cited in BA van der Kolk, 'The compulsion to repeat the trauma: re-enactment, revictimization, and masochism', *Psychiatric Clinics of North America*, vol. 12, no. 2, 1989, pp. 389-411.

had been together for a year.' Liz's new partner rolled his eyes and smiled. My wife and I were a bit taken back, but he wasn't at all. He knew how the story was going to end. Liz went on to explain how harmful her previous relationships had been, and if she had chosen the things that she was attracted to—if she had gone with the familiar pattern—she would have got the same sad, heartbreaking result. She knew what her new partner was like. He was a decent and loving person. She knew that she could not stick with immediate attraction to a dangerous partner. The excitement, the boom and bust, the fear then the break, the apologies, the excuses, then the reconciliation and closeness, was not a pattern that she wanted to continue with.

All of us who have been through troubled relationships when we were younger are at risk of involving ourselves in harmful relationships as adults. The relational scripts have already been laid down and when our anxiety is elevated, the previously learned patterns of behaviour and thought become activated by that state of arousal. We do what we tended to do when we were younger.

Our subconscious has its way with us, this is true; but it is also true that in our adult years, a lot of us begin to question whether what we have experienced was as normal as we had thought. We question ourselves and we consult others for their viewpoints. We become flexible in our thinking and see things from different perspectives. We make comparisons with friends and draw new conclusions—or more accurately, and this is the point I'm trying to emphasise, we make new comparisons and draw new conclusions *because* we have new friends. New insights are born out of the collaboration between safe, interested and understanding friends who bring new perspectives and ask penetrating questions. They become the 'new normal', and only when we openly reflect and talk about our history with them can we properly weigh up what has happened and whether or not we need to change.

For those of us in a situation where insight is low and there is ambivalence about the need to change, the journey will be long, not short. If this is your situation, then establishing your pyramid of support will be helpful for you, though it may need to come from a more conscious or intentional part of you. Your insight and motivation to change will follow later.

What to do if you can't change the proximity of relationships and it is unsafe

A significant number of us have high proximity to unsafe people and this appears fixed, or at the very least is difficult to change. You might be married to someone who is unsafe, or live with a sibling who is unsafe, or you might work with or for someone who is unsafe. Virtually all of us will have to contend with this sort of situation at some time. We will have to face this situation; it can't be avoided.

Facing others can be provocative and many unsafe people react poorly to even the most delicately handled confrontation. This appears likely when the person in question has a history of escalating quickly to yelling, name-calling or, worse still, shoving and other physical violence. Being honest with ourselves is the key: if you think they are not capable and not willing to face the situation with you, then postpone any big decisions about your relationship for the time being, and instead focus on increasing the FID (frequency, intensity and duration) with others who you think could be safe. Meet with a professional person who can help you to develop an action plan.

Nothing is more important at these times than to have friendships and contacts who provide safety. Building a small community of people around you that comprises caring professional people (like a General Practitioner or a psychologist or psychiatrist) and wise, stable friends to advise and support is crucial. These situations can be very serious, and they require careful and considered responses. It is only when we establish new connections with people who can support us that we can have the strength to break away from or build better boundaries around people who are volatile. Cautious wisdom will be both a guide and a friend. Facing and addressing our social situation is necessary, but facing slowly and in a piecemeal way with the support of trusted friends and professional people will be vital.

Pause and review

- In order to recover and flourish, we need to build a pyramid of support. The inclusion criterion for admission to your pyramid is the same as the exclusion criterion: safety. We need safe, loving people in our lives—people who connect and understand; people who keep confidentiality and don't control us.
- After we have gathered safe people around us, we need to 'dose up' on those people. Just like an antibiotic, we need to have a frequent, intense dose over a prolonged period of time.
- Face, forgive, focus on the future and have fun. These are ongoing processes that nourish our relationships. This dynamic is most appropriate for those relationships where there have been small declines in safety but there remains good potential for change.
- Sometimes we are not even aware of what is happening. We get hints but we remain unaware of the sort of relationship we have. We have to spend time reflecting on previous patterns if we are going to be released from the cycle of relational distress.
- Sometimes the people we are with aren't safe at all and they aren't responsive to our plea for safe connection. It is at these times that we need to build a solid pyramid around us, one

that might include professional people such as psychologists or psychiatrists.

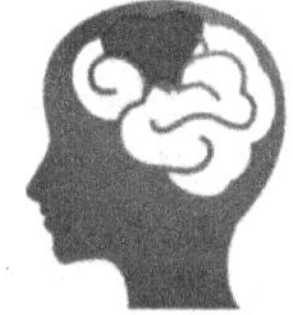

Have there been times in your life when you operated in the mode of 'repetition compulsion'?

Are you still in that mode?

What is the prognosis if your relational pattern does not change?

If you are no longer in that mode, how did you get out of it?

We have been taking large strides forward in recent chapters. We have been speaking about the need to properly establish a pyramid of support. We discussed in Chapter 6 the advantage we have in establishing the vertical part of our pyramid. In this chapter, we have shared how important it is to establish the base of the pyramid: getting the horizontal connections right.

The threat that lurks just beneath the water, lying in wait for us as if we are unsuspecting swimmers, isn't the lack of spiritual connection, nor is it the lack of connection with others. It is the lack of connection with ourselves. Without that, we are prone to repetition compulsion and vulnerable to unravelling when circumstances change.

A limited connection with ourselves limits the extent to which we can benefit from the pyramid we create. We may have faced and forgiven, and now be having fun, but deeper connection with others will depend on whether or not we understand and reveal ourselves to interested people. If we have no insight, no emotional language to convey our internal experiences, then the interested other will be short-changed by the experience and so will we.

Given that connection with others is contingent on our own

connection with ourselves, it is vital to focus on our internal connection and build it up. We simply cannot have connection with others if we don't understand ourselves, but understanding ourselves is contingent upon being connected with ourselves. This is the topic to which we now turn.

8

Connection with self (people heal themselves)

Of all the connection points—the vertical with God, the horizontal with others and the internal connection we have with ourselves—it is this latter connection point that is all too commonly in short supply. It is not unusual to find someone who can be connected spiritually and connected with others and have almost no connection with themselves. Fortunately, having worked through the previous chapters, we are in a position to remedy that situation.

In many respects, we have now been primed for this chapter. Seeing the connection consequences (betrayal, poor self-esteem, shame and alienation) can alert us to injuries we might find when we look inward. We are going to use what we have previously discussed to increase our understanding of ourselves.

For many of us, we now seek to employ a skill that we may never have cultivated. To reflect on oneself, or introspect, comes to most people via time and training. It is hard, and I have empathy for those who struggle to do it because I myself have struggled to do it. But it is worth it. Socrates knew that. So important was this process, that he told us that life wasn't worth living if we didn't do it. I don't know if this is strictly true, but you can see his point. It is important. It led him to make the injunction, 'Know thyself.'

The Bible speaks with equal emphasis. In the Old Testament book of Proverbs, we are told to guard our hearts 'above all else'. The proverb indicates that this is a top priority. Why? Because 'everything you do flows from it'.[1] Our thoughts, our behaviours, our moods and our bodily reactions all flow centrifugally out from our hearts. But we can't guard what we don't know, and we can't know what we haven't connected with. Our potential for true healing is limited by the extent to which we are connected to ourselves. That is why an Austrian Jewish philosopher said, 'We can be redeemed only to the extent to which we see ourselves.'[2]

Having reasonable expectations about how easy it will be to connect with ourselves will be important. The rate at which we develop a connection with ourselves varies according to three aspects of our social history:

1. **The way we had our emotions reflected back to us when we were young.** Remember our discussion about 'mirroring'? Our ability to get a sense of what is going on for us is caught up in the nature of what gets reflected back to us. Knowing ourselves depends on whether or not the image reflected back to us was distorted by the caregiver: was their mirror cracked, warped, scratched or cloudy?
2. **What our caregivers modelled to us.** Caregivers who told us what they were thinking and what they were feeling modelled to us how we might get to know ourselves,

[1] Proverbs 4:23.

[2] This quote is commonly attributed to Martin Buber. He was a prolific author, and it is hard to know exactly which text this quote comes from, because it is very rarely referenced within a specific text. This entry on *Goodreads* is typical: <https://www.goodreads.com/quotes/482049-we-can-be-redeemed-only-to-the-extent-to-which>

and their modelling of this behaviour provided us with a language to capture our own emotions. By revealing these ways of thinking and behaving, they conveyed to us that we can do the same.

3. **Whether the caregiving we received was active and constructive.** Remember Shelly Gable's recommendation that we talk to each other in 'active and constructive' ways in Chapter 2? This way of relating leads us to build an understanding of ourselves and constructively respond to ourselves in a way that is directly linked to that understanding.

Intrapersonal connection—that is, connection with ourselves—is to a large extent dependent on our history of interpersonal connection. Like many skills, the skill of introspection depends on caregivers having the time, energy, curiosity, interest and attitude that might help it to develop in the younger people in their care. A sense of wonder from trusted loved ones is indispensable in the process of developing a connection within ourselves.

Hopefully, some of you might be able to cut yourselves some slack in light of this. When we let our history of relationships create expectations, we can create more reasonable expectations for ourselves. Maybe you haven't been connected with yourself, but is that surprising when you look back on your significant relationships? A degree of self-compassion and patience with yourself will make your journey smoother.

There are other reasons why we don't connect with ourselves, though. When we have a heart-related injury, we do not naturally move towards it. There is a reflexive action that occurs at the mere thought of it. Like touching a hot stove, without thinking we violently jerk ourselves away from thinking and talking about it. Emotions are big, bossy and often negative by their very nature. They threaten us with loss of control when we speak of them. The four connection injuries (betrayal, worthlessness, shame and alienation) are profound in their depth and power, and it is no wonder that many of us become phobic about them and think it best to leave them alone lest they overcome and overwhelm us.

Our reluctance to connect with our emotions is what psychologists call 'affect avoidance'. Out of concern for our sleep, for our own productivity during the day or for relationships around us, or even just because we don't want to feel bad, we say to ourselves, 'Leave it in the past'; 'Why talk about the bad things?'; 'Look to the future.' We can feel an immediate relief upon saying this, but this strategy cheats us of safety in the long run. When we avoid it, we have failed to resolve it. As a result, avoidance may not always be possible. Reminders occur like a bad friend whom you keep running into. The bad friend pops up in this place and that place. Familiar smells take us back. *Deja vu* is not a quaint concept, and nostalgia is on the nose. Many of us hate to be reminded of something in our past, but when we say, 'Leave it in the past', we are really resigning ourselves to be indefinitely plagued by a nasty form of reminiscence.

When reminded in this way, some of us are not even able to put words to the feelings that we have. This can be because our emotions have become under-regulated or because they have become over-regulated.

When our emotions are under-regulated, we feel way too much all at once. We avoid the feeling because our experience of it is that we lose control of our emotions. It is simply too much. The sheer size and weight of our emotions lead us to fear them, and when we do experience them, their power drowns out our ability to consider and label the emotions we have.

For others, we can't label and consider our emotions because our emotions have become over-regulated. When asked to comment on what we feel, a blankness looms. This is the end product of over-regulation—emotional agnosticism. We become so good at putting the feelings aside, we end up feeling nothing. Our feelings aren't big and threatening; they are non-existent. It is almost as if we've lost an emotional pulse.[3] Or at least so it seems. The physical symptoms still speak—about fear, about anger and about sadness.

Whether or not you are over-regulated or under-regulated, labelling your emotions is indispensable in the healing process, but you need to show some grace towards yourself if you are finding it difficult to do.

If your caregivers showed an interest, if they modelled how to use emotional language, if they were active and constructive in the way they spoke, if they were a 'clean' mirror, if you were read stories that explored the inner lives of others and if you don't have big emotions that you react to like touching a hot stove, then introspection and gaining a connection with yourself will take only a little time and effort.

If, however, you did not experience these things, then it will take longer. That in no way means that you can't develop the skill; it only means that you need to be patient with yourself as you develop it.

How would you describe your experience with your caregivers as 'mirrors'?

To what extent do you think your caregivers had emotional literacy?

How did they take an active and constructive interest in your emotional life?

[3] As mentioned in Chapter 5, this impairment has a name: alexithymia. It is a condition in which people are unable to put words to feelings. People with this condition can recognise emotion in others, but can't recognise it in themselves. Louis Cozolino notes that 'patients with alexithymia are also described as having concrete or stimulus-bound cognitive style restricted imagination, and lack of memory for dreams.' L Cozolino, op. cit.

Even though the road towards self-understanding is long, we cannot jettison the journey. Not knowing who we are puts us at the mercy of circumstances and unresolved feelings, but it also puts deep connection with others beyond reach of people who love us, because others can't understand us if we don't reveal ourselves to them, and we can't reveal ourselves to them if we have nothing to reveal.

Our goal is to connect with ourselves. We can do this by integrating our feelings with our thoughts, bodily sensations and behaviours. By doing this, we can see how all of these experiences come from our hearts. Once we have done this, we can link together a series of similar events in time to form a story.

When you do this, this will be 'your story', or more accurately, the story of you. It is by this story that you and others can know you, and when you have this story, you and others can be more deeply connected. If you can do this, you will be able to 'see' yourself and will be better able to 'be seen' by others.

Every one of us reading this book will recognise ourselves in a mirror, but not every one of us will know who we are. Not knowing our essence is linked to a range of distressing mood, behavioural and cognitive symptoms. In order to know ourselves, we will need to connect with ourselves. If we don't, we won't understand ourselves. Neither will anyone else, except God.

It doesn't have to be this way. We can remedy this lack of self-knowledge. Identifying key events can get you started. These events gathered into a narrative help comprise your own story. Even if you don't tell others about them, just writing about your experiences can impact you in positive ways.[4]

[4] JW Pennebaker & RS Campbell, 'The effects of writing about traumatic experience', *Clinical quarterly*, vol. 9, 2000, pp. 17–21.

I'll show you how I help others to do this in therapy.

Bill is 35 years of age. He works in IT as a programmer. He has been married to Janet for 13 years.

He came to therapy because he noticed that his mood had deteriorated since his child began school. This was a puzzle, because Bill dearly loves his son, and his son had been so excited about starting school and becoming 'big'.

I asked Bill how he would describe his mood during the weeks since his son started school.

He replied, 'Nervous.'

I asked him how he was last year and the years preceding his son starting school.

He said, 'Flat.'

With his guidance I started to draw up the graph below. I put in a theoretical normal line (the horizontal axis) and this became his timeline. I put in a waterline and said, 'If you fall below this line, you might consider that you've become depressed … that is, you've got a range of symptoms such as considerable amounts of unhappiness, loss of positive feelings, worthlessness and possibly even suicidal thinking.'

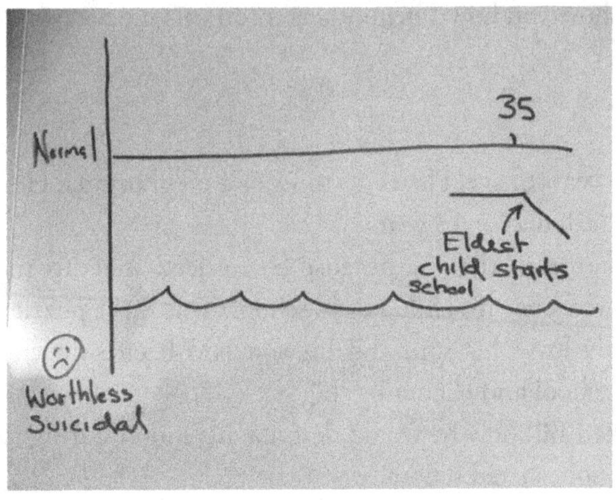

Figure 20. Chronology 1

Bill told me that he didn't feel like he was depressed at the present time, but he was once.

'When was that?' I asked.

'Just after I got married.'

'That is puzzling,' I replied. 'You told me earlier that Janet was a decent person.'

'She is,' Bill explained. 'On our honeymoon she told me that before we got married she had been unfaithful to me. She said she didn't want to tell me until after we had got married because she didn't want to lose me. I felt broken. It was with one of my friends.'

'That sounds difficult.'

'It sure was,' he said. 'I was down a lot of the time. I felt worthless.'

'How were you before you got married?' I asked.

'Yeah, I was doing well. I'd finished university and I'd got a job. It wasn't well paying, but it was a great start. I was playing sport with a local soccer team. They were good days.'

I knew then that most likely he had suffered a depressive episode at the age of 22, and that he was feeling normal prior to getting married, so I drew a line that descended from the normal line, down under the waterline.

I wondered whether he had never quite recovered from the news he was told.

'After the honeymoon, did your mood go back to normal?' I asked.

'Partly, but that was because of medication ... I don't think I've been the same since.'

When I asked that question, I knew that the line could come up, but wasn't going to return to the 'normal' line again. This was the 'flatness' that he was experiencing prior to his son starting school. I wanted to check how he was feeling earlier in his life. I knew that he was doing well before he got married, but I just wanted to make sure there was nothing earlier in his life that had upset him.

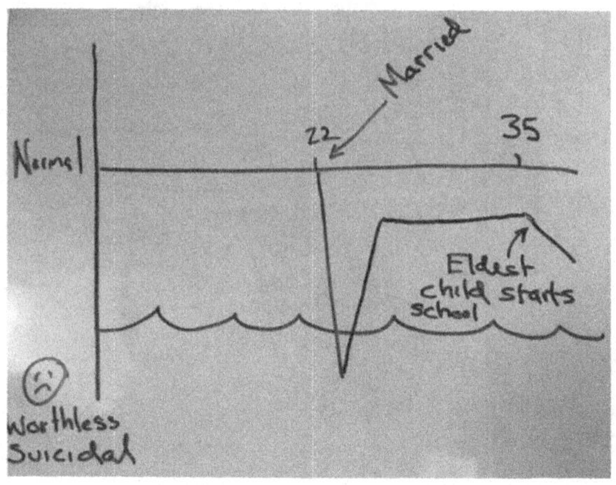

Figure 21. Chronology 2

'Were you okay in your teenage years and back into primary school?' I asked.

'For the most part,' he replied. 'When Mum and Dad divorced I took that really hard. I thought it was my fault, that Dad didn't love me enough to stay, that I wasn't enough for him. My mood wasn't as bad as then [he pointed to the dip in his mood at the age of 22], but it was tough'.

I was glad I asked. Even though it was tough when he was little, he had shown me that it wasn't as tough as it was when he was 22, so I put in a smaller dip in the graph. I knew that he must have bounced back at some point though …

'You said before that the years prior to you and Janet getting married were good, so I'm thinking that your mood must have recovered at some point after Mum and Dad divorced?' I asked.

'Yeah, you are right. It took me a couple of years, but one of my friends took me to church when I was 14. I really felt God's love and the love of friends. It was exactly what I needed. I forgave Dad, even though he didn't visit me much. I seemed to take it in my stride.'

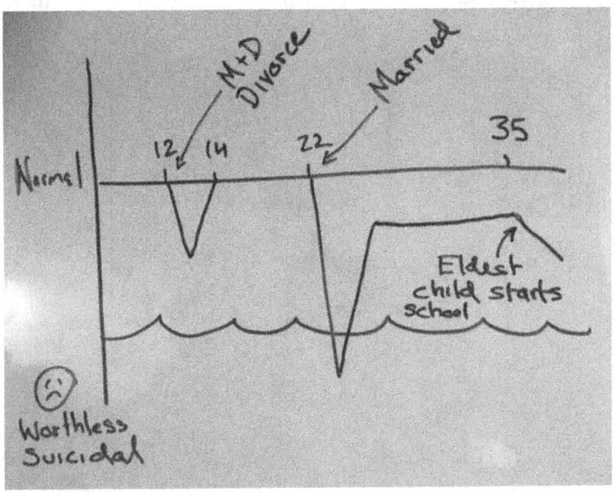

Figure 22. Chronology 3

I now had the clear impression that when he was 12 he found it difficult when Dad left but recovered well. From a diagnostic perspective, I wasn't too worried about that time of his life, but there was an impression that he endured a major depressive disorder at age 22. Unfortunately, it looked as though the condition never went into full remission. The anxiety that he felt with his son going to school had exacerbated the poor mood that was preceding it.

Transparence and collaboration are key aspects of all effective therapy. I am always talking to myself when I'm with people. Little phrases echo through my mind, reminding me of the policies I've put in place for myself—phrases like 'Be curious, don't be clever', 'Ask, don't tell' and 'Be with them, let them establish what is true of them.' So there I sat with Bill, with these words bouncing around inside of me. I wanted to check with him how I was interpreting his history.

'It seems obvious that medication was helpful after you got married, but it also looks as though something has lingered. Is that right?'

'Yes.'

'What is that?'

'I love Janet. In fact, I've wondered if I love her too much. She has stuck by me, and I have no reason to think she has been unfaithful. It is just … to this day, I wonder if I'm good enough for her. I wonder if she might want to leave. If she did I'd feel rotten.'

I was relieved that I had listened to my self-talk. He was really opening up at a heart level and I was keen for this time to be productive for him. I wanted him to connect with himself.

'Is there a link, then, between 22 and 12?' I asked.

Bill paused. 'I don't … maybe. No. Oh … It is almost as if being single was easier …'

There was a pause. Bill disengaged from me. He seemed to look at a distant object to the side of me, down near my feet. His hand came up to support his head, like it had suddenly become heavy. His words slowed down and the tone of his voice dropped.

'No-one leaves you when there is no-one close to you, they can only leave when they are near,' he said.

'So now, why have you become more anxious about your son?' I asked him, leaving him to put the final pieces of the puzzle together.

'I don't know,' he replied, as if a little exasperated.

Then there was a longer pause, as we both gave him permission to think and feel. In time, his exasperation gave way to his curiosity, but I wasn't sure whether the silence was as productive for him as it could be, so I asked him a question.

'Bill, what is the worst thing in your mind that could happen to your son at school?'

'Oh, that is easy. I get images in my head after I drop him off at school. Images of people excluding him at lunch, not wanting to play games with him. That is why I try so hard, almost too hard, to engage with him when I pick him up from school. I know he is tired, but I almost pester him with questions in order to show that I'm interested in him. I want to show him that I'm not going to abandon him.' His words were picking up in speed.

'You don't want people to leave him?' I ask.

'No, of course not,' he said with a tone of surprise, as if that was a silly question. 'What sort of a dad would want that …'

He stopped, placed his head in his hands and cried.

And the link between the present and the past was complete. He didn't want his son to endure what he had endured.

Bill's parents had trouble relating to each other all through his early schooling and he was constantly scared about them leaving him. When he was young, he felt like it was his role to keep them together. He felt guilty when they decided to divorce, as if somehow he was responsible for it, but he also felt that he was not good enough for his wife. She was and had been a loving partner for 13 years—she had just made one mistake like so many of us do in our early twenties. Bill knew that. He knew that she loved him and that he should forgive her, but he was haunted by the thought that he was not enough for her. He didn't want his own son to go through what he was feeling. He didn't want him to feel like he wasn't good enough for his dad or wasn't good enough for his school friends, and again Bill was taking too much responsibility for keeping relationships together. He was becoming anxious about what might happen as his son spent more time with friends at school; he was scared of what might happen to his son if his son trusted other children and they betrayed him. School reminded Bill of the fear that he had felt when he was young and the fear that he had felt that his wife might leave him. He projected this fear onto his own son. The irony was that his own son was really happy with school, wasn't worried about such things, and knew full well that his own father would never abandon him.

My eldest daughter had a Barbie wand. She is a teenager now, so the wand has long since been relegated to an op shop donation bin. The wand was pink, was about 35 cm long and had a long shaft with a star on the end of it. When you pressed a button, the star flashed and made a sound like a harp being strummed. When she was little she used to press the star and turn her siblings into frogs or princes. I told Bill about the Barbie wand. I asked Bill how much difference it would make to his life if we could wave the magic Barbie wand over himself and undo his heavy sense of unworthiness, blame and abandonment.

'The difference would be huge!' he said.

We know we aren't dealing with anything peripheral here. To know what is on our hearts is to know our substance, and to change our hearts is to be changed substantially. To put it simply: what is in the heart is the heart of the matter. To change someone's heart will make a 'huge' difference. Bill's response illustrates the genuine need that exists in many of us to have our hearts healed, and it also illustrates how strategic it is to address this area of our functioning. Change your thinking? Sure, that is a good idea. Change your behaviour? Sure, that isn't such a bad idea either. Change your heart? Now that is a *great* idea, because both your thoughts and your behaviour flow from it.

We venture towards this goal of having a change of heart, not only because it is strategic, but because it is biblically sanctioned and even mandated. When the writer of Psalm 42 became aware of his emotional distress, his response was to look more closely at it. He quizzed himself: 'Why, my soul, are you downcast?' he asked.[5] Again and again he asked himself, 'Why?' But why does he ask why? I think this is plain for all: he wanted to understand himself. The Psalmist asked these questions in the hope that by connecting with himself, he would achieve personal insight. This is how our spiritual forebears dealt with distress: they sought to connect with and understand themselves.[6]

Knowing how strategic connection with ourselves is, and knowing the potential impact it can have if we get it right, it seems wise to turn our attention to *how* we might set a new growth pattern in motion. This is what we are going to do now.

Eight things you need to do to gain a connection to yourself

Our journey in this book has taken us through what connection is (a binding), what it is like to go without connection (injuries of omission like loneliness), and what it is like to have disconnection (the presence of bad connection like physical or sexual abuse). We have discussed how relationships can hurt us in profound ways, producing betrayal, worthlessness, shame and alienation. These connection injuries spill over into other sectors of the heart. When injured in this way, we label ourselves in ways that create new and horrible identities, hopelessness and despair.

All is not lost, though. Far from it.

We have been nurturing a garden. We have been creating a

---

[5] Psalm 42:5.

[6] Of course, this is not all the Psalmist does. He also sets himself a direction to become connected with God: 'for I will yet praise him,' he says. The thread of his recovery is characterised by the pursuit of these two things: connection with himself, and connection with God. These two activities are co-occurring and you can see these themes recurring in Psalms 42 and 43 ('Why, my soul, are you downcast?' and 'Put your hope in God, for I will yet praise him').

relational environment that is looking good for growth. The soil has been tended and the pH is just right. It is dark and rich, and full of nutrients. We have got the hose ready. Surrounded by horizontal warmth and safety, saturated by vertical love, connection with ourselves is the only connection point we are yet to establish. When we do this, the connection that we have with God and others only becomes magnified because our own understanding of ourselves bolsters the connections that we have with others.

First, I'm going to suggest six primers that, when they are in place, can help us to connect with ourselves. These primers underwrite (but don't entail) a good connection with ourselves. They put us in a good position to let it happen.

1. Develop a new attitude

A crucial ingredient in change is to have a new attitude to the connection process. A constructive attitude will help to foster the self-connection process. It *is* good for you. If you do it, you *can* prevent decomposing and you can prevent overreacting. If you have a positive attitude, you will act with interest and respect towards yourself. So many of us rip into ourselves psychologically. Some of us actually hate ourselves. Some of us completely ignore ourselves. Only active interest and empathy towards ourselves will help. Empathy is required for the process, because it is only via uncovering the truth and accepting ourselves that change can occur. Carl Rogers once said, 'The curious paradox is that when I accept myself just as I am, then I can change.'[7]

[7] C Rogers, *On becoming a person: a therapist's view of psychotherapy*, Houghton Mifflin Company, Boston, 1961, p. 17.

2. *Make time to connect with yourself*

In this time-poor society, we discard self-connection because other people and other issues scream out urgently demanding immediate attention. We come to the end of a week, and we think 'I was too busy' to do this or that. But we always make time to do what we think is important. It is time for you to prioritise connecting with yourself. No priority = no time allocated = no connection.

3. *Be open to new thoughts and perspectives*

A full tank of curiosity is essential. Without wonder, there is no chance that we will uncover the information we need to respond to ourselves in helpful ways. Many of us grew up with caregivers who weren't interested in our thoughts and feelings. If we don't show an interest in ourselves, we are just treating ourselves in the same way our caregivers did.

4. *Find a quiet space*

Having prioritised the task as important, having assigned time to do it, and possessing an attitude of openness, our next step is to find a quiet space. Loud, demanding noises muffle our own whispering voice. Surely my mother spoke with profound psychological insight when she yelled at my already yelling brother, sister and me, 'Will you kids be quiet? I can't hear myself think!' We can't hear ourselves think when *people around us* talk so much, and we can't hear ourselves think when *we* talk so much. Our ability to hear our own voice is bolstered by decreasing the white noise that surrounds us and ensuring the stillness of our own tongue. It does not have to be perfectly quiet, though. Some of us benefit more if there is some white noise around us, like when we are sitting in a coffee shop. Others require something in their hands to fiddle with, or a ball to throw, or a drawing to do. Whatever your strategy to help you connect with yourself better, do what is most productive for you.

5. Change your physical environment

A change of geography is often required, not just because it can remove us from the noise, but because it removes us from the typical cues for mental habits. The busy, cluttered places in which we live and work often create an urgent state for our minds, ushering us to the same thoughts and behaviours that are familiar to us. Go for a walk. Go for a drive. Have a swim and sit on a beach. Whatever or wherever the physical environment is that helps you to reflect, seek it out and do it by yourself.

6. Observe

We have now taken the initial steps needed to reduce the noise and primed ourselves to perceive in new ways. We need silence around us to hear the voice within us. We have reduced the volume of other people's voices, but we also need to turn down the residual echoes that can bounce around the chambers of our minds: what other people think, what other people want from us, how others feel about us and who other people think we are. We need to turn up the volume on our own voices. We need to consider our own experiences. What is on our hearts is often revealed in emotional language. We need to ask, 'What do I feel about me?' Then, simply observe. Recognise the physical symptoms and consider how they might inform you about how you think of yourself. Observe the thoughts and images that go through your mind. How are you tempted to behave? Do you want to withdraw? Do you want to fight? Are you tempted to fake that you are okay? A helpful way to approach this is to join together the different domains of our functioning (i.e. be SMART). In the present, consider what triggers the emotions, and link those emotions with how you cope when you experience those emotions, what you think, and your physical reactions. All of these aspects (thoughts, feelings, actions, body symptoms) of our functioning are prisms through which we might see into our hearts.

These points will help you discover 'what' it is that you are experiencing as you contemplate what is on your heart. Now we are going to consider 'why' we are experiencing it. It is time to look for an explanation of that state. Like the Psalmist in Psalm 42, we ask, 'Why, my soul, are you downcast?'[8] The linking up of physical, emotional and mental domains is important in its own way, but a richer explanation will incorporate how these experiences come from the heart and how the heart is linked to historical events as well—just like Bill and I did. Your task is to understand yourself in a deeper way. Insight can come from focusing on your present functioning as mentioned above, but it is deeply enriched by seeing the heart and linking the heart with your own history.

Now that we have clarified the six primers (attitude, time, openness/curiosity, quietness, geography, observation), we turn our attention to how we actually do connect with ourselves. Sometimes connection with ourselves can take time, but it can sometimes happen quite quickly.

7. Locate it in your heart

We can use the information from the SMART process to go deeper. We want to look through those experiences to explain those experiences. Have you been experiencing omission (loneliness) or commission (nastiness, aggression)? Do you experience betrayal, poor self-esteem, shame or alienation? How would you quantify it?

[8] Psalm 42:5.

Perhaps those labels aren't quite right for you. If so, how might you describe your experience better? Have you put a label on yourself: 'I am ______', or 'I am a ______'? Ask yourself a question like, 'What do my emotions, my actions, my physical reactions and my thoughts say about what might be going on for me at a deeper level?'

You know that you have located what is on your heart when your answer to that question explains your mood, your actions, your physical reactions and your thoughts. For example, if you said, 'They say "I'm an idiot"', then this would explain why you get angry at yourself and why you have negative thoughts about yourself.

8. Link what you've discovered to times in your history

Now we have a lead to chase. Whatever happened to you in your heart, ask yourself whether you can trace it back to other events in your personal history. Tell the story: consider the observations that you've made about yourself in point six above. How did that pattern of thoughts, feelings, behaviours and physical symptoms start? Link the present to the past, or your heart with your history.

Have you had a similar experience in the past? Who were you relating to when you first had that heart issue? Was there an event? What was that time of life like for you? How would you describe it? Did that feeling improve and then resolve only to come back more recently (like Bill with his little boy starting school)? Or did it start small and get progressively worse? At those times, in those places, what was happening to you at a heart level?

Picture yourself back there. Put yourself in that room; sit at that school desk; think of that person whom you were with at the time. Now link the past events with the present. *How does* the past link with the present?

The reason why we connect with ourselves is so that we can achieve a better understanding of ourselves. The reason we do this is that it is only when we connect and understand ourselves that we will be able to respond to ourselves in a helpful and constructive way. We will be using these steps in the next chapter, as they are the starting points of the transformation process.

As you find insight, it will not be surprising at all if significant feelings well up within you. Do not be surprised—after all, heart issues are emotional. It is very appropriate to adopt self-care strategies at times like this. Arrange time to unwind afterwards, and consider writing out any insights you have gained, or any observations you've made that are interesting to you. This is important because labelling gives us control, but also because insight is slippery, and without documenting it, we may find that the insight escapes us later on.

Every so often, I sit with people who think they are doing well, but they are not. They have a bravado about them, and with an air of confidence tell me that they don't need to see me anymore.

A lot of the time, I sit with people who think they are doing poorly when they are actually doing well. They think that because they find a heart-level injury, that is confirmation of doing poorly. It isn't.

If you feel bad because you've perceived a deep connection injury coupled with an identity label, then you are on the way to healing. Be encouraged. Your insight and understanding of yourself is one of the most promising indications that your future will be a lot better than your past.

Now that you've seen your heart from the *outside in*, look at your behaviour, thoughts and choices from the *inside out*.

I think I must have been quite naïve when I was studying Clinical Psychology. I sat in a class in Sydney with twenty other twenty-somethings. We learnt, among many other things, about

Albert Ellis's 'rationality'.[9] As a student, I thought that in the future I would be taking each client through a sequence that would reveal their corrupt and emotionally provocative thinking. I thought that once they told me what they thought, I would show them that the way they thought was 'irrational', and that this so called irrationality was what had led to their difficulties with anger, depression or anxiety. Then, when they could see what they had been doing, the people who came to see me would become enlightened like me and would get better because of their improved rationality.

I was so wrong.

It's turned out to be the opposite of what I predicted. I spend most of my time reminding people of how rational they actually are. Given what has happened to them in their relationships, and given the nature of their heart-level injuries, it is more than understandable that they think, act and physically react in the ways they do. I tell them that if I had been through what they had been through, I'd be the same, think the same, act the same and feel the same. They're understandable; they're normal; they're human.

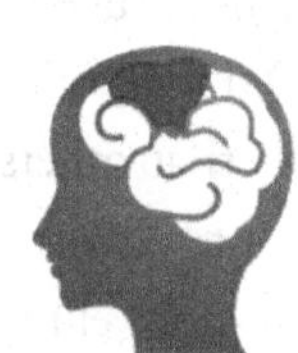

Can you make sense of the way you feel, act, think and physically react?

If so, how?

If not, what is in your heart and history that might help you to explain these things?

When we sense just how understandable we are, we might experience an 'aha!' moment. We might exhale in a way that signifies relief. The 'aha' moment is a leap of insight that makes sense of the

[9] Rational Emotive Behavior Therapy, founded by Albert Ellis, identifies the cause of distress to be the irrational thoughts we have. Its influence is waning a little, but the impact of this form of therapy was significant at the time at which I was in training.

SMART experience. Sometimes it happens; but if it doesn't, don't get discouraged. The insight doesn't always come easily to us. Just keep on wondering.

All of our symptoms become understandable when we come to terms with not just our hearts but also our history. Our hearts are created by those significant relationships in our past and what is in our hearts flows centrifugally out of them in irresistible ways. Of course those situations troubled us. Why wouldn't they? Why wouldn't our moods, actions, reactions and thinking be influenced by what we have been through? People have hurt us and our hearts have been broken, and our thinking, acting and physical reactivity is different. That *is* rational. The restless discontentment, irritability, irascibility, loss of energy, sadness and anxiety flow centrifugally out of the heart. We cope by fighting, by fleeing or by faking. Our thoughts automatically offer interpretations that are negative. We become vigilant; our bodies don't switch off. Like a cat with its back arched up and its fur standing on end, we are ready for what we think could happen, or like a dog scurrying away with its tail between its legs, we avoid what we expect.

We can find ourselves living in a state of readiness. We see danger far off, but it never feels far off. We brace ourselves for it, and relive it. Urgent relational dramas demand immediate solutions. Old memories feel like 'only yesterday'. We become stuck, and the skills that others develop to thrive (to persevere, to tolerate distress, to be patient, to persist in the face of challenge, to confront others, to delay gratification) elude us because we are too busy using skills that we developed to survive (to read danger, to predict and avoid it or to fight against it).

'People's minds are developmentally specialised toward local environmental conditions'[10] wrote Frankenhuis and de Weerth. They note that children who have endured stress adapt in ways that are helpful to them. What they are saying is that the way

[10] WE Frankenhuis & C de Weerth, 'Does early-life exposure to stress shape or impair cognition?', *Current directions in psychological science*, vol. 22, no. 5, 2013, pp. 407–412.

we behave isn't dumb—it is adaptive. People who have grown up around danger find that it is much better to be looking out than looking in—better to predict when Dad has been drinking than to introspect. As a result, we can know the danger, and this keeps us out of it. There have been times when we predicted we were in danger but we weren't, or when we thought that people were not interested when they really were. This is unfortunate, but false positives are better than false negatives. Better to over-predict than under-predict, or over-protect than under-protect. We think, 'That person hates me' and we find out that they don't, but assuming that they do hate us is better than assuming that they don't, because if we assume that they don't hate us and we get it wrong we will feel terribly betrayed. At least we can be prepared if we live with our guard up. Why wouldn't we do all these things? Nobody wants to get hurt again.

I do not want to normalise all behaviour and thinking, though. The goal is not to be so lacking in compassion that I say, 'You are normal … it is normal … have a good life.' It is to be so connected and understanding of every person's journey that it becomes explicable. The people who have missed out on good connection or endured the nastiness of disconnection are not weird or defective. They are normal people who have endured things that they never should have. The task, as it has always been, is to see the patterns. The core senses that we carry around with us, the heart-level injuries, explain our thoughts, actions and reactions.

It *is* understandable, but the cruel reality is that what was so good for survival is bad for recovery. The way we thought, acted, reacted and felt was helpful at the time, but it creates further problems down the track.

The energy of what is in our hearts flows centrifugally outwards, but unfortunately the petals of the 'Heart Flower' (see Figure 9 in Chapter 4) bend back into the heart, confirming and consolidating the injury. We need to change from the inside out, but we also need to change the way we think, act and react to calm our hearts. We will tackle this problem in the next chapter.

Pause and review

- Connection with ourselves is biblically mandated but the skill is developed by our relational upbringing. That is to say, the Bible wants us to do it, our spiritual forefathers did it, but it is limited by the extent to which our carers modelled it to us and encouraged us to do it ourselves.
- Our ability to connect with ourselves is bolstered by a positive attitude, an openness to experience, time, a change of geography, finding a quiet space and making quiet observations of the way we operate.
- Deep connection with ourselves involves using the observations of 'SMART' to consider what is in our hearts, and linking what is in our hearts with our histories.

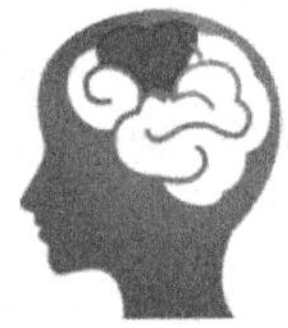

Are you connected with yourself?

What has been your attitude to connecting with what is in your heart?

Do you make sense to yourself? What is one thing you can do to connect with yourself better?

In Chapter 6, we outlined how we might cultivate a closer spiritual relationship. In Chapter 7, we discussed how we can foster better relationships with others. In this chapter, we have developed some ideas about how we might be better connected with ourselves. In doing so, we have now nurtured the three-point connection process.

What we have not yet discussed is personal transformation, or *how* people change. How can we use these connection points in the change process? What steps are involved in the change process? These issues are the focus of our attention in the next chapter.

9

In, back, up, forward

The answer to the question 'How do people change?' varies depending on who you ask. If you ask a Cognitive Therapist, he or she will tell you to focus on changing your beliefs; if you ask Behaviourists they will tell you to change your behaviour; a Somatic Therapist will help you focus on your body; and if you ask a person of faith, he or she will tell you that God changes people. Typically, the therapist or the person of faith will encourage you to focus on one domain of human functioning and stop there. We are not going to neglect these individual areas—rather, we are going to use each area in our quest to be transformed.

The process we are going to use is a four-step process that I created to help people traverse the crucial stages of personal transformation. I call it '*In, back, up, forward*'.

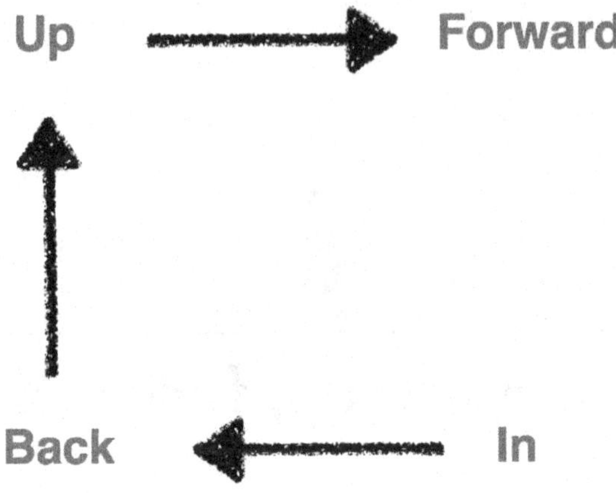

Figure 23. The four-step transformational process

The transformational process starts with reflecting on a situation that is frequently provocative for you. You may have already gathered up information on this sort of event in Chapter 5 when we first used the 'SMART' approach, or more recently in Chapter 8, but you might also choose to use a new situation. When you have one, you can begin the process of *in, back, up, forward*:

In

Like opening a door to a room deep in our own house, we go *in*to our hearts. We are going to be SMART here, using the information we have gathered in the SMART process. The place to start is with our emotions because, as we have discussed in Chapter 5, emotions are the primary way in which the heart communicates. Facing them can be hard, so we will have to be wise. Face your emotions with someone who you believe to be loving, wise and safe (remember the criteria for safety from Chapter 7). Strive to re-experience the emotions in safe ways.[1] Collect the emotions and speak them out. Now turn your attention to the other areas of your SMART functioning so that you can gain a better understanding of your experience.

> **Situation**: What was the situation that troubled you?
>
> **Mood**: What were the feelings that you experienced?
>
> **Action**: How did you behave when you had those feelings? Did you say anything at the time?
>
> **Reaction**: What physical symptoms did you experience?
>
> **Thoughts**: What thoughts went through your mind? Did any images, pictures or memories come to you?

---

[1] Many therapists who use exposure therapy speak about a 'window of tolerance'. The window contains moderate emotions only. We don't want to be over-aroused (hyperaroused) nor do we want to be under-aroused (hypoaroused). If you feel too much, you'll overshoot the window and that won't be good for you; in fact, it will only secure your injuries. First of all, it is vital to remember that you have choices. You can choose to face what has upset you. You don't have to. You might choose to talk about only a part of it, or you may choose to talk about it only for a couple of minutes. You are in control. If you decide to face it and you are overshooting the window, approach the memories in a piecemeal way and try using a long, slow exhale. Use the SMART strategy; stay connected (use eye contact) with the person you are talking to as this will keep you in the present (try stating your age, the date, where you are and who you are within the present moment); and give yourself a little more distance from the trauma. Don't undershoot the window either. If you don't experience much emotion, you won't re-engage the old feelings enough for them to find expression. If that is you, focus on gathering up information and patiently persist with the task of putting words to feelings, bodily reactions and memories. Speak in the first person. If you undershoot the window, the heart-level disturbances will only lie dormant waiting to be triggered at another time.

Look through each of the SMART domains to the functioning of your heart. Remember the connection injuries that we outlined in Chapter 4? Look for the connection injuries now (betrayal, worthlessness, shame, alienation), and their accompanying identity tags ('I am a ______' or 'I'm ________'). Name the injuries that are located in your heart, and see how the injuries flow centrifugally out into your actions, reactions, mood states and thoughts. Take your time to slow down and consider. This is where it gets interesting, because this is where you might see how the heart explains the way you function. Does what you've come up with explain what you've observed in each domain of the SMART acronym? If it doesn't, you may need to persevere a little. If it does, you will feel a small 'aha' moment of clarity.

Back

Link what is in your heart with your history. Go down the stem of the 'Heart Flower' to a time when the flower was younger. Ask yourself these questions:

- When have I had this before?
- Who was I with?
- What does this remind me of?
- Is there an image that comes to mind?
- Is there a metaphor that could explain my experience?

Put yourself back there. Describe it—not necessarily the incident itself, but perhaps the aftermath of it. What do you see? What do you hear? What is it like for you back there and back then? These experiences are the original 'bacteria'.

Link the past with the present. Our task is to connect with our own narratives and find the heart-level experiences that are linked together within them. If we have done that, we have completed an understanding of our hearts; but if we are to find positive change, we must bring our hearts and our history to the 'antibiotic'.

Up

The God of the Bible is the ultimate antibiotic. We have already brought some of the 'pyramid of support' together in the first two parts of this book, but at this stage the whole pyramid comes together. Even though there is both horizontal and vertical connection in this stage, I have called this stage 'up', as opposed to merely going 'out', because going to the cross is the cardinal feature of the personal transformation process for Christians.

Before you do, remember that you are approaching not only a God of purity, but a God of pure love. You are safer than you'll ever fully realise and more loved than you know. Engage with your heart and put yourself at the foot of the cross. Look up and ask God to be with you. Notice the disparity. Back there and back then, amongst the bacteria, you sensed that you were unsafe, either by omission or commission. In the present situation, at the present time, that old sense of threat doesn't exist. Look vertically to God while you look horizontally to the people in your pyramid. The violence isn't there, the yelling isn't there, the nastiness isn't there, the bad attitudes aren't there, and the neglect or inattention aren't there. Whatever it is that hurt you, notice that it doesn't exist in your relationships.

Now look for the positive thing in the present that you may not have had in the past. The absence of love and care back there in the past has now been remedied. It was missing back then, and you may have been living in a vacuum of love and support, but if you have built your pyramid well, you should see the presence of love in the present. We need to sense the presence of this, because we know that relationships can heal us when they're both connected and safe. The researcher John Briere calls the process of healing by positive relationships 'counter-conditioning',[2] but really it is about love and connection. Pure empathy and loving connection without reservation provides the aspirin to settle all our inflammation. The love we experience in the present helps us to come to peace with the lack of connection and the disconnection of the past. Keep one foot in the past, and one in the present. Go *up* to the cross. Sense the hurt, and, although it sounds a little clichéd, 'feel the love'.

We have now covered three parts of the *in, back, up, forward* sequence. Going 'in' to our hearts and 'back' into our histories leads us to connect with ourselves. Pulling together our pyramids, and in particular going 'up', increases our horizontal and vertical connection.

Many of us are hurt because of others, but many of us remain hurt because we take our value and identity from others. Who we ask to give us value and identity is who we worship, and if that is others and they let us down, then we have outsourced the solution of our hearts to the wrong people.

At other times, we have depended on ourselves to heal our hearts, but we have failed. We have relied on ourselves to give ourselves value and identity, but we have fallen short.

Whether we have worshipped someone else or we have worshipped ourselves, our challenge is to take our idols and give them to God. We connect with our hearts and our histories, and we go 'up' and say sorry for asking ourselves or others to heal our hearts knowing that God is the only one who can do that for us. This is one of the most demanding and productive opportunities: to repent when we are hurting, to say sorry when we are depressed and anxious, to apologise when we are broken. Only when we do this can we let go of the past and look to the future.

---

[2] JN Briere & CS Scott, *Principles of trauma therapy: a guide to symptoms, evaluations and treatments*, Sage Publications, Los Angeles, 2006.

Forward

This is the final step and one that is dear to me, because if going in, back and up are done properly, often going forward is very natural. Because we are centrifugal people, all categories of SMART functioning are changed when the heart changes. Nonetheless, it is not always altered in a seamless way and we have to integrate our thoughts and actions in a way that is in accord with having a new heart.

Many of us know what our hearts should be. We should feel forgiven, we should not be thinking toxic thoughts, and if we really were confident about who we were in Christ we wouldn't avoid some situations and we wouldn't physically react to things the way we do. We may have gone *in, back and up*, but there are thoughts, actions, physical reactions and feelings that keep the old state of heart intact. We want to undo the feedback loops and change these to accord with the new heart that we have been given. Consider this question:

As someone who:

- takes no value or identity from what you have or haven't done
- takes no value or identity from what others have or haven't done to or for you
- has value beyond measure, a trust that is beyond doubt, and a sense of honour and belonging that is unshakeable in God

... how might you think and act differently today?

This last step is important, and much of Cognitive Behaviour Therapy (CBT) focuses on this. CBT goes 'in' just a little, hardly ever goes 'back', never ever goes 'up', but always goes 'forward'. It looks for the maintenance factors for your distress. Resolving the thoughts and behaviours that maintain distress is a must, and CBT is right to address them.

Remember our Heart Flower in Chapter 4 (Figure 9)? We used it to illustrate the way thinking, behaviours and physical symptoms flow out naturally from the heart. This is an important aspect, though it is important also to recognise, as we did earlier, that the petals flow back into the heart to keep the heart injuries in place (the broken lines). There might be interpretations that need to be reworked (learning not to take things personally) and there may be coping behaviours that need to change (learning not to avoid things that make us anxious).

This is why we hurt for so long. Many of us remain upset for years, even decades, after an event or series of events, because the heart-level injury is maintained by how we act, react, feel and think. These maintenance factors have to be discarded.

Moving 'forward' represents a participatory step in the process of heart-level transformation. Sometimes we have to cultivate new habits with our thoughts, actions and physical responses so that our hearts can stay repaired. When our hearts are changed properly, new thoughts, physical reactions, behaviours and feelings naturally flow out. There are times when we need to make sure that these responses occur, otherwise our old injuries will be maintained.

We need to react differently, so becoming aware of and directly manipulating our physical reactions will help.[3]

---

[3] Progressive Muscle Relaxation is a technique that involves systematically tensing up and releasing different muscles in the body. It has been shown to induce a sense of relaxation and has been particularly helpful in the treatment of insomnia, Generalised Anxiety Disorder (which is characterised by difficult-to-control worry about many different issues), headaches and Panic Disorder. Start by doing your own body scan: notice which parts of your body hold tension. Squeeze the muscles together and make them tense. Hold the tension for 5–7 seconds. Relax the muscles and notice the change in tension. Do this two or three times. Discontinue immediately if you get cramps or if you have a sense of feeling out of control. This strategy should not be seen as *the* core strategy to treat other anxiety problems such as PTSD, specific phobias and Social Phobia.

We need to act differently by facing others, not fleeing from them or fighting with them.

We need to distance and detach ourselves from our mood states by putting a time code on the feeling (i.e. 'This is the feeling I had when I was 14') so that we can stop the reliving.

We need to change our thinking by reframing situations and seeing challenges as opportunities to grow, not as catastrophes that have set us back 'yet again'.

Having said this, some modern therapies seem at times to be a little … soulless. I'm sure I'd be seen as the Dark Lord of Psychologists for confessing this, but I stand by the comment. Such soulless therapies fail to fully recognise the roots of psychology. The word 'psychology' literally means 'the study of the soul' and this is what psychology originally sought to examine (from the Greek, *psyche* means 'soul' and *-logia* means 'study of'). The soul is not a tangible thing, but it is an experience that emerges from our amazing capacity for relationships. Our empathy for each other, our ability to know each other's stories, and our ability to gain a sense of another person's lived experience and capture it all with words endow us with an amazing capacity to relate not just to each other but to a deity.

Who we are as people is the amalgam of all the relationships we have had. We are broken and made by relationships; deformed and reformed by them. People are relational in their very essence. People aren't in their essence thinking beings, nor are they doing beings—even though we both think and do. We are primarily relational entities, soulful and sentient to the core. We are centrifugal in that we change primarily from the inside out. Most of us are spiritual, most of us sense that symptoms are symptoms of something, and all of us have a past.

I was reflecting on this towards the end of my Christmas holidays in Sydney. I was there seeing family and friends. The day after I got back, I sat down and I remembered a book from long ago. I searched through multiple cupboards at home and couldn't find it. I knew I had lent it to a friend but I was sure he had given it back. I drove in to work and found it on the bottom shelf in my office. In a chapter entitled 'Cognitive Contributions to Soul', it said 'the experiences of relatedness to others, to the self, and most particularly to God … endow a person with … a soul.'[4]

I remembered the pyramid of support. And it occurred to me, even at this late stage of writing, that in this book we have been using our souls, and the souls of others, to heal our hearts.

Time and time again I have gone *in, back, up and forward* in my life, and on many occasions it has been very moving, even life-changing—like that time with my friend John, when he asked me whether I ever thought that God delighted in me the way I delighted in my daughter. I went into my heart, I wondered about my past, I connected with God's perspective. I don't expect that it will be always therapeutic, but I do it because I know God wants me to worship him, and I know that my heart needs me to worship him.

There are times when I wonder why, despite following the template of *in, back, up and forward*, nothing has changed in my heart. It is at these times that I decide to focus on the first step, that of connecting with myself (going 'in'). I try to remain curious about my own functioning via each of the domains in the SMART

[4] WS Brown, 'Cognitive contributions to soul' in WS Brown, N Murphy & HN Malony (eds), *Whatever happened to the soul: scientific and theological portraits of human nature*, Fortress Press, Minneapolis, 1998, p. 102.

acronym (i.e. I ask, 'I wonder why that situation is provocative? I wonder why that mood keeps coming up for me? When I take that action, what does that tell me about what is on my heart? What does my physical reaction say about what I'm sensitive to at a deeper level? What do my thoughts suggest to me about me?'). Only when I do this can I come to understand why the process of change has been slower for me than it has been for others.

Pause and review

We have developed a four-step process:

- In: look at what is in your heart through the prism of your situation, mood, action, reaction and thoughts.
- Back: link the present with your past—link what is in your heart with your history.
- Up: take your heart to God. Ask him to give you trust/self-esteem/honour/belonging, a new identity, and hope. Repent of trying to get value and identity on your own or via others, and place your injuries at the foot of the cross. Turn your back on them, and walk away.
- Forward: change the way you think, act, react and feel to align with your new heart.

Have you been worshipping others or yourself in the sense that I have described here?

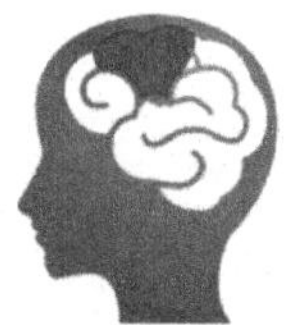

Have you asked God to give you trust, self-esteem, honour and a new sense of belonging to him?

What thoughts, actions, physical reactions and feelings need to change to be more 'in synch' with your new identity in Jesus?

In the chapters preceding this one, we have reestablished our relationships with God (Chapter 6), with others (Chapter 7) and with ourselves (Chapter 8). Establishing a secure relational framework like this is essential for the change process. As previously mentioned, it is a little bit like putting the scaffolding around a building prior to a renovation.

In this chapter we have mapped out a pathway forward. We have been outlining how we might use these connection points to recover and grow. If we can go *in, back, up* and then *forward* in relationships, change is more than possible—it is likely.

10

Change is not only possible: it is likely

When you look back on your history, there are things you can't change. We can't change the fact that mothers were cruel, that dads were indifferent, that cousins, boyfriends or bosses were spiteful. We can't change the fact that girlfriends were unfaithful. We can't change the fact that an uncle was cruel, or that a friend was mean-spirited. We can't change the fact that that we were lonely. We can't change the fact that people weren't interested in us.

These are the facts of history and, unfortunately, we live in their shadow.

So what *can* you do as you face the future?

Bad moments of disconnection need not determine your future. They can be terrible experiences, yet we need to see beyond the events that characterised these times, and see the pattern and journey that our hearts have taken since those events. When these bad events and bad people broke our trust, destroyed our sense of self and left us without hope, our hearts were broken. The events of disconnection themselves are not the problem; it is that these events injured us in a deep way. That is the crucial issue. The problem isn't that these things have happened; the problem is that these things got to our hearts.

Bad moments of omission are not what determine your future, either. The determining factor, again, is whether or not those times got to your heart. We cannot change the bad things that have happened, but we can—and this is the good news—change whether they get to remain in our hearts. The only thing we *can* change is the most important thing *to* change. This is the cardinal feature of those who have recovered: the people who have been through lack of love or disconnection and recovered are those who no longer bear the injuries in their hearts. They haven't changed their past, but nor do they need to.

You can do what they have done. Change, recovery and growth can happen in all of us. Sometimes it happens quickly and sometimes it happens more slowly, but it always happens by setting up a new supporting pyramid of safety and warmth, and going *in, back, up and forward.*

Bad relationships have been endured by many of us, yet many have found a way to trust, to love and be loved by others again. We have thrown off labels given to us by others and have been relabelled by God and others as 'worthy' and 'lovable'. We have regained a sense of direction and purpose, and we have hope. For those of us blessed to have found a way to recover, our way out has been determined by the extent to which we have relegated bad relationships to the past. The bad times have become memories that fail to haunt us because we've found a new temporal context. They are 'back there and back then' memories. Those old experiences don't plague us. They don't intrude into the present. They are psychologically impotent and part of an old story that is separate from us. They don't define us at a heart level: they've failed to leave their mark.

By now, your social climate may have changed or may be in the process of change. Looking around your pyramid of support (see Figure 17 in Chapter 7), you might recognise a structure that can hold you. When your pyramid is reconfigured and characterised by safety, warmth and understanding, you are ready. You may not be healed quickly, but you are set up to be healed.

We have connected with others and the promise of a new heart is found in those around us. A new heart is created by a God who cares and by friends and family who love us. Only when we are surrounded by connection can that old ache of omission be healed. Only when we are surrounded by connection can the wounds of disconnection be dressed and recovery begin. When loving relationships soothe us by the active and constructive interest of compassionate attunement, a new identity comes to pass. We say, 'I am loved' or 'I am lovable', because we notice the way others are responding to us. When we are near and known, accepted, understood, and enveloped by those whose intent is that we flourish, hurt will begin to pass. Then, when we are connected in such a way, we can foresee betrayal changing to trust and worthlessness changing to self-esteem. When the loving connection leads us to be clear of moral wrongdoing our shame will change to honour, and when loving connection leads to new roles our sense of alienation will change to belonging.

Now we step into the connections that heal us. The more open we are in safe and attuned environments, the more it will happen naturally. The negative thoughts that we think, the nasty things that we say, and the fighting, faking and fleeing are patterns of the past that become fractured by a new heart that feels loved, safe and whole.

This is how therapy works. It works by reliving your previously experienced disconnection in the presence of safety, and reliving lack of connection in the presence of someone who cares for you. What is back there is brought into the present. The darkness is brought into the light.

Being connected with and being known in your vulnerability is the antidote for all betrayal, worthlessness, shame and alienation. If the bacteria of connection injuries are brought into contact with the antibiotic of loving connection with humans and with a

Creator God, then deep, heartfelt healing emerges from the hurt. Relationships have broken us, but relationships are the making of us.

All things unspoken remain untouched. The memories and experiences remain embodied, waiting to be activated by the next *deja vu* moment that sits around the corner. Conversely, nothing that is spoken is left untouched, and if we can speak out the hurt into an environment of safety and love then those old hurts become washed by their immersion in love, and hope is summoned by the sense that those injuries may well be something that can remain in the past.

Sally, who you might remember from the first chapter, learnt to connect better with herself. She found that the more she did, the easier it got. When she confessed to her husband the things that she thought made her dirty, she saw not only a new side of him, but a new side of herself:

> I discovered something, but I feel like I may have already known it … just how much he has always cared for me, that I mean something to him, that maybe I'm acceptable to him … but I only got a sense of it when I opened up.

She learnt to open up more to her husband and those close to her.

Ben found some people at church whom he trusted to open up to. He told some friends quietly one night over beer that he had been struggling with porn. At the time, he felt that he was going to be overcome by emotion, but he was so grateful for their response:

> One of my mates said that he has struggled from time to time, and the other just said that he was so sorry that I had been doing it tough, and that he felt bad because he hadn't asked more questions.

When I asked him what that was like, he added:

> You know, I wasn't expecting it because I thought I was just making a confession, but the surprising thing was the day after I told them, my loneliness left me. I think it was not the beginning of love, because I always knew that Mum loved me, but it was the beginning of feeling loved again, of feeling worthwhile again. I think I felt fully known. It was what I hoped for from my Dad when Mum died.

Tony found his people. Retirement was tough and he knew that the loss of a role was bad enough, but looking back it occurred to him that he never knew how much he was depending on that role in order to belong.

'I used to say to people "I'm an accountant" like that would establish my credentials and would lead people to value me,' he said. He found new depths of spiritual connection because he was startled by his own realisation that his role was something he was using as leverage to obtain value and acceptance from others. He took his old role to the foot of the cross and left it there. In his quiet times, he reconfirmed that God was who he worshipped, not his ability to engineer his own quest for belonging. He worried less about what people thought of him as a retired person and found little ways to serve and love others around him.

Samantha knew that she had been betrayed by William. When she connected with herself she saw that she had been duped by charm and made dizzy by it. She saw that her response of remaining quiet gave William permission to be cruel towards her.

'My self-respect was eroded by my willingness to keep the peace,' she confessed. She said that she used to believe that she had to be subservient in a way that she thought her spiritual tradition wanted her to. I asked her to check with her pastor to see whether that was what was expected of her. She was shocked by the response:

> My pastor said, 'Absolutely not!' when I asked him if I should just accept and love William in spite of the way he was behaving. He told me that I should 'expect respect', that I can 'expect love, and any form of cruelty, any form of destructive or manipulative behaviour is entirely unacceptable'. He wanted to check back in with me and his wife to talk about how safe I felt.

When I asked her about the impact of that conversation, she replied:

> Well, I realised that even though I got confused, my intuitions were right ... I wasn't made to be a doormat. But it is better than that ... my pastor asked me whether or not I thought this is what God wanted for me ... I knew my prayer life had dropped away but I didn't know why. When he asked me that, I realised that I thought God was like William ... insecure, needing my absolute submission. My pastor told me what Jesus was like, that he wasn't insecure, that he could be trusted, that he wanted me to have freedom and safety ... without knowing why, I just started praying again, about anything, about everything.

With better horizontal and vertical connection, she became clearer about her boundaries. We spoke at the time about how cautious wisdom was required, and she learned to approach William carefully and calmly. Putting in boundaries made William's behaviour worse, so she told him that they would stay separated until such time as he stopped blaming her and took full responsibility for his own behaviour.

In all of these cases, the healing was set in motion by connection—connection with God, with others and with the self.

Relationships hurt, but relationships also heal.

You are now standing at the edge of a new adventure—one that wasn't even possible before. Sally, Ben, Tony and Samantha simply weren't free to navigate a direction of their own choosing until they first recognised the heart-level injuries that they were carrying. With their connection injuries healed, an opportunity arrived.

Connection makes us who we are

Who we are as people is dependent on connection. Being such highly relational beings, we grow when we are together in safe loving relationships, and we decay when we are not. We are made for genuine and meaningful connection with others and we are incomplete, even injured, without it. Connection with others not only provides us with an opportunity to recover from old hurts, but to flourish because of a growing sense of trust, self-esteem, honour and belonging. Yet there is something else too, something unexpected. Remember how with disconnection the damage flowed out and over the edge of the connection cup and into other areas of the heart? The same thing works with connection. The positive impact fills us up, and the positive impact flows up and over into the other areas of our hearts, too.

To illustrate this, I will share with you an example from a counselling session. It shows how relationships devoid of the nurturing qualities of real connection create the way we think and act. It also shows that it is only in the presence of loving, actively interested people that we are filled up and provided with the exciting prospect of just being ourselves.

Recently, I sat with a lovely guy named Euan. He is in Christian ministry. If you met Euan, you would think him personable and interesting, as I did. I had met with him five or six times prior to the meeting I am about to share with you.

When we sat down together, I asked him how he felt after our discussion the week before. He said that he felt really good. He said, 'When I left here I just started praying—I felt free to be totally honest with God, then I thought, "I remember that I used to be like this when I was young."'

I asked what happened next.

'When I got to the car park I crossed paths with people I had never spoken to before, and I thought, "I wonder how they would respond to my being open and honest?"'

When Euan had this experience in the car park, he was suddenly transported back to his earlier years. When he was younger, speaking from an honest place would always be met with rejection. He would either be ignored or be ridiculed. As he grew he learnt to keep his mouth shut and guard everything he said. The lack of disclosure meant he could avoid being rejected for what he said, but the absence of interest from others sowed a belief into his heart: 'I'm not allowed to be myself; it is too unsafe.'

The bottom line for Euan, as it is for all of us, is that you can't be yourself until your need for connection has been addressed. It is only when you feel that you can trust, you are worthwhile, you feel honoured and you belong that you can go about the business of being honest about what you think. If your heart isn't full of connection you'll sacrifice honesty at the altar of connection, because the need for love trumps the need to be truthful every time.

We think of family as a natural place of nurture and for many of us it is. But for many reasons, the patterns of close and caring connection that should exist between child and parent can fail to develop.

People like Euan grow up with an anaemic experience of relationships. Euan's family was always arguing. His father was a well-respected professional, but around his family he was as emotionally volatile as he was intelligent. His parents often fought heatedly. No-one in the home was keenly interested in Euan or in what he had to say.

At home, when his mum and dad argued, everyone would retreat to their bedrooms. At a time in his life when his opinions were becoming more informed and insightful, he found that his parents weren't interested. On many occasions, he wanted to talk to his dad about the way he treated his mum, but he knew that his dad was too emotional and would soon flee such discussions. Better not to share.

Why aren't we honest with others? The simple answer is that it is sometimes not safe enough to do so. To be ourselves, we need safe connection. Being free to be ourselves and disclose what we think and be who we are is only possible when we are immersed in safe, loving connection with others. Not everyone is fortunate enough to live in an environment where they receive positive affirmation and loving responses to what they share. The words of our African brothers and sisters are true: 'I am because of others.' If connection in the close relationships around us is damaged, it will be difficult to learn to be who you truly are. The good news is that when you are around others who do love you, you can be yourself.

Euan cultivated a close spiritual relationship and cultivated relationships based on mutual interest. He married a warm and loving lady and he became free to be himself. His cup of connection had been filled up and it spilt over the sides, filling up his identity. The last I heard, he was doing a post-graduate degree.

This is the beautiful vision of connection that is both ordinary and extraordinary—a vision of the way things can be if we relate to each other the way that God wants us to. The realisation of that vision is not only possible: it is, in fact, probable if our attitude is right.

For the vision to be realised, we will be required to live according to our better nature. We will need to be gentle, kind and interested in each other.

It is an enchanting vision because it sees the beauty of love as a realisable goal. It sees people as mysteries who can be better understood; it sees each person as worthy of love and understanding; it acknowledges the power of people to heal another; it sees the potential of the divine to change us; and it gives us the hope that no matter our past, we have the capacity and the opportunity to recover and heal from deep injury.

It starts with eye contact and a smile. It involves changing the way we treat people who we are acquainted with but don't know well: greeting the guy who gives me a coffee and thanking that woman in the traffic who lets me into her lane. It involves the way we interact with people we already know well—showing an interest in their lived experiences, and opening up to friends when they show an interest in us. It involves treating people as ends in themselves, humanising them, connecting with them and understanding them in such a way as to make them whole by our love and acceptance of them.

Then the benefits spill out over the top of the cup of connection into other sectors of our hearts. We see the green shoots of identity begin to grow, because we are safe enough to be ourselves. The confidence builds as we make choices and our direction becomes established, and positive relationships secure for us what we have longed for—trust, self-esteem, honour and belonging.

Benefits flow centrifugally out of the heart into all of our being. When we are connected, the body's inflammation subsides, the brain stays healthier, the mood stabilises, and our behaviour settles.

The benefits spill out and onto all the people we mix with. The benefits impact families, communities, churches and workplaces. When we are interested in others, and when we take an active and constructive approach to understanding and empathising, others benefit.

Then the cycle starts again. Other people feel our connection, it spills over into other sectors of their hearts, it spills over into their bodies, their brains, their moods, their behaviour, and back into their relationships with others.

From birth, we strive for connection, and upon attaining it, we are nourished by it. We are created with this thirst; we were born with this need, and the desire to be cared for never really leaves us. We find wholeness in the love of other people and our hearts are filled up by them. In connection with someone who is warm and caring we find resolution of betrayal, worthlessness, shame and alienation and we find the promise of trust, self-esteem, honour and belonging.

Our hearts get hurt by disconnection. Our hearts get healed in connection. We hurt, then we heal. A three-point connection is the answer.

POSTSCRIPT

I want to thank you for giving me your time. I'm grateful for the vulnerability that you have allowed yourself to experience by considering your own heart. It is an act of courage to do so, and I'm impressed by your willingness to do so.

For me, the privilege of entering into that space is always accompanied by a very deep sense of honour and wonder. It reminds me of Moses taking off his sandals as God spoke to him through the burning bush (Exodus 3:5). Speaking to people at a heart level is like walking on sacred ground. It is not a place to throw my weight around, but a place to be in awe, and to be mindful, slow to speak and full of gratitude—a time to 'take off [my] sandals'. Thank you for letting me into that space.

Five years after starting this book, the importance of its message is still impressed upon me. Only the other day, I had the opportunity to speak on the radio in Queensland about connection, then two weeks later a new person came to see me. He had been listening to the radio program, and he wanted to come to my practice and meet me because he felt that I understood him. The truth is that I had never met him until that point; it was just that I spoke about the heart and the importance of connection.

Now having spent so much time writing, I'm going to do what I ought to do. I'm going to talk with my wife, teach my eldest child how to drive and practise volleyball with another child; and when I go to bed, I'll say my prayers asking God to fill my heart with his love.

ACKNOWLEDGEMENTS

I am the recipient of wisdom and education both formal and informal. For this wisdom I feel both grateful and undeserving. I am grateful to my parents Sue and David who loved me with patience as I took my time stepping up to maturity. My 'Heart Flower' started well in life because of you both.

I am in debt to the wisdom that Dr John Warlow has bestowed on me over many years. It is a wisdom that he both inherited and developed himself. Much of the work here is informed by his thinking and I am privileged to have been part of conversations with him over many years.

I'm also blessed to have been part of a community of lively and intelligent people who contribute to my life in the Living Wholeness network: Dr Johanna Lynch, Andy Pocock, Peter Hayton, Peter Janetski, Ashleigh Withers, Daphne Austin, Deanna Pitchford, Dr Jill Warlow, Peter Brown and Dr Carolyn Russell. It is on these shoulders that I stand.

I have benefited greatly from the support of Leone Drew, not only because she is a very skilled grammarian, but because she has been an example to me of holding close to her saviour, not because of her suffering but in spite of it.

I am so thankful to the fabulously talented Paul Harvey who created the Heart Magic Eye image and the Heart in Mind website and has made countless other gestures of goodwill towards me.

I am very fortunate to have the good company of Dr Alan Headey at Heart in Mind whose conversations so often inspire me to continue the work we have started.

I'm very thankful to Karen Lucas, my 'comma princess', for her help with grammar. I'm flattered to receive artistic input from the prodigiously talented Cath 'Rosie' Rose and Andrew Nobbs at Covenant Christian School. They must take full credit for the cover design.

I'm so happy to receive straight-talking advice from my dear friend Rich McNee ('I don't care what university he comes from').

To my gym buddy and long term friend Rich Petterson, I'm thankful for the recurring questions about when I'm going to finish.

I'm thankful for the support of my brother Matthew who has given constructive advice about early parts of this book.

I'm privileged to have very insightful feedback from Richard Niessl. I am also thankful for the recently departed Tony Andrews whose willingness to help and encourage me was breathtaking.

I need to give full credit to Chris Hardie who created the Heart in Mind logo: thanks for sharing your design talent.

I am also very grateful for the support, laughter and theological guidance of my dear friend, the Reverend Neil Scott.

I cannot overlook the incredible and insightful help of Associate Professor Jill Willis who selflessly took time out during her long service leave to review my work and ensure that it had a more coherent structure.

I am in debt to Lisa Neale in Sydney and Hanna Nate from WestBow Press for doing an expert job helping me through the editing and publishing process.

To my wife, Kylie: we are equal, we are different, but no—you have never been indifferent. I'm so grateful to our Maker for our partnership at work and at home. For your talented and intuitive way with words, I cannot thank you enough. I am thankful for the deep connection that we share. I can't imagine life without you, and nor do I ever want to.

For the many clients who have poured out their hearts to me and taught me more than they know: thank you for the courage to come and for showing me the importance of connection.

APPENDIX A: THE NEED TO FACE WHAT IS IN OUR HEARTS

The non-negotiable needs of our hearts—to be accepted, to belong, to be loved and to have purpose—demand our careful attention. If the longings of the heart are attended to, we are more likely to be psychologically healthy. Our mood will be more settled and less reactive, and when our mood is calmer we can think more clearly.

Connection, direction and choice are our deepest psychological needs, and if we are to flourish, grow and enjoy psychological balance and wellbeing, they must be met. Only by keeping these needs in our awareness—that is, by keeping them 'in mind'—can that be made possible. I'll give you three reasons to help motivate you in this journey.

Three reasons to understand your heart

The different sectors of the heart are connection, direction and choice. Each of these domains has profound psychological significance. I want you to sense that these areas of your functioning are worthy of your time and attention. Devoting yourself to understanding what is in your heart will lead to dividends that will pay off for years to come.

Why?

Here are three reasons:

1. Your heart explains your struggles.
2. Your heart is your hidden substance.
3. Living with your heart in mind will help to avoid partial answers.

1. Your heart explains your struggles

Our hearts do not exist in isolation from the rest of our being but constantly interact with all other parts: our bodies, behaviour, mood and minds. The heart is implicated in our everyday experience of life. At any particular time, what is happening in our hearts explains much of what we experience, think, do and feel. When it looks as though our hearts could break, we become physically nervous. When our hearts do break, we become depressed and withdrawn. When our hearts are full, we're happy and tend to be focused, energetic and fruitful. The state of our hearts governs and therefore provides the explanation of much of our functioning. Our feelings, thoughts and behaviours can be indicators of what is on our hearts.

Steve was a semi-professional athlete. He was simply striking by his sheer physicality. Despite an outward appearance of having direction, control and success in his life, he had a damaged heart and was struggling. Bullied in his childhood by his father, and enduring a volatile connection with his stepmother, he was left feeling sensitive to others, uncertain about himself, and insecure in his relationship with his partner.

I had met with him about 10 times when we devoted almost an entire visit to talking about his heart. I explained to him that we all have 'heart' needs that are not only legitimate, but must be met if we are to flourish. His heart-level needs had been left unmet. Particularly in childhood, his heart had not been nurtured, and this had set him on a path in adulthood of disturbing uncertainty about himself and his relationships.

The following visit he returned and slumped in his chair, not in defeat, but reclined and relaxed.

'I get it,' he said, opening up his hands as if to the sky. He continued:

> Last week you explained that I need connection and safety, I need to be understood and I need to be given choices. I don't think I had those things growing up. I've decided that I've had enough of people who don't do that for me in my life, and I've decided that is what I'm going to do for my partner.

The outworking of the solution can take time, but the point is that the heart is significant in our functioning. If it is struggling for any reason, our whole being will be negatively impacted. As a result of the simple step of turning towards his heart, Steve was able to increase his understanding of his history and validate the hurt that he had been experiencing. He reported that his mood had improved and that he now had clearer direction in his relationships.

2. Your heart is your hidden substance

Though unseen, every heart is precious, intricate and extraordinary. Not knowing that or believing otherwise does not change that reality. The heart of each person is completely unique—so remarkable, that seeing into a person's heart is a sacred process.

Making the transition from the superficial to the depth of a person is what happens when we gain an insight into this normally unobservable reality. It is humbling and can be sad, joyous and poignant all at the same time. It is an authentically profound experience and is difficult to explain, because the experience is so right-brained: few words, lots of emotions and a sense of getting in touch with the reality of understanding another self.

An example that illustrates the experience of seeing into someone's heart is watching Susan Boyle's audition on Britain's Got Talent. (If you haven't seen this, I encourage you to look it up on YouTube.) A middle-aged lady dressed in a very ordinary, middle-aged way walks across the stage and takes her place in front of the judges and a large studio audience. Her unimpressive physical appearance belies her talent. The crowd is put off. They think she won't amount to much. However, neither the crowd nor the judging panel knows what is to come. They can't see her talent. They don't know her. The moment she delivers the first few lines of 'I Dreamed a Dream', everyone is awestruck and overcome with respect. We judge, we assume, but ultimately we are left feeling ashamed for being so superficial.

When Susan Boyle sang we were all humbled, even thankful for the lesson in humility. This is what it is like to see into someone's heart. We are humbled, almost embarrassed, for being superficial; for seeing only the physical. And so we should be. People *are* beautiful, awe-inspiring entities no matter who they appear to be on the outside, but we only fully understand that when we see people at heart level. What is true of others is true of you. You are beautiful; your uniqueness is sacred. By better understanding your heart, this reality emerges. This is your essence.

There are so many things that can blind us to our own essential beauty, just as there are many things that can distract us from seeing it in others.

For example, you may have a friend who ... well ... let's be frank ... smiles too much. Every time you meet with her, her greeting seems a little over the top. She uses an excess of eye contact. She holds onto your arm when she says hello. She says that she has been missing you, though you suspect this may not be true. She might use compliments that make you feel a little claustrophobic. Others think she is a faker. She never reveals anything negative about herself to others. Instead, she likes to focus on other people, and does this by asking questions like, 'How are you—really?' She presents only the happy side of herself. She is pleasant, but you don't feel like you know her.

One day, it aggravates you that she keeps asking you how you are. The tax department has been going through your history, and they keeping asking you what you did and when you did it, and now you meet with your friend and she is asking you what you did and when you did it. You ask her to stop. It isn't as if you don't want to be with her; it is just that you want some peace.

You're fine with this interaction but she is not. She apologises. You don't know why. You do want to be with her, but you don't want people meddling in your affairs. She says, 'I should go.' This is unexpected and you ask her why. She says, 'Because I'm no help to you.'

In a moment of insight, you ask her, 'You think I only like being with you when you are helpful to me?' She nods as the fear and sadness rise up in her body.

'Is that why you are always so keen to find out how I am and what I've been up to?'

'Yes,' she replies, 'and I get scared that if I'm not bright and happy, I'll be a burden to you, so I always try to ensure that I make you and others feel good.'

You realise that she isn't the faker other people believe her to be. She actually isn't intrusive either, though she copes with her own vulnerabilities by being intrusive. She is simply fearful: fearful of not being loved, fearful of being useless to others. Her entire history lights up in your mind. Previous difficulties become illuminated and explicable. Others have concluded that she is pretentious and even overbearing. You now know that she is neither of these things, but you understand how people may have come to this impression. You see through her coping strategies and into her heart—into her essence. You see her caring nature, her frailty and her driving need to be affirmed. She just wants to be loved. That is all.

This is the end point of a treasure hunt. You have seen into her heart and found the true substance of your friend, and it feels so precious. The secret unlocks compassion and a new way of relating, one that promises to be profoundly nourishing for you both.

In this moment, she is properly understood, and entirely vulnerable. The next step will be the making or breaking of the relationship.

We are not what we do. That is not our real substance. We are not what we have, nor are we our qualifications or our outward appearances. Our real substance is not to be found in the external, visible factors of our life. It is found in our hearts, and our hearts are the products of our relationships.

This is good news for some. If we have been loved and understood in a deep and comprehensive way, then our hearts have been nurtured and our substance will be in good shape. We will have a true sense of who we are and where we are going in life, and we will know that we have choices. For others, the news may not be so good. If we haven't been connected with, loved and nurtured, then our hearts will be deprived and struggling. We may live in constant fear of others because we have been horribly mistreated and that mistreatment has made us believe that we are 'disgusting', 'worthless', 'defective' or 'a failure'. We may be trapped in a cycle of constantly striving to feel better about ourselves. We may be wired to believe that if we progress in life, achieve status, acquire money or power, find a partner or have children, we will find fulfilment. There is nothing wrong with any of these things in themselves. They are all among the many options and blessings in life. However, like the coping strategies mentioned above, none of them will fix a wounded heart. Part of us may want to believe that they will deal with our inner pain, but as strategies for healing, they are counterfeit and ineffectual.

We need to stop doing things. We need to see through the worldly solutions with their urgent and compelling demand for attention. The glossy promise of a heart-level solution beckons us to 'do' and the dopamine[1] kicks in and our brains become giddy with the promise of having our hearts healed.

There is only one real way of ensuring the health of the heart. We need to turn towards it and learn to understand what is happening at that level of our being.

3. Living with your heart in mind will help to avoid partial answers

Those who have never been particularly mindful of their hearts may feel sceptical about the need to delve into matters that have always seemed abstract or irrelevant. It probably appears easier to continue unchanged, accepting the occasional patch of heartbreak, disappointment or grief without giving it much thought. What difference would it make to learn to walk with the 'heart in mind'? Aren't there quite simple guidelines available that would direct us in life and bypass the need to take this inward journey?

People have no shortage of advice on how to live life more effectively. Often the advice can be framed as being courageous or heroic. It is not unusual, for example, to hear someone give the encouragement to 'tough it out' or 'just get on with things'.

A great many, though not all, in the psychological community would offer general advice along similar lines: 'We simply need to think differently or stay more relaxed, or be more flexible or adaptive.' If you are struggling, this encouragement, though helpful, may not resonate because it does not respond to the depth of what you've been through or the pain that you bear. It does not come close to actually dealing with deep wounding and you would probably feel that it requires you to pretend that your pain does not exist.

The broader Christian community places the focus of positive human functioning elsewhere. It highlights not the need to merely

---

[1] Dopamine is a neurotransmitter in the brain that has a role in reward and motivation.

'tough it out' but instead the need to 'get on with the business of being like Jesus'. Likewise, this encouragement, though helpful, may not resonate because it is not connected with your story at a heart level.

Both of the encouragements above are helpful, but simple guidelines are not the recipe for flourishing in life, because they overlook the deep needs that we have. The encouragement to be spiritually aligned to Jesus is always applicable, but unless the 'bacteria' meet the 'antibiotic' (see Chapter 9), the energy to do so will never come from our hearts and we are left with a dutiful spiritual walk, one that fails to nourish us or give us energy.

Dealing with the heart involves an understanding of its functioning on a day-to-day basis. Living each day trying to be more relaxed and/or trying to be more like Jesus will not produce insight into our hearts. We must understand the state of our hearts to enable us to live in such ways. The ongoing health of our hearts can be ensured only if we understand what is needed to make us whole. Healing from both past and future injuries depends on our ability to uncover and face the pain of those incidents. Living by secular and or spiritual platitudes may well make us more functional, but if we neglect the daily functioning of that unique, extraordinary and central part of our being, then it will come at great cost. We will find ourselves living a precarious existence, susceptible to reminders of unresolved issues from the past.

APPENDIX B: 'SMART'

Situation: What were you doing and who were you with when you became troubled?

Mood: What feelings did you experience at the time?
Think of as many different emotions as you can and identify which emotions you felt. Give them an intensity rating (mild, moderate or severe).

Actions: What did you do or say at the time? How did you cope?

Reaction: How did your body react?
(Consider heart rate, breathing, dizziness, pain, fatigue, etc.)

Thinking: List any thoughts, pictures, memories or images that came into your mind at the time.

APPENDIX C: THE FEELINGS LIST

When feelings are elusive, it is often helpful to have a look at a list of them and consider whether you are experiencing any of them. Here are some suggestions:

- ☐ Hurt
- ☐ Scared
- ☐ Worried
- ☐ Anxious
- ☐ Fearful
- ☐ Humiliated
- ☐ Embarrassed
- ☐ Angry
- ☐ Sad
- ☐ Demoralised
- ☐ Bereft
- ☐ Listless
- ☐ Furious
- ☐ Joyful
- ☐ Content
- ☐ Concerned
- ☐ Pessimistic

Printed in the United States
by Baker & Taylor Publisher Services

Printed in the United States
by Baker & Taylor Publisher Services